T0305071

Japanese Multinationals in Europe

NEW HORIZONS IN INTERNATIONAL BUSINESS

Series Editor: Peter J. Buckley
Centre for International Business,
University of Leeds (CIBUL), UK

The New Horizons in International Business series has established itself as the world's leading forum for the presentation of new ideas in international business research. It offers pre-eminent contributions in the areas of multinational enterprise – including foreign direct investment, business strategy and corporate alliances, global competitive strategies, and entrepreneurship. In short, this series constitutes essential reading for academics, business strategists and policy makers alike.

Titles in the series include:

Multinational Enterprises, Innovative Strategies and Systems of Innovation
Edited by John Cantwell and José Molero

Multinational Firms' Location and the New Economic Geography
Edited by Jean-Louis Mucchielli and Thierry Mayer

Free Trade in the Americas
Economic and Political Issues for Governments and Firms
Edited by Sidney Weintraub, Alan M. Rugman and Gavin Boyd

Economic Integration and Multinational Investment Behaviour
European and East Asian Experiences
Edited by Pierre-Bruno Ruffini

Strategic Business Alliances
An Examination of the Core Dimensions
Keith W. Glaister, Rumy Husan and Peter J. Buckley

Investment Strategies in Emerging Markets
Edited by Saul Estrin and Klaus E. Meyer

Multinationals and Industrial Competitiveness
A New Agenda
John H. Dunning and Rajneesh Narula

Foreign Direct Investment
Six Country Case Studies
Edited by Yingqi Annie Wei and V.N. Balasubramanyam

Japanese Multinationals in Europe
A Comparison of the Automobile and Pharmaceutical Industries
Ken-ichi Ando

International Joint Venture Performance in South East Asia
Craig C. Julian

Governance, Multinationals and Growth
Edited by Lorraine Eden and Wendy Dobson

European–American Trade and Financial Alliances
Edited by Gavin Boyd, Alan M. Rugman and Pier Carlo Padoan

Japanese Multinationals in Europe

A Comparison of the Automobile and Pharmaceutical Industries

Ken-ichi Ando

Associate Professor, Department of Economics, Shizuoka University, Japan

NEW HORIZONS IN INTERNATIONAL BUSINESS

Edward Elgar
Cheltenham, UK • Northampton, MA, USA

Published by
Edward Elgar Publishing Limited
Glensanda House
Montpellier Parade
Cheltenham
Glos GL50 1UA
UK

Edward Elgar Publishing, Inc.
136 West Street
Suite 202
Northampton
Massachusetts 01060
USA

A catalogue record for this book
is available from the British Library

ISBN 1 84376 655 8

Printed and bound in Great Britain by MPG Books Ltd, Bodmin, Cornwall

Contents

Figures

Tables

Acknowledgements

This book is based on my PhD thesis, undertaken at the Department of Economics, University of Reading, UK. First, I would like to express my gratitude to my supervisors in Reading, Professor Geoffrey Jones and Dr Matthias Kipping. Professor Jones supervised my MA dissertation at the Graduate School of European and International Studies in 1990/91, and when I started my PhD research in 1996, he and Dr Kipping always gave me their kind guidance, help and encouragement. Without their generous support, this book may not have reached fruition.

I also benefited from the various comments of those outside Reading. In Europe, under the Programme for the Doctoral Tutorial in International Business of the European International Business Academy (EIBA) at Stuttgart, Germany, in 1997 I received much constructive advice from Professor John Dunning, Professor Peter Buckley, Professor Jean-François Hennert, Professor Daniel Van Den Bulcke, Professor Bernhard M. Yeung and Professor Stephen Young. Their comments on my PhD research plan were invaluable.

I also owe a great debt to scholars in Japan. Professor Takao Sasaki supervised and guided me towards an academic life, when I studied in the undergraduate and graduate schools of Hokkaido University. Professor Akira Kudo invited me to the European Studies Workshop at the Institute of Social Science, Tokyo University. The discussions with Professor Kudo and others at the workshop facilitated the completion of my work.

This book is based on unique information obtained from interviews with personnel at multinational enterprises, trade unions and ministries, the internal materials of multinationals, and so on. Because of confidentiality, I cannot list the names of the interviewees, but I am grateful for their generous help.

I would like to acknowledge the financial support that I received from various sources. The scholarship from the British Council in 1990/91 enabled me to study for my MA in Reading. The University of Reading and EIBA provided financial support for me to attend the doctoral tutorial and the conference of EIBA in Stuttgart in 1997. I received a grant from the Ministry of Education, Japan, in 1999–2000 (MEXT KAKENHI 11730026) and another one from the Japan Society for the Promotion of Science in 2003–04

(JSPS KAKENHI 15530182), which enabled me to conduct a series of interviews in Europe and Japan.

Finally, I would like to thank my family. My wife, Alice Izumi Horiuchi, always gives me her smile and her love. Our children, Tomohiro and Naomi, put new life into me. Without them, I could not have finished my work.

All the gratitude, however, does not reduce my own responsibility for this book.

Ken-ichi Ando

1. Introduction

This book investigates the strategy and management of Japanese multinational enterprises (MNEs) in Europe, where business conditions have been changing under the development of the European Union (EU).[1] The emergence of the Japanese economy (Preston, 2000; Matray, 2001) and the development of European integration (Neal and Barbezat, 1997; Gillingham, 2003) are the main forces behind the tri-polar structure of the global economy, along with the central role of the US. The interface between Japan and Europe initially concerned trade or trade friction, but has shifted more and more to include foreign direct investment (FDI), especially from Japan into Europe. However, the relationship between Europe and Japan is less close than that of either with the US, and there has been little analysis of the subject. This justifies the examination of Japanese MNEs in Europe. The uniqueness of Europe should also be kept in mind. That is, the European economy, which is not that of a single country, but an integrating economic entity under the EU, prompts MNEs to search for appropriate strategy and management policies. This is also true for the case of Japanese MNEs, and will be examined through a comparative investigation of auto and pharmaceutical MNEs.

This chapter is structured as follows. The next section looks at the general feature of Japanese FDI (1.1), and we then turn our attention to the unique character of the European economy developing under the EU (1.2). From a comparison of Japanese FDI and European integration (1.3), three main themes of discussion emerge (1.4).

1.1 JAPANESE FDI

Japan has been one of the significant direct investors in the world economy since the 1980s (Basu and Miroshnik, 2000). The stock of Japanese outward FDI grew dramatically from \$19.6 billion in 1980 to \$331.6 billion in 2002, and was ranked sixth in the world (UN, 2003, p. 262).[2] Nevertheless, due to the low rate of FDI against its GDP or gross fixed capital formation, the present situation is not recognised as Japan's normal position, which is as the second largest economy in the world. Therefore, a UN report suggests that

'[Japanese] investment abroad grew ... and is expected to keep growing' (UN, 2002, p. 43).

Indeed, the growth of Japanese FDI in the 1990s is not as impressive as in the late 1980s, mainly due to the poor economic performance of Japan itself. The accumulated FDI for the five years between 1991 and 1995 was $196.8 billion, which was lower than the $227.2 billion between 1986 and 1990.[3] Even though the total Japanese FDI between 1996 and 2000 increased to $259.4 billion, its share in the outward FDI of the world declined from 11.7 per cent in 1990 to 4.9 per cent in 2002 (UN, 2003, p. 253). The point to be emphasised, however, is that Japan has started to follow other developed countries with regard to international production, in spite of the less favourable conditions of its domestic economy (UN, 2000, pp. 38–40). Furthermore, the aggregate data does not distinguish the activities of each Japanese MNE. This is especially important, since in the 1990s, Japan divided companies into 'winners' and 'losers', even in the same industry. For example, Toyota and Honda recorded their highest profits in the late 1990s, while Nissan, Mazda and Mitsubishi needed a capital injection from the foreign competitors Renault, Ford and DaimlerChrysler, respectively, in the same period.

Japanese FDI illustrates not merely the quantitative change during the 1980s and 1990s, but also the qualitative change. The geographic change of Japanese FDI is remarkable, and Europe is at the centre of that change. Japanese FDI to Europe increased steadily from the late 1980s, although it started more than a hundred years ago (Mason, 1997). As a result, the European share of Japanese FDI rose to 35.5 per cent in the five-year period between 1997 and 2001, from 14.1 per cent between 1949 and 1979. In 2002, Europe was now the largest recipient of Japanese FDI flow with 41.4 per cent, exceeding North America 23.1 per cent and Asia 15.3 per cent. Since the manufacturing sector gradually increased Japanese FDI into Europe during the last two decades to 2001, its share accounts for 32.9 per cent of total FDI in Europe in 2001. As a general trend, four industrial sectors, that is, chemicals, machinery, electrical and electronic equipment, and transport equipment, have retained their importance in FDI into Europe.

The survey conducted by the Japan External Trade Organisation (JETRO) also supports the development of operations by Japanese MNEs in Europe (JETRO, 2002). The total number of manufacturing subsidiaries in Europe and Turkey was 984 at the end of 2001, indicating a more than fivefold growth from 171 subsidiaries in 1983. The increase can also be seen in the number of research and development (R&D) and design centres. In 2001, there were 387 R&D centres and 83 design centres, rising from 187 and 35, respectively, in 1989, which are the oldest available figures. These facts suggest that Japanese FDI into Europe may be motivated by complicated factors on both the supply and demand sides.

Thus, Japanese FDI into Europe does not develop in static circumstances, but rather in the dynamic situation under EU integration. This warrants further investigation.

1.2 EUROPEAN INTEGRATION

Europe is a unique economic entity, due to regional economic integration under the EU, which is one of the most important factors when we consider the European economy. European integration originated from the European Coal and Steel Community (ECSC) set up in 1952, which aimed at establishing a common market for coal and steel among six countries–France, Germany, Italy and Belgium, the Netherlands and Luxembourg. The successor organisation was the European Economic Community (EEC), which extended the competence of the Community to all economic areas from the narrower one of the ECSC. In spite of the existence of a looser approach through the European Free Trade Association, the EU increasingly represents the European integration movement (Urwin, 1991; Heater, 1992; Neal and Barbezat, 1997; Gillingham, 2003).

It is often said that the development of the EU has three aspects, 'deepening', 'widening' and 'enlargement' (Pelkmans, 2001). The 'deepening' refers to the establishment of a freer internal market. Following the ECSC, the EEC established a customs union in the 1960s, which eliminated internal customs tariffs and quotas, and introduced common external tariffs (Hine, 1985). The new movement of European integration was brought about by the Single European Market (SEM) programme addressed by the Commission in 1985 (Commission of the European Communities, 1985; Hoffmann, 1989; El-Agraa, 1994; Lucarelli, 1999), which planned to abolish the remaining non-tariff barriers (NTBs) in the EU by the end of 1992.

The 'widening' is the extension of the policy scope of the EU from internal liberalisation. Typical examples are the Common Agricultural Policy, the regional policy and so on. Launching the single currency, the euro, in 1999 was the most notable progress made by European integration in the 1990s. Eleven of the fifteen member states adopted the single currency with inter-bank operations from 1 January 1999, although some member states like the UK did not participate in the project despite fulfilling the Maastricht criteria.[4] Even though the euro had initially depreciated against the US dollar, the UK pound sterling and the Japanese yen, the euro area has been experiencing big changes, including more severe competition (Meeusen, 1999; Valencia, 2000).

The geographic area of the EU has enlarged through the increase in the number of member states. The EU originally started with six countries, but then expanded to fifteen member states. After the UK's failure to join the EU in 1961 and 1967, the UK, Ireland, Denmark and Norway were finally approved for membership in 1973, but Norway failed to ratify its entry following a national referendum (Nicholson and East, 1987). The second enlargement was realised in the 1980s, despite the hesitation of the EC Commission due to economic reasons (George, 1985). As a result, Greece became a member of the EU in 1981, while Spain and Portugal were welcomed in 1986 (Nicholson and East, 1987). The collapse of the East European bloc by the early 1990s made the neutral countries reconsider their foreign policy. Austria, Finland and Sweden entered the EU, while Norway again rejected the membership by referendum. Shifts to a market economy qualified the former planned economies of Eastern Europe to apply, and the 2002 Brussels Summit agreed to the membership of ten Central and Eastern European countries from May 2004.[5]

This summary suggests that Europe shows its own dynamic movement towards a freer and wider market under the EU. The process of regional integration itself has not been harmonious, and includes numerous disagreements among European countries, such as the failure of the UK membership in the 1960s, the division of the EU member states over a single currency and so on. Such dynamics, however, have their own significant locational conditions for firms in general, and for MNEs in particular. This is also true for Japanese MNEs in Europe.

1.3   INTERFACE BETWEEN JAPANESE FDI AND EUROPEAN INTEGRATION

The mutual relationship between Japanese FDI into Europe and the development of European integration will now be examined, in order to introduce the key themes of this book. According to Dunning (1988, 1993), three factors are considered in a firm's decision to invest abroad rather than to license or export. The first is competitive advantages, enabling the company concerned to compete against indigenous firms on foreign soil (Hymer, 1976). The second is internalisation capability, whereby the firm can organise un-tradable resources such as knowledge, information and technology more efficiently within its own organisation than market (Buckley and Casson, 1976; Rugman, 1981; Hennart, 1982; Caves, 1996). The last is locational conditions, which cannot be obtained through trade (Dunning, 1988, 2003). The combination of these three factors enables and leads a firm to invest abroad, rather than merely to export or license, and we should reconsider them in the context of the changing economic conditions in Europe.

The European economy shows a unique development in the process of European integration, and has diversified features on both the demand and the supply sides. For the last-half century, the EU has increasingly become an integrated market from a patchwork of national markets. The framework for a business, however, is not merely constructed by establishing the regulations for the market at the European level, but could be a more complicated configuration among the interested parties including the company, labour, the state and so forth, as Whitley (1992) suggests. National characteristics of demand and consumers' taste persist, and differ one from the other (Niss, 1994). The integration of labour markets is a far-reaching (or unrealistic) object, while the quality and skill of the labour force and industrial relations are different in each country (Lane, 1989, 1995). There is an immense variety of government regulations and infrastructure among the member states, which should be harmonised *ex ante* or *ex post* (Siebert, 1990; Sun and Pelkmans, 1995). In addition, the introduction of the euro indicates that the formal process of EU integration itself can vary among the member states according to their preference, since some countries such as the UK opted out of the single currency programme. Thus, the development of the EU is an asymmetrical process rather than a simple path of integrating the national economies into the EU.

The asymmetrical change of the locational conditions in Europe influences firms both within and outside Europe. This means that the locational advantages should be assessed from the perspectives of both the European and national economies. An MNE, therefore, has to decide which location within Europe is the most appropriate for its own business objectives. MNEs transfer not only investment capital, but also intangible assets, such as technology, management methods, business knowledge and information (Caves, 1996; Enderwick, 1996; Lall, 1996). This is closely influenced by the investment method. Furthermore, MNEs have to upgrade their own organisation, in order to fully and efficiently conduct the foreign operation (Stopford and Wells, 1972; Bartlett and Ghoshal, 1989). The internalisation school of foreign direct investment (FDI) emphasises this point. At the same time, the general locational conditions of the host economy are constantly changing. This is especially true in Europe, and MNEs have to adjust and adapt themselves to the changes. From this perspective, the development of Japanese FDI into Europe is not simply a matter of expanding facilities, but each MNE has to make some serious decisions and to undertake the restructuring and re-organisation of its European operations.

1.4   CENTRAL THEMES

The above considerations give rise to three fundamental and mutually related themes to be addressed in this book. The first theme is *in which country* Japanese MNEs should invest. The asymmetry of the EU economy poses a difficult question for MNEs, in addition to the questions common to other regions. That is, once an MNE decides to invest in Europe, it must further consider the location within Europe in which to invest.

The second theme is *which method* Japanese companies have chosen to invest in Europe. Here, it is worth further emphasising the dynamic change of the entry mode by MNEs. The dynamic changes in the European economy brought about by European integration have been gradually changing the locational conditions, and the MNEs themselves have also improved their own ability to adjust to such changes. The method for tapping into new ventures can be different, and the entry mode itself is influenced by the conditions in Europe as well as the capability of the MNE. Therefore, the entry mode will be analysed in the context of the dynamic time series, both of European integration and of the MNEs.

The third theme concerns *how* Japanese MNEs operate their business from the pan-European point of view. Assuming the asymmetrical and continuous change of the locational conditions, this is a more serious issue for MNEs in Europe than anywhere else. Moreover, because of their relatively brief experience in international operations, and their relatively identical character in the domestic economy, this is more critical for Japanese MNEs than for their US or European counterparts. Therefore, the management of Japanese MNEs will be investigated from the European perspective, as opposed to the national one.

These are the three central themes that this book will address, and it should be borne in mind that each of them is closely related to the others. Each theme is individually important, and there is some accumulation of independent research, as we shall see in the next chapter. However, this does not add up to a study of the inter-relationships of the themes. The investment decision and method are connected with the location of each facility, while the development of FDI by an MNE may not automatically guarantee that it will concentrate all of its facilities in a single European country. The diversity of the locations necessitates further co-ordination among the subsidiaries from a European perspective. For an MNE, it is quite natural to continuously assess these three issues, and each decision substantially influences the operation in Europe. Therefore, the above three themes will be addressed, bearing in mind the mutual relationships.

NOTES

1. The EU changed its name from the European Community (EC) in 1993 following the ratification of the Maastricht Treaty. The EC itself was a result of the Brussels Treaty in 1967, which united three Communities, that is, the European Coal and Steel Community (ECSC), the European Economic Community (EEC), and the European Atomic Community (Euratom). Throughout this book, we shall generally use 'EU' to suggest not only the EU itself, but also the EC and the EEC before the Maastricht Treaty in 1993.
2. The UN data are quite different from those published by Japan's Ministry of Finance (MOF). The latter are based on notification and were $767.0 billion. For the international comparison, the UN data are used here. The International Monetary Fund (IMF, 2000) based on data from the Bank of Japan gives $401.6 billion, which is the accumulated stock between 1977 and 1999 for Japan.
3. The data are calculated in US dollars based on the average dollar–yen exchange rate from the data published by Japan's MOF, which is expressed in Japanese yen. The original data can be obtained from the home page of MOF, http://www.mof.go.jp. The MOF data may well be larger than the actual FDI because of the notification basis. However, the revival trend in the second half of the 1990s from the decline in the first half can also be recognised from the IMF data.
4. The eleven participating countries are Austria, Belgium, Finland, France, Germany, Ireland, Italy, Luxembourg, the Netherlands, Portugal and Spain. The non-participants are Denmark, Sweden, the UK and Greece. Among the last four, the first three voluntarily stayed out of the single currency programme. Greece did not fulfil the Maastricht criteria in 1998, but it made great efforts to gain membership, and it succeeded in becoming a new member in 2001.
5. The new member states from 2004 are Cyprus, the Czech Republic, Estonia, Hungary, Latvia, Lithuania, Malta, Poland, Slovakia and Slovenia.

2. Literature Survey

2.1 INTRODUCTION

Three fundamental and mutually related themes of Japanese MNEs in Europe are to be investigated in this book, that is, the location within Europe, the entry mode in the context of internationalisation, and the management from a pan-European perspective. They are quite important issues for understanding MNEs, and there has already been much research on them. But, it is also true that there are some gaps in the research concerning Japanese cases in Europe. This can be explained by the relatively new phenomenon of Japanese FDI into Europe, and the limited availability of data and information, especially compared with US cases. This chapter will summarise the literature, and clarify the points to be examined.

The structure of this chapter is as follows. The next three sections will look at the theoretical and empirical work on the three central themes, namely, the FDI location (2.2), the entry modes in a time series (2.3), and the cross-border management at the European level (2.4). A summary of the literature will indicate the detailed questions to be analysed (2.5).

2.2 THE LOCATION OF MNES UNDER REGIONAL ECONOMIC INTEGRATION

Since we are interested in the asymmetrically changing environment in Europe under the EU for the strategy and management of MNEs, it is natural to start with location. Firms investing abroad have to find the most suitable country for carrying out their strategy, and some theoretical and empirical research has already been conducted. Vernon's product life cycle theory suggests that the location shifts unilaterally from the most- to the least-advanced economies (Vernon, 1966, 1979; Markusen, 1985). Thomsen and Nicolaides (1991) use the approach of the product life cycle model when they analyse Japanese FDI into Europe. The main purpose for applying this model, however, is to suggest the impact of the protectionist pressure by the EU and member states on the investment timing of Japanese MNEs, rather than on the FDI location in the EU. Similarly, the macroeconomic approach by Kojima (1978) suggests a change of the location from developed to less-developed countries in the context of the comparative advantage theory of international trade, although his argument is criticised as not being analytical, but normative (Buckley, 1983) or by the ignorance of the protectionism impact on FDI (Strange, 1993). Indeed, both Vernon and Kojima were interested in the location pattern of FDI between developed and less-developed countries, with the emphasis on the wage cost difference. It is worth asking whether the different wage levels in Europe influence the location of Japanese FDI.

The 'new international trade theory' offers a different insight into location from the conventional trade theory. In contrast to the traditional customs union theory (Viner, 1950; Robson, 1987), the new international trade theory associates three elements, that is, international trade, scale economy and location (Krugman, 1990; Markusen, 1995; Venables, 1995). If the trade costs including the tariffs and non-tariff barriers are low, and the economy of scale is big enough, then firms concentrate economic activities in a certain location in order to benefit from the economy of scale. According to Baldwin (1994), who applied the new international trade model to the EU, we would expect the EU to accelerate the process whereby firms in a certain industry concentrate in a smaller number of locations; this is called the 'agglomeration effect'. Here, the existing production centre is likely to be the preferred location due to the external economies.

Empirical research has been conducted to assess the agglomeration effect on FDI, but the results are diverse. Some results are supportive of the agglomeration effects theory: previous investment in the same industry, intermediate inputs and pure technological spillover are significant factors (Head et al., 1995), while the quality of infrastructure, the degree of industrialisation, labour costs and market size have positive impacts (Wheeler and Mody, 1992). On the other hand, other research found no evidence of agglomeration as a general phenomenon in the process of completing the SEM programme (Dunning, 1997; European Commission, 1997c; Dluhosch, 2000). Indeed, Japanese FDI into Europe tends to concentrate in the UK, Germany, France and the Netherlands in value terms, while Spain would be included by the employment criteria (Thomsen and Nicolaides, 1991; Yamawaki, 1993; Nicolas, 1995; Thiran and Yamawaki, 1996). From the historical studies on Japanese companies in Europe since the nineteen century, however, Mason comments that 'there has been a shift in Japanese FDI in Europe from geographical concentration to geographical dispersion' (Mason, 1994a, p. 31).

This research provides some interesting points, but other conditions such as demand, created resources and institutional factors are ignored. Therefore, we should take a wider perspective. The eclectic paradigm of Dunning (1988,

1993) is a suitable basis for looking at Japanese FDI from a wider perspective. Dunning maintains that a combination of three advantages enables a firm to invest abroad: the ownership-specific advantage, the internalisation advantage and the locational advantage. In the absence of any one of these, the company in question does not invest, but rather exports or licenses. Although it is not a formal economic model with predictive capacity,[1] Dunning's paradigm provides an appropriate framework for detailed empirical research. For the purpose of this present book, we need to consider Dunning's locational advantage in more depth.

In this context, Porter (1990) explains the basis of international competitiveness, since MNEs need to maintain the competitive edge abroad. Porter proposes that a combination of factors decides the international competitiveness of an industry in a country: the resource conditions, the related and supporting industries, the demand conditions, and the firm's strategy, structure and rivalry (Figure 2.1). The first factor is the endowment of the natural and created resources such as skilled labour, while the second is the accumulation of industries supplying the materials, parts and components, and supporting services for the particular industry. The size and nature of the demand in a country influences the competitiveness of the companies in the industry. The fourth factor includes the creation, organisation and management of the company itself, but Porter especially emphasises the rivalry among companies to strengthen the competitive advantage of the industry in a country. In addition, government policy and chance are mentioned as forces influencing the above four factors.

The argument of Porter's Diamond provides a helpful basis for considering the locational advantage for FDI,[2] and each factor should be reassessed as a locational advantage for inward FDI while paying due regard to European integration. In the context of European integration, non-tradable resources explain the inward FDI in a certain country within Europe. The labour force is one of the most typical examples of a non-tradable resource. Some scholars confirm its importance for FDI location (Friedman et al., 1992; Yamawaki, 1993),[3] although other investigations show the opposite result (Veugelers, 1991). The existence of related and supporting industries is an attraction for foreign firms to invest in a certain country; this is similar to the agglomeration model. However, relatively, European integration could reduce the advantage of one country over others in this regard because of the possibility of pan-European procurement. For example, Wells and Rawlinson (1992) investigate the impact on suppliers of Ford's introduction of Japanese-style production, but do not find any evidence of agglomeration. This suggests that Ford makes use of suppliers from a pan-European perspective.

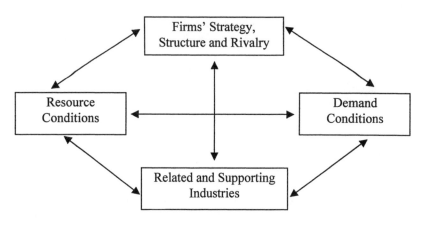

Source: Porter (1990, p.72).

Figure 2.1   Porter's Diamond

The demand factor is important, but the significance between quantitative and qualitative aspects should be appreciated. It should be emphasised that European integration has a double meaning in terms of the quantity of demand. An integrated Europe becomes a more attractive location for FDI (UN, 1993), although it does not explain why a certain country in Europe is chosen. At the same time, however, the small countries in the integrated area can be relieved of the disadvantage caused by their small domestic market size. The establishment of Belgian plants by US auto MNEs in the 1960s is a typical example (Hu, 1973),[4] although according to other research the size of the host country's domestic market is still an important determinant (Yamawaki, 1993). Furthermore, the demand factor also has a qualitative aspect. 'Globalisation' or 'Europeanisation' does not mean that people in different countries have the same taste for the goods in question, but rather that national differences in preference are still considerable, even among the EU member states (Hood and Young, 1983; Baden-Fuller and Stopford, 1991; Dunning, 1993; Niss, 1994; Rugman, 2001). Thus, the qualitative factors of demand should be kept in mind.

Rivalry is especially emphasised in the fourth factor by Porter, and European integration strengthens the competitive pressure within the EU.[5] Rivalry can be a factor to accelerate the inward FDI into the integrated area. However, it could affect the member states indifferently, and this means that rivalry would have little effect on the FDI into a certain country within the integrated region. The role of the government is particularly crucial here in the context of European integration, since the situation in Europe is characterised by the co-existence of national governments and the EU (Raines and Brown, 1999). As national policy is influential mainly within the country in question, the government policy factor could make a difference in the locational advantage among the member states. For example, national governments can provide economic aid (Hill and Munday, 1992), a different tax system, environmental regulation and so on, even within the EU (Friedman et al., 1992). Thus, European integration requires MNEs to simultaneously monitor both national governments and the EU (Aaron, 1999; Loewendahl, 2001), although other empirical research does not find support for government factors having an influence on FDI (Veugelers, 1991).

Some additional issues concerning the location are not fully examined by the above models. The expansion of R&D sites abroad is reported in some research (Howells, 1990; Dalton and Serapio, 1998). This new aspect of FDI into developed countries leads scholars to widen the perspective. It is important for MNEs to supplement the lack of home-country facilities by tapping into the scientific, technological, managerial and other capabilities of the host economy through foreign R&D facilities. Such FDI can be called 'knowledge-seeking' investment (Pearce, 1997; Peters, 1998). Other research has investigated the significance of technological capacity among European countries on the FDI location (Dunning and Cantwell, 1991; Pearce and Papanastassiou, 1996; Cantwell et al., 2001), although this research lags behind that on manufacturing.

At the same time, company conditions also influence the FDI decision. Risk-reducing considerations lead a company to favour familiar countries in the early stage of FDI (Davidson, 1980). The parent firm's size and performance are important factors for the locational decision. The larger the company, the more easily it can invest abroad, while the better the business performance of the company, the more easily it can make difficult decisions concerning FDI (Kravis and Lipsey, 1982).

This section has looked at the theoretical approach to the location theme, and shown the results of the empirical research on the determinant factors for the MNE's location from the various viewpoints. The first three theoretical approaches focus on the locational theme from supply-side considerations, while Dunning's eclectic paradigm gives a wider perspective. The locational advantages based on Porter's Diamond were examined, with an emphasis on European integration. The knowledge-seeking approach model sheds further light on the new phenomenon of FDI, and broadens our perspective from manufacturing to non-manufacturing activities such as R&D. The empirical studies, however, do not always test the same variables, or support the same factors with other research.

2.3 THE ENTRY MODE IN THE SEQUENTIAL PROCESS OF INTERNATIONALISATION

When a firm invests abroad, it has to face the crucial decision on the entry mode. There are generally three modes for MNEs to invest in foreign business: greenfield investment, acquisition and joint venture.[6] In addition, it is impossible for any large enterprise to simultaneously establish all of its business facilities in a large market like the EU. This certainly makes entry into foreign markets a sequential process, which could involve a mixture of different kinds of entry mode. An MNE would choose one of the three entry modes based on an assessment of the advantages and disadvantages of each entry mode (Buckley and Casson, 1998). This section will look at various factors affecting the entry mode.

First, the financial cost is an important factor directly affecting the decision. A joint venture is clearly the cheapest method among the three, because it shares the capital of the new business entity. It is more difficult to estimate the difference in the financial costs between greenfield investment and acquisition (Vasconcellos and Kish, 1998). If the qualitative nature of the entry mode is ignored, the absolute financial cost is not meaningful. The conditions of the stock market, which change daily, influence the cost of the acquisition. The existing facilities obtained through the acquisition cannot be as advanced as those of the greenfield investment, and the differences between them could be significant.

Further significance can be indicated on the qualitative aspect for considering the choice among the three. As Hymer (1976) pointed out, competitive advantages are crucial for an MNE to survive and expand abroad. The internalisation theory can provide a basis for considering how MNEs minimise their costs to maintain competitive advantages in foreign countries.[7] The company-specific advantages are closely related to the knowledge of the MNE, whose market is not always perfect and often does not exist at all. Since the entry mode influences the organisation of the foreign subsidiaries, it would show how an MNE internalises the knowledge and other intangible assets at the point of going abroad (Root, 1987; Caves, 1996, ch. 3).[8]

Thus, it is crucial for the foreign business that the subsidiary is effectively and efficiently controlled and managed. The control over the foreign interest may well show a unique preference among the three entry modes. In this context, a greenfield investment is the best solution, since a company can construct the organisation from scratch as it wishes. On the other hand, a joint venture is the least attractive solution because of the sharing of some intangible assets, which could be eroded from the MNE in question to the partner. An acquisition lies somewhere between these two solutions. Even if the acquiring company can escape the problem caused by consulting with a partner, it might still face conflict with the remaining staff from the acquired company. The statistical research on the entry mode, which uses R&D expenditures or the cultural distance dummy as independent variables, is not always in accord. For example, Hennart and Park (1993) showed a significant positive relationship of R&D intensity to greenfield investment, but Kogut and Singh (1998) found a similar relationship to joint ventures. Kogut and Singh further indicated that cultural distance supports the superiority of joint ventures and greenfield investments over acquisitions.

At the same time, MNEs need to internalise local knowledge for their success abroad. MNEs should attain knowledge of the host economy both before the investment and during the operation there. Knowledge of the local economy including the regulatory framework can be gained through a joint venture or an acquisition more easily than through a greenfield investment. This is because the joint-venture partners or the acquired company already possess local knowledge. An acquisition may well be better than a joint venture, since the acquiring firm can access freely and fully the knowledge accumulated by the acquired company. There is a preference for joint ventures, when firms seek local firm resources, or seek to enter an unfamiliar market (Hennart, 1991). On the other hand, when the FDI into the same product area does not need as much local knowledge as in other cases, greenfield investment is chosen more often than acquisition (Hennart and Park, 1993).

Further additional factors affecting the entry mode decision include uncertainty and risk, and the speed of entry. With regard to these factors, greenfield investment is likely to be the least attractive because it would intensify the downward pressure on the market through its own additional production capacity (Caves and Mehra, 1986). Under conditions of low market growth, acquisition is preferred to greenfield investment (Caves and Mehra, 1986; Zejan, 1990; Hennart and Park, 1993). A joint venture is less exposed to risks than an acquisition, because of sharing the business with the partner; this is especially confirmed with regard to FDI into less-developed countries (Beamish and Banks, 1987). The speed of entry is another consideration of MNEs. A greenfield investment consumes the longest time to start up the business, while an acquisition makes all the necessities available for the MNE from the acquired company. A joint-venture partner provides some necessities, though not all of them. Thus, the speed of entry is the fastest with an acquisition and slowest with a greenfield investment. The joint venture lies somewhere between the two (Hennart and Park, 1993).

Last but not least, acquisitions and joint ventures have their own problem; the appropriateness of the target or partner company. Without a potential target company for the acquisition or the joint venture, a company has no choice other than greenfield investment (Zejan, 1990). In addition, the capability of the company to be acquired or to become a partner is not always sufficient for the business strategy of the MNE. In such a case, the MNE itself has to supplement the shortcomings.

Table 2.1 sums up the above discussion regarding the relationships between the three entry modes and the factors influencing the decision. Note that the same factor influences each entry mode differently, but the same number of 'minuses' (shown by ' – ') does not imply the same degree of importance between the different factors. Rather, it implies the following. Knowledge, for example, may well be the weakest advantage for greenfield investment, followed by joint ventures, and the best for acquisitions. The disadvantage of greenfield investment with respect to the knowledge factor, however, is not the same as the disadvantage caused by the entry speed for greenfield investment, or the same as the control factor disadvantage of a joint venture. For a greenfield investment, it is not implied that the uncertainties and risk costs are three times as much as the control costs. Even within the same cost, the difference between the entry modes does not reflect the ratio of the significance. In summary, Table 2.1 roughly shows the order among the three entry modes within the category of a particular factor.

Table 2.1   Influencing factors and entry mode

	Financial costs	Control	Uncertainty and risk	Knowledge	Entry speed	Target availability
GFI	– – –	–	– – –	– – –	– – –	n.a.
AQ	– –	– –	– –	–	–	– –
JV	–	– – –	–	– –	– –	–

Note:
GFI: greenfield investment; AQ: acquisition; JV: joint venture; n.a.: not applicable.
The disadvantages increase as the number of minuses (–) increase.

Note that the comparison of the entry modes is static in nature, but the actual decisions are made in the process of the internationalisation of the firm in question. Thus, an examination should be made of the internationalisation process model enabling an assessment to be made of the importance of the knowledge in the context of the dynamic development of a firm (Johanson and Wiedersheim-Paul, 1975; Johanson and Vahlne, 1977).[9] The internationalisation of a firm is a process of trial and error in its own operation history. Prior to the foreign operation, companies have little knowledge of the economic, legal and social conditions of the target market, and therefore experience a large 'psychic distance'. The internationalisation process aims to develop both an incremental accumulation of knowledge, and an increasing commitment to the foreign operation by the company concerned, in order to reduce the psychic distance. The present knowledge and commitment is not only the result of previous operations, but also affects the perception of the opportunities and risks concerning the next expansion of business. Some empirical research made clear the nature of the knowledge accumulation, which is influenced by its duration (Eriksson et al., 1996), and is the first step towards the internationalisation (Eriksson and Majkgard, 1998). The longer an MNE operates abroad, the more 'experiential knowledge' it can obtain. Such knowledge itself affects the appreciation of the costs brought by internationalisation (Eriksson et al., 1997). Furthermore, the difference in the internationalisation strategy between client-following and market-seeking strategies is clearest at the early stage, but later becomes lost (Majkgard and Sharma, 1997). In the context of entry mode decision, the implication of the accumulated knowledge can change in the firm's internationalisation process.

Here, the foreign entry of an MNE should be considered from the perspective of the internationalisation process model summarised above. The selection of the entry mode by an MNE is likely to change from one stage to another in the process of its internationalisation. The importance of obtaining knowledge from a local firm through a joint venture or acquisition would decline in the later stage of the internationalisation process, when preference for greenfield investment would be greatest. The same can be applied to the case of uncertainty and risk. The choice of the entry mode might well be expected to shift towards greenfield investment. Empirical tests using the diversification variables do not always support this expectation, however. For example, Agarwal and Ramaswami (1992) do support it, while others like Hennart (1991) found the opposite result.

On the other hand, early entry influences the knowledge of the company, and affects the perception on the foreign operation in the following stage. The success of the entry could make the next one easier, while failure would lead the MNE to be more cautious in the next attempt (Padmanabhan and Cho, 1999). At the same time, the accumulated knowledge enables the MNE to control the subsidiaries more easily, and reduces the control costs of the acquisition. Therefore, a shift from greenfield investment to acquisition can be expected along with the internationalisation process (Caves and Mehra, 1986; Zejan, 1990). Similarly, Woodcock et al. (1994) confirm the superiority of greenfield investment over the other two alternatives, and the superiority of joint ventures over acquisitions. Thus, any assessment of the relationship between the internationalisation process and the choice of entry mode with regard to the cause and the result should be treated with caution.

In spite of scant research exclusively examining the entry mode in the auto or pharmaceutical industries, there are nevertheless some historical works, case studies and other material. The automotive MNEs started by exporting and moved to local production for serving foreign markets. At the beginning, the national distributors that imported and sold cars in the host country were, in general, local firms rather than the wholly-owned entities of MNEs. Success in this field might well produce a shift to full ownership (Wilkins and Hill, 1964; Mullineux, 1995). Johanson and Wiedersheim-Paul (1975) investigated the case of Volvo, whose manufacturing sites were established in countries that had sales subsidiaries. The entry mode, however, indicated a company preference even among American MNEs, at least in Europe. With respect to the entry of US car MNEs in the early days, Ford generally adopted a greenfield investment approach (Wilkins and Hill, 1964), while General Motors acquired the UK and German companies, Vauxhall and Opel, respectively (Sloan, 1965). Note that the same entry mode does not guarantee the same result even in the same country. For example, Peugeot still produces cars in the UK at the plant acquired from Chrysler in 1978, but the latter suffered a business failure at the plant bought from Rootes (Church, 1986, 1994). Further, Johanson and Wiedersheim-Paul (1975) investigated the change from full ownership of foreign production to a joint venture by Volvo in the 1970s.

On the other hand, the pharmaceutical industry also shows its own unique pattern of foreign entry. Macarthur (1991) discussed the preference for licensing-out to a local partner by Japanese pharmaceutical MNEs until the late 1980s, since when acquisitions and joint ventures have become more popular for entering the European market, but he does not analyse the reasons for the choice in depth. On the other hand, European and American drug MNEs entered the Japanese market mainly through joint ventures with Japanese companies. However, from the 1990s, foreign companies in Japan dissolved the ventures and became independent (*Yakuji*, various issues). Although the acquisition of Japanese firms by foreign companies is still rare,[10] the preference for full ownership can be recognised. Penner-Hahn's (1998) unique study of the internationalisation of basic research by Japanese pharmaceutical MNEs investigates not only the entry mode for foreign research, but also the development process. The results, however, do not confirm any systematic sequence of setting up the R&D facilities among sponsored, collaborative and fully-controlled facilities, especially for established firms whose main business is prescription drugs. In addition, the results indicate the different incentives for international R&D between established and new entrant firms, which conduct business mainly in the food or chemical sectors.

Finally, Yamawaki (1994) investigates the general pattern of Japanese MNEs' entry into Europe and the US. Concerning entry mode, companies generally preferred greenfield investment to acquisition or capital participation in both Europe and the US, although Yamawaki does not analyse the determining factors. Furthermore, he finds in both entry modes that FDI into Europe is mainly based on a horizontal strategy rather than diversification. The preference for greenfield investment for horizontal entry into Europe is echoed in Hennart (1991), which supports the opposite case, that is, a preference for joint ventures for diversification.

This section has summarised the choice of the three entry modes while paying special attention to the internationalisation process model. Various factors influence each entry mode differently, but the problem here is that their mutual comparison is quite difficult, even in a static situation. The dynamic perspective based on the internationalisation process model adds other complicated possibilities.

2.4   PAN-EUROPEAN MANAGEMENT

The appropriate decisions for the location and entry mode do not guarantee the success of the FDI. Management should contribute to the good conduct of the business in the host economy. How to manage the operation of subsidiaries, however, raises various questions. There are different types of business practices and systems around the world, as Whitley (1992) maintains, and an MNE always has to cope with the frictions and opportunities presented by these. A number of studies have been done in each aspect of management,[11] but this section will focus on the very nature of MNEs' own management.

Since MNEs allocate their assets in more than one country, the 'multinationality' of their own resources is a benefit that only MNEs but not domestic firms can enjoy. Kogut (1983) clearly explains the three benefits that MNEs exploit from multinationality. The first is obtained from arbitrage of the institutional differences among the countries. MNEs can reduce costs through the appropriate allocation of their resources in different governments' regulatory frameworks such as taxes and incentives. The second benefit comes from learning about informational externalities through the international business, while the final benefit can be derived from joint production in marketing and/or manufacturing.

Like Kogut, various scholars approach multinationality from different academic interests, although they do not always use the term of multinationality. For example, from intensive historical research, Wilkins (1974) explores the fact that American MNEs had already reached a situation of enjoying multinationality at a very high level until the 1960s. At the first stage which she refers to it as 'monocentric', the FDI is very simple, while the second stage sees a change to a 'polycentric' structure of the foreign business. The big US MNEs construct a 'conglomerate' organisation for the foreign operation, which must be controlled effectively. Dicken (1992b) presents a model of multinationality along with an organisation of the product units from the viewpoint of the economic geography. Figure 2.2 shows the development of multinationality based on the arguments of Wilkins and Dicken. From the viewpoint of multinationality, the foreign subsidiaries and affiliates are not a mere branch of the parent, but a substantial part of the organisation for constructing the sources of global competitiveness.

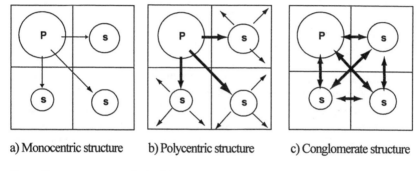

a) Monocentric structure   b) Polycentric structure   c) Conglomerate structure

Note: P: parent company, S: foreign subsidiaries. A vector depicts flows of capital, goods, services, information and so on.

Figure 2.2   Development of multinationality

In order to realise the benefits of multinationality, the crucial question for the MNE is how to manage the relationship between the parent and the subsidiaries, and that among the subsidiaries. Thus, the management of an MNE and its evolution have attracted academic interest. The classic work by Stopford and Wells (1972) found two courses for MNEs evolving from domestic companies to a global matrix grid structure, which is not necessarily reality but represents an ideal situation. One is to extend the product division, which is suitable for a company with a diversified product portfolio, and manage the subsidiaries along with the products of the MNE. The other is based on a regional division, which fits a company that depends on relatively few products, for conducting the foreign operation based on regionally divided areas of the world such as North America, Europe and so forth. Furthermore, it is suggested that neither of the two management types is permanent, but each is a transitional stage towards global matrix management.

Subsequently, Bartlett and Ghoshal (1989) investigated the different pattern of the parent–subsidiary relation, and suggested the ideal development of a future MNE. The present types are classified as the multinational, global and international corporations. The first has the most independent and autonomous subsidiaries, which give the MNE high adaptability to the local requirements. The subsidiaries of the second type, which is the most centralised, rely on an efficient parent. The third one retains its competitiveness by transferring the parent's knowledge and technology to the subsidiaries. The transnational corporation, which is the ideal for the future, should pursue all three objectives simultaneously, that is, flexible adaptability, global efficiency and knowledge transfer. Global integration and local uniqueness go hand in hand, and MNEs need to gain the benefit of multinationality by adapting their organisation and management.

The problem of how to manage an MNE can be addressed by considering the answers to unique questions being asked about the European situation. Europe is changing rapidly in terms of the market, regulatory and institutional environment, especially driven by European integration under the EU. Europe is a microcosm of the rapidly changing global economy. Does Europe give MNEs the opportunity to obtain the benefits of multinationality? If the answer is positive, how do MNEs realise the benefits of multinationality? The new trend of research in the 1990s is to answer these questions.

Stopford and Wells have been criticised for their insistence that regional management is not permanent, but transitional toward the global matrix grid structure. For example, Morrison and Roth (1992) suggest that there is a limit, when US MNEs, which possess subsidiaries with historically long experience and autonomy, pursue centralisation of operations. Rather, the regional solution enables them to utilise the capacity and resources of the subsidiaries. Morrison et al. (1991) and Hirst and Thompson (1999) also disagree with the discussion on globalisation. Under growing regional pressure from, for example, the SEM, US managers reassess the regional alternative. The regional strategy forces both the parent and the subsidiaries to resolve some challenges for restructuring the organisation, in which the division of roles, tasks and competences should be negotiated and changed between them. Blackwell et al. (1991) point out both the requirement for co-ordination and the danger of the one-size-fits-all approach. It is critically important for MNEs to maintain the balance of competence between the global and the local (Morris, 1991; Amin, 1993). At the same time, MNEs should bear in mind that the balance of competence is likely to be different from one function to another, between business units, and within the national organisation.

From this summary of the literature, it is evident that an MNE should also seek the benefit of multinationality at the regional level, rather than simply at the global level (Rugman, 2001). In fact, in order to manage the foreign operation, some MNEs have set up their regional headquarters on a geographic basis. Figure 2.3 is the revised structure of the 'conglomerate structure' shown in Figure 2.2 (c). This indicates that the regional headquarters has some competence and takes over the responsibility for the region from the parent, and the latter controls mainly the former rather than all of the national subsidiaries. To the extent that regional management is an appropriate resolution for MNEs, at least for the foreseeable future, the research interest serves to direct the organisational and managerial features of MNEs in Europe.

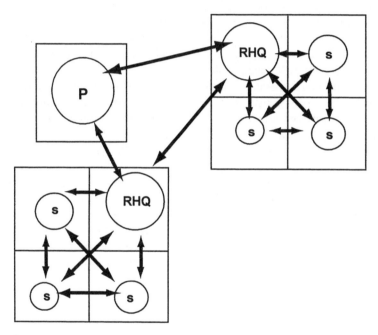

Note: P: parent company, RHQ: regional headquarters, S: foreign subsidiaries. A vector depicts flows of capital, goods, services, information and so on.

Figure 2.3   Multinationality at the regional level

Research on the European headquarters (EHQ) of firms reflects the academic interest concerning the management from the regional perspective. Researchers used to take US MNEs as the representative sample, but recently they have started to include Japanese cases. This is mainly because of the historical fact that US MNEs have already had long operating experience in

Europe, while Japanese MNEs are relative newcomers. Previous work raises some interesting issues. First, the reasons for establishing an EHQ are examined empirically. For example, in a comparative study Shutte (1997) analyses Japanese EHQs as well as the regional headquarters of European MNEs in Asia, and finds two common reasons for their establishment: the internal difficulty of management by the parent; and the external environment that makes MNEs understand the similarities in a certain region. Yasumuro (1992) also finds that Japanese MNEs establish an EHQ mainly because of the external environmental factor, that is, the EU's single market.

It has been found that the establishment of an EHQ leads to a reorganisation of the regional operation. According to the empirical study by Sullivan (1992) on US MNEs, the reasons for establishing an EHQ and the internal and external factors influence the organisation itself. Further, the organisation of MNEs should be constructed from a blend of formal and informal structures. However, the EHQ is not simply a microcosm of global management within a geographically limited area, according to Lehrer and Asakawa (1999). EHQs are not always given full competence from the parent company but some operations, such as basic research, are unbundled from the pan-European perspective operation. In other words, the importance of centrally directed co-ordination is high in upstream operations such as R&D, while it is low in downstream operations such as sales-related business. Thus, there is agreement on the importance of adjusting the organisation and management in the process of integrating the regional operations. The interactive design among centralisation, formalisation and enculturation is crucial for the organisation and its adaptation in the MNE (Sullivan, 1992; De Koning et al., 1996; Shutte, 1997).

The managerial objective of the EHQ is clear from the reasons for its establishment, that is, efficient management at the European level, whereas the findings on the organisation and its development indicate that efficient management is not the simple task of merely constructing a microcosm of the global operating structure within Europe. Rather, an EHQ has to actively find, nurture and redeploy the resources of the MNE in the context of its own global management (Lehrer and Asakawa, 1999). Furthermore, Japanese MNEs face human resource management issues due to the large difference between European and domestic conditions (Yasumuro, 1992), although this is also one of the most important questions for MNEs in general.

2.5   KEY QUESTIONS

The summary of the previous literature raises detailed questions concerning the main theme of this present book. Answering the questions would surely fill the gaps in the research. First, there is a tendency in the previous work to investigate cases concerning the US. This is a common feature of the three main themes, largely due to two reasons: the long history of outward and inward US FDI, and the availability of the most advanced data. It is safe to say that Japanese FDI into Europe is still a relatively uncultivated area for academic assessment. Some pioneer works have been mentioned, but they are generally not as comprehensive as those on FDI by or into the US. Therefore, it is important to confirm the situation of Japanese FDI into Europe with respect to the three themes in this book.

Second, the existing research tends to focus on production facilities, and pays little explicit attention to the non-manufacturing activities of manufacturing MNEs. However, the present activities of these MNEs range from local production to other areas, that is, the sales-related operations including logistics, R&D and, of course, the regional headquarters. Some research has already addressed non-manufacturing activities such as R&D, as mentioned above (Pearce, 1997; Peters, 1998),[12] but it is still true that the present method of analysing the location and the entry mode of the non-manufacturing facilities falls far behind the conventional approach to the manufacturing sites. Thus, non-manufacturing facilities, as well as production sites should be investigated, and this approach will be taken in this book to examine the location and the entry mode.

The third point concerns an analysis of the factors that determine the decisions concerning the location, the entry mode and the establishment of the EHQ. The analysis regarding the location will be done in two stages, by examining first, whether Japanese FDI follows the predictions of some theories emphasising the supply-side conditions, and second, the actual reasons for the location by Japanese MNEs. The extension of the Vernon-Kojima approach may suggest that the FDI into the EU would be directed to less-developed member states as an export centre. In reality, the early research expected that Japanese FDI would increase in the comparatively disadvantaged sectors like chemicals to less-developed member states in the EU, such as Ireland and those in southern Europe (Sekiguchi, 1979; Darby, 1996). On the other hand, the new international trade theory suggests the agglomeration of Japanese FDI into the core of industry in the EU. If such tendencies cannot be found, then it is likely that more complicated conditions are influencing the decisions on the location, as the eclectic paradigm suggests. Even if the predicted phenomenon occurred, the reasons for its occurrence will be thoroughly investigated.

Regarding the entry mode, the various factors may well have an influence, but the empirical tests are contradictory. This is partly because some industry- and/or company-specific factors affect the decision making. This investigation will look at the entry mode at the company level, so that the determinant factors can be examined in more depth. Then, the question whether the industry- and/or company-specific factors show some commonality will be addressed. Furthermore, the analysis will pay attention to the context in which the determinant factors affect the decision making. The internationalisation process model suggests that the accumulation of 'knowledge' in the company concerned is the important context. Most of the literature summarised above, however, looks at the factors at a certain point in time. Thus, the entry mode will be explicitly considered in a time series. Again, the point to be remembered here is that the locational factors are changing, as well as the companies. This is especially true and important for analysis of the entry mode into Europe due to European integration. Therefore, both the determinant factors concerning MNEs' internationalisation process, and the changing environmental conditions of the host economy in a time series of the EU will be analysed.

As to management at the European level, the actual operation of the EHQ will be examined in detail. Recognising the importance of regional management and the establishment of the EHQ requires a suitable operation from a pan-European point of view, rather than operations from a national subsidiary or from the parent in Japan. The particular business area, and how the EHQ co-ordinates with its business partners in Europe will also be investigated. Here, the important but missed point in the previous literature is the co-ordination with non-equity partners. Since the entire business and geographic area is not fully covered by their own subsidiaries, the co-ordination of MNEs with the non-equity business partners as well as within the company group will be examined. At the same time, it is crucial to point out the problems created by the establishment and operation of the EHQ, and their solutions. Even if an awareness of the importance of the region leads to the establishment of the EHQ, this does not automatically guarantee better management than before. Indeed, some research surveyed in the last section reports the significance of the process of integrating the national management into the European body. However, it is likely that there will be various obstacles to pan-European management. Successful management in Europe needs more than the establishment of an EHQ, but most literature fails to consider this point. Thus, the problems faced by the EHQ and how it resolves them will be analysed.

The questions concerning the three main themes will be investigated in depth in the following chapters. This naturally requires a suitable methodology, which will be explained in the next chapter.

NOTES

1. In his more recent work, Dunning called the model a 'paradigm' rather than a theory.
2. Porter's Diamond is generally used to consider the national competitiveness of the home economy regarding not only trade, but also the FDI. For example, Jones (1993) uses Porter's Diamond to explore the home-country basis of multinational banks.
3. The Vernon-Kojima approach also follows in the same line of this argument.
4. Hill and Munday (1992) also confirm that the size of the local economy does not affect the regional distribution of the inward FDI into the UK.
5. This point is repeated in the EU reports on the impact of integration. See Cecchini (1988), Emerson (1992) and European Commission (1996).
6. Indeed, serving foreign markets includes licensing-out, export and FDI. Exports and licensing will be examined in the section on the investigation of Japanese MNEs, since both of these are sometimes closely related with the FDI into Europe. Concerning the selection among exports, licensing and FDI, the eclectic paradigm of Dunning (1988, 1993) provides useful insight.
7. The internalisation theory was first proposed by Coase (1937), and developed further by Williamson (1975, 1985). Some scholars (Buckley and Casson, 1976; Rugman, 1981; Hennart, 1982; Caves, 1996) apply it to the FDI theory.
8. The main interest is not necessarily the entry mode, but the organisation; however, see Stopford and Wells (1972) and Casson (1990).
9. The internationalisation process model is the expansion of the theory of the growth of a firm to the international dimension. Concerning the theory of the growth of a firm, see Penrose (1959).
10. There are a few cases of main Japanese pharmaceutical companies being acquired by foreign ones: full acquisition of Banyu by Merck in 1984; 35.88 per cent share of SS Seiyaku by Boehringer Ingelheim in 2000; and Chugai by Roche in 2001. On Banyu, see Giga et al. (1996); on SS Seiyaku, see Jihou (2000). Roche agreed to acquire Chugai, the tenth largest Japanese pharmaceutical company, at the end of 2001 (*Financial Times*, 11 December 2001).
11. Some important issues and research results are the transfer of the production method (Kenney and Florida, 1993), human resource management (Tung, 1990) and the impacts of cultural factors (Mead, 1998).
12. For the opposite case of FDI from the non-manufacturing to the manufacturing sector, see, for example, Hennart and Kryda (1998).

3. Methodology

3.1 INTRODUCTION

In order to investigate the main themes by answering the questions raised in the last chapter, the Japanese auto and pharmaceutical MNEs will be compared. This chapter explains the methodology for our research. Each of the three themes, that is, the location, the entry mode and management from a pan-European perspective is addressed. It is important to understand the strategy and management of Japanese MNEs chasing a moving target – Europe in the process of regional integration. It is not appropriate to analyse them independently, but to bear in mind the mutual relationships. Furthermore, the focus is not limited to the manufacturing sites, but is directed at all facilities of Japanese MNEs in Europe. This theme setting inevitably requires a suitable methodology, including data collection. At the same time, the method itself provides the uniqueness of this book. Thus, the research methodology will be explained in detail.

This chapter is structured as follows. The next section illustrates the reasons why the auto and the pharmaceutical MNEs were chosen for the comparative case studies (3.2). The explanation for the selection of the MNEs concerned will be given in the third section (3.3). The last section describes the unique approach to collecting the data and information adopted for this book (3.4).

3.2 COMPARISON OF THE CASE STUDIES OF TWO INDUSTRIES

First, case studies at the company level are inevitably required for our research interest, mainly because the aggregate data cannot fully resolve the themes of this book. Although the aggregate data of Japanese MNEs' facilities in Europe are available from various sources, such as the Japanese MOF, JETRO and so forth, they are inappropriate for considering the mutual relationships both among the facilities of a certain MNE and among the three key themes. For example, some MNEs possess all facilities from R&D, manufacturing, sales and marketing to the regional headquarters, while others have only some of them. The timing, the order and the location of the investment in Europe can differ from one MNE to another. Such differences are deeply based on the strategy and the decision making of the MNE in question, and influence the management in Europe. Aggregating the data at the industry or the macro-economy level, however, makes the differences less clear cut. Thus, the company-level analysis is quite crucial for our research.

Comparative analysis is very useful in answering the questions raised by our themes. The differences among the cases help to clarify the factors influencing the decision making of MNEs, while the similarities beyond the industries enable us to understand the fundamentally important factors involved in European FDI. The case studies of the automobile and the pharmaceutical MNEs enable us to clarify the differences and similarities in the European strategies and operation of Japanese MNEs more than any other two industries. This is mainly because of their different position in the world economy.

It is well known that the Japanese automobile industry has been leading the change from mass production to flexible production system since the 1970s (Altshuler et al., 1984; Womack et al., 1990). Japanese auto MNEs could have increased exports using a flexible production system, but that had led to protectionism in the US and Europe. Consequently, from the 1980s, Japanese auto MNEs started to invest, so that they could avoid the pressure of protectionism. In this process, it became clear that the flexible production system was transferable from Japanese soil. US and European competitors have also worked hard to introduce, adapt and further improve the flexible production system. Consequently, the competitive edge of Japanese auto MNEs is no longer incontestable. Rather, most Japanese automobile companies need a capital injection from US and European competitors.[1] Competition with local companies is fiercer in Europe than in the US, as the difference in the market share of Japanese manufacturers suggests. Japanese cars enjoyed 11.4 per cent and 35.3 per cent of the market share of new car registrations in Western Europe and the US, respectively, in 2002 (SMMT, 2003).

In contrast, the Japanese pharmaceutical industry is positioned in the completely opposite situation from the motor vehicle industry. Pharmaceutical imports by Japan were ¥713 billion in 2001, largely exceeding exports worth ¥331 billion (Jihou, 2003, p. 156), although the trade gap has narrowed. However, the balance of licensing-in and -out has shown improvement during the last two decades. The number of license-out agreements with foreign companies has exceeded that of license-in since 1980, and the balance of royalty fees has remained near equilibrium since 1985. Indeed, it turned black for the second half of the 1990s (Jihou, 2003; JPMA, 2003). Some research has suggested that the Japanese pharmaceutical industry could become a global player (Reich, 1990), but an innovative capacity for inventing new drugs is the key factor in turning such a possibility into reality.[2] At the beginning of the 1990s, only a limited number of Japanese companies had such potential (Sapienza, 1993). At the same time, Japanese pharmaceutical companies have been excluded from the global consolidation. In the 1990s, US and European pharmaceutical firms pursued mergers and acquisitions of competitors in and out of their own countries. Japanese firms, however, had been excluded from this global trend of mega-mergers among the drug companies in the 1990s. Two exceptional cases are SS Seiyaku and Chugai, which were respectively acquired by Boehringer Ingelheim in 2000, and by Roche in 2001. Thus, the Japanese pharmaceutical industry has not played a leading role, but rather has been marginal and passive on the world stage.

The selection of these two industries for the comparative case studies provides some additional benefits for the main themes, since the Japanese pharmaceutical industry is a comparatively disadvantaged sector. FDI from a comparatively disadvantaged sector is generally little investigated in the literature. This is mainly because competitive superiority against the indigenous firms in the host country is assumed as a premise.[3] Reflecting this, the analysis on Japanese FDI tends to look at competitive sectors such as the auto, and the electrical and electronic equipment industries. This is also true in the case of Europe. The previous research has emphasised the importance of both the pressure of protectionism and the growth enhancement effects of EU integration, especially under the SEM programme (UN, 1993; Clegg and Scott-Green, 1999). However, previous literature has ignored certain significant factors. Some sectors of Japanese industry have never faced protectionist pressure from Europe, but have increased their FDI. The pharmaceutical companies are a typical example, and they will be analysed in comparison with others that have already been examined. Macarthur (1991) and Kanavos (1996) investigated Japanese pharmaceutical FDI into Europe, but both of them emphasise the domestic factors in Japan, and there is little analysis of the locational advantages that Europe provides for Japanese pharmaceutical MNEs. The findings of this present book through a comparison with the auto MNEs should also help to plug this gap.

In addition, the analysis of the auto and pharmaceutical MNEs is useful for the purpose of examining strategy and operation. Both of these industries provide their products to final consumers, but are influenced the least by other industries. Therefore, they can independently set their own strategy. On the other hand, for industries supplying intermediate goods to other industries, 'following the customers' is one of the most influential factors for decision making regarding FDI. For example, Sachwald (1995b) examines some cases of Japanese chemical companies that invested in Europe based on the follow the customer strategy. In such cases, the FDI is the dependent variable of the customer's decision, rather than the result of its own decision making. Even if the auto and pharmaceutical MNEs are interested in their final customers in Europe, their decision making is less affected by other industries. In other words, these two industries are suitable for examining the strategy and management of Japanese MNEs, with regard to their own decision making.

The comparative case studies of Japanese car and pharmaceutical MNEs will elucidate their strategy and operation in Europe. This is because of the clear difference of their positions both in the world market and towards Europe, and their relative independence from other industries. The next section describes the companies selected from these two industries.

3.3   SELECTION OF THE COMPANIES ANALYSED

This book analyses three companies, Honda, Nissan and Toyota, from the auto industry, and four MNEs, Fujisawa, Sankyo, Takeda and Yamanouchi, from the pharmaceutical industry. This section clarifies why they were chosen, and the advantages and disadvantages of an analysis of this relatively small number of companies.

The selection is based on the length and depth of the companies' involvement in Europe in each industry. There are eight motor companies producing passenger cars, and three companies that specialise in commercial vehicle assembling in Japan. Those selected are the top three in Europe among the eight passenger car producers, although the market share of each producer is still relatively low. For example, Toyota, with the top market share among Japanese cars, had a 4.4 per cent share in Western Europe in 2002, while Nissan had 2.5 per cent in 2002, down from 3.8 per cent at its peak in 1993 (SMMT, various issues). In addition, all three are deeply committed to the European market not only through local production, but also through other facilities besides manufacturing.

The other companies were not selected, because of their limited operations in Europe. The next two largest automobile companies, Mazda and Mitsubishi, are excluded from the analysis. Mazda has been under capital participation by Ford, the US company, from 1979, and that has made it difficult for Mazda to pursue its own strategy in Europe. Indeed, some of the Mazda badged cars in Europe are supplied from the local Ford factory. In contrast, Mitsubishi had been independent until 2000, when it received a capital injection from DaimlerChrysler, a German–US company. In 1991, Mitsubishi set up a joint-venture car production programme with Volvo, the Swedish company,[4] in the Netherlands, and assembly began in 1995. The activities of Mitsubishi in Europe, however, are limited to this joint venture.

Thus, it was also excluded from the analysis.

With regard to the pharmaceutical industry, four MNEs will be examined to address the main themes. This industry is much less concentrated than the auto industry. There are the 'big' 14 and the 'middle' 18 companies for prescription drugs, but they are much smaller than the global top 10 companies. For example, Pfizer's turnover is $26.6 billion, more than three times larger than the sales of Takeda, the biggest drug company in Japan, with $7.85 billion in sales in 2001 (Scrip, 2003, pp. 48, 223). In spite of fluctuations in sales that are faster and bigger than in any other industry due to the commodity-specific nature of medicine, four companies had more than ¥100 billion foreign turnover in 1998, and these are the selected companies for this study. Eisai follows the four, but its turnover was only about ¥70 billion, and its main European operation actually started from the mid-1990s with a relatively small stake, the university laboratory in University College London. Furthermore, the four companies have their own development facilities, and sales subsidiaries in Europe, as well as in the US. Others are still at the stage of focusing on the US market more than on Europe. Thus, Fujisawa, Sankyo, Takeda and Yamanouchi are the four companies that will be investigated.

The limited number of companies examined enables a more detailed analysis to be made. Since the necessary data and information are not always available from public sources, they were collected from each company, and included a series of interviews. That makes the research unique, but at the same time it is a time-consuming method, which will be explained further in the next section. The problem of using public source material can be explained by some examples. The Directory of Toyo Keizai is the most often used data source of Japanese MNEs. It lists three subsidiaries of Yamanouchi in Europe, but, according to this investigation, the actual number is 19, even excluding the holding company. JETRO has surveyed the operation of Japanese manufacturing companies in Europe from the early 1980s, but it tends to look at the production side. The non-manufacturing aspects of manufacturing companies are no less important than production, and therefore an examination of the entire operation is required. Thus, the JETRO survey is insufficient. In addition, the differences among companies in the same industry cannot be distinguished from the aggregated data. Therefore, the company-level comparison is the strongest point of this present study.

However, we should also be aware of the constraints on this approach. In order to conduct a precise investigation at the company level, we are looking at just seven companies. This is a relatively small number of samples, and might well be the cause of bias because it is influenced heavily by the findings from one or two MNEs. For example, the share of the food sector in Japanese FDI to Europe increased from 2.0 per cent in 1998 to 74.1 per cent in 1999 because of the acquisition of the tobacco business from the Nabisco group by Japan Tobacco. Comparative study at the company level can make clear the differences as well as the similarities, but it may not be possible to generalise our findings due to the possibility of such bias. It should be emphasised that it is difficult to establish a general model using only a few samples. Nevertheless, a precise examination of the research themes enables an assessment of the strategy and operation of MNEs towards the regionally integrated economy. In other words, the deeper understanding gained from a small number of case studies can be a strong basis for academic development in the future, as Eisenhardt (1989) maintains, even if this has some limitations for generalisation.

The most advanced MNEs regarding European business were selected from Japanese car and pharmaceutical industries and that has its own advantages and disadvantages for the analysis, compared with the aggregate data analysis. These points will be borne in mind during the research.

3.4   DATA AND INFORMATION

The intention to examine the central themes at the company level requires the adoption of a suitable method for data and information collection. Most of the original data and information used in this book were collected directly from the companies themselves: through a series of interviews and examination of the publications of the companies concerned. At the same time, secondary sources are not ignored, but are rather used to confirm and supplement the original data. This section explains the method used for gathering the original data, which also constitutes the originality of the research.

Concerning the first original data item, the author conducted a series of interviews at the seven companies between 1997 and 2003. These interviews were conducted with personnel not only at the subsidiaries in Europe, but also at the parent offices in Japan. Because of confidentiality, the names of the interviewees cannot be listed. Those responding to the request for an interview are from the middle and top levels of the companies. In some cases, presidents of the European headquarters welcomed a personal interview to discuss European strategy and management. In other cases, the interviewees provided the follow-up information by letter or e-mail.

The interviews were not limited to the seven MNEs, but included related third parties. The UK subsidiary of an American company responded to an interview request. Officials of the trade unions of some UK factories and the central offices of two British trade unions were also interviewed. They gave their assessment of the situation and described the historical relations with

Japanese MNEs in general, and the car MNEs in particular. Personnel at the European office of the Japanese Automotive Manufacturers Association in Brussels also explained the historical development of Japanese car companies in Europe. The London office of JETRO, the Japanese Ministry of Health and Welfare (MHW), the industry association of Japanese pharmaceutical manufacturers, and European Business Community in Japan also provided much useful information on the Japanese and global pharmaceutical industry. Without these interviews, the assessment of Japanese MNEs may have been biased towards the company's point of view. In other words, the interviews other than those with personnel at the seven MNEs were helpful in evaluating the MNEs as neutrally as possible.

The interviews were conducted on the basis of open-ended questions, rather than a questionnaire style. The latter would be better for statistical analysis, but that is not always appropriate with respect to the research themes. The emphasis is on the decision making and the affecting factors, which are likely to be both different and similar from one industry to another, from one company to another, and from one point in time to another. At each interview, the interviewer, that is, this author, asked general questions concerning the three main themes, let the interviewee answer such general questions, and, if necessary, confirmed the details of the response. Even though each interview had been carefully prepared, there were some important instances where the interview turned in an unexpected direction. In most cases, this helped the interviewer to understand the European strategy and operation of, and the environment for, the MNE in question, and positively extended the perspective for interviews on subsequent occasions, or with other companies.

The merits and demerits of the series of interviews are that most of the interviewees were Japanese, both in Europe and in Japan. As a Japanese, himself, the interviewer was given more opportunities to interview Japanese companies than foreign companies. [5] The communication between the interviewee(s) and the interviewer was quite smooth, since there was no language problem. It is impossible to judge, however, whether the interviews with Japanese staff are biased to the company position or the preference of the parent office, unless interviews with non-Japanese individuals are also conducted. It is necessary to bear this in mind, when considering the implication of the interviews. Where possible, confirmation of the statements made in interviews was obtained using information from other sources, such as newspapers, magazines and interviews with others.

Another primary information source was the publications of the MNEs themselves. These include annual reports, subsidiary brochures, in-house journals, internet home pages and so on. Some of these are produced for the purpose of public relations, others are for the employees within the company and the company group. They are useful for clarifying the company situation. The annual reports do not always directly provide the information concerning the research themes. However, following a series of annual reports makes it possible to establish the turning point of the business. At the same time, the published materials helped to clarify the questions asked in the interviews. For example, the ownership structure did not always reflect the management structure, and that led the interviewer to ask about the method for managing the subsidiaries.

The weaknesses of these kinds of published materials are their availability and reliability. The public relations materials are relatively easy to obtain, either from the company directly or through access to the internet home page. However, they tend to emphasise the positive and favourable aspects of the company; unfavourable information is often omitted from such publications. In addition, the data and information are not always up to date. The number of employees in one European subsidiary of a company varies from one publication to another, even though these may be published in the same year. On the other hand, the in-house materials are more reliable with regard to accuracy, since they are often used for or based on managerial decision making. Because of their importance, however, availability is limited. Some companies provide such information, but considerations of confidentiality prevented direct quotations. Nevertheless, they are very useful sources for understanding the strategy of the company concerned.

The primary source material was collected for the purpose of addressing the main research themes, but it has certain limitations. Therefore, data and information from newspapers, industrial magazines and semi-published materials such as research reports of public organisations, as well as statistics from public and semi-public sources were also used. Indeed, it is undeniable that these also have their own constraints, but the primary and secondary source material can complement each other.

Finally, the data and information used in this book also determine the nature of the analysis as being qualitative rather than quantitative. The sources varied depending upon the information, due to the collecting method, while the data was not always obtained in a comparable form. As a result, the analysis is qualitative, rather than an attempt to judge the statistical significance of the hypothesis. However, it is hoped that this book will make a serious contribution from the methodological point of view.[6]

NOTES

1. Only Toyota and Honda among 11 Japanese car companies have no capital injection from foreign companies, except for Daihatsu and Hino, which are members of the Toyota group.
2. Reis-Arnd (1987) shows an increase in Japanese-origin new drugs, but these tended to be 'me-too' drugs, rather than innovative ones.

3. This seems to be a kind of tradition of FDI theory stemming from the seminal work of Hymer (1976), who first identified on the difference between FDI and international portfolio investment as the emphasis on control over the competitive advantages of the company in question.
4. The passenger car division of Volvo was acquired by Ford, and now it is a subsidiary of the US car MNE.
5. Ford UK and Germany, and Opel, the German subsidiary of GM, declined the request for an interview with the author.
6. Miles and Huberman (1994) strongly and persuasively point out the significance of qualitative data analysis.

4. Preliminary Comparison between Automobile and Pharmaceutical Industries

4.1 INTRODUCTION

The main themes to be addressed have now been established, and the methodology for the investigation explained. Chapters 5 to 7 will analyse each of the three themes in turn. Before undertaking that task, this chapter will outline the background for Japanese MNEs operating in Europe. No company is free from industry-specific features when establishing strategy and conducting operations in Europe, and Japanese MNEs are no exception. Japanese car and pharmaceutical industries are in quite opposite positions in the global market. More general differences between them, however, can be distinguished at the industry level. However, environmental factors are also significant for the decision making of MNEs. This is the major concern of this present book, represented by the advance of European integration under the EU. Furthermore, the company profile affects the European strategy and management of the company concerned.

This chapter is structured as follows: first, the general character of both the auto and drug industries is outlined (4.2); second, the development of the EU in these two industrial sectors is followed (4.3); and third, a general description of each MNE is given (4.4).

4.2 GENERAL CHARACTER OF THE INDUSTRIES

Since both the manufacturing and non-manufacturing facilities of Japanese car and drug MNEs in Europe will be investigated, it is convenient to begin by looking at the relationships among the main business activities in each industry, including research and development (R&D), production and sales-related business (Porter, 1985; Dicken, 1998). Each industrial sector has its own priority among the three, with a different emphasis from one industry to another, due to industry-specific factors including technological elements. The priority among the three naturally affects the strategy of MNEs, even if none of them can influence strategy independently from the others' considerations. At the same time, good mutual relationships among the three have to be maintained. Therefore, in order to understand their strategy, the general character of the auto and pharmaceutical industries will be examined from this perspective.

4.2.1 Automobile Sector[1]

The automobile sector was one of the leading industries of the twentieth century, from the aspect of production, as well as with regard to the impact on people's lives. When Ford introduced mass production of the 'Model T' in the early part of the century, sales increased substantially and the production process was seen as the most important factor for a motor company with respect to competition. The mass production system could dramatically reduce production costs through economies of scale. As a result, most of the small companies were swept away, and the industry became more concentrated. In the US, the so-called 'Big Three' remained, while each large country in Europe possesses one or two national champions (Chandler, 1990). Even if Japan seems to be the exceptional case, with eight independent passenger car producers until the late 1990s, the number of manufacturers still shows a high concentration.

Not only is the production process important, its transformation has more significant implications for the industry. It is well known that mass production faced severe competition from the late 1970s from a new production system in Japan, referred to here as the 'flexible production system'. Its main feature is to manufacture a greater number of different models of cars, with fewer units of each, at a lower cost and in a shorter time than with the mass production system. Many factors underlie the flexible production system, such as the introduction of robots, just-in-time parts and components delivery, and so on. The most fundamental factor, however, is to involve all related parties, from the factory workers to the suppliers, in the efficiency and quality improvement activities. This seems an easy task, since all concerned parties are heavily influenced by the performance of the assembler. However, mass production could not appreciate this, or even imagine such co-operative involvement of workers and suppliers (Altshuler et al., 1984; Womack et al., 1990).

The flexible production system originated in Japan, but has expanded all over the world with further development. Because of its competitive advantage, flexible production has replaced mass production in two ways. First, both US and European carmakers have intensively tried to introduce flexible production in their own factories (Starkey and McKinlay, 1993; Fridenson, 1995; Musso 1995). Even if the introduction process is not easy due to the necessity of changing the traditional manufacturing method, including labour management, failure would mean the closure of the plant or bankruptcy. Therefore the success of the introduction is a question of survival. The other route is through Japanese companies that transplant the flexible production system through FDI of their own (Wickens, 1987; Garrahan and Stewart, 1992; Kenney and Florida, 1993; Mair, 1994).

Further changes of the production system can be seen mainly in Europe in the 1990s, when the common platform production system was introduced. This aims to produce a greater number of different models with economies of scale and scope. With the common platform production system, the basic engineering structure, that is, the platform, is constructed using the same type of engine and chassis, thus reducing the development costs per car. What the final consumers recognise as differences, such as the body, the internal equipment and accessories and so forth, however, should be differentiated to provide more models from the single type of platform. The combination of the introduction of the flexible production system and the development of the common platform production system has enhanced European and US manufacturers and made competition more severe, especially in Europe. Because of the improvement of automobile producers in Europe, including US MNEs, Japanese car exports to Europe in the 1990s did not show as dramatic an increase as expected at the beginning of the decade. The market share of Japanese cars including the local production in Western Europe was 10.8 per cent in 1989, 11.8 per cent in 1998 and 10.4 per cent in 2001 (SMMT, various issues).

Along with the production process, both R&D and sales-related business also have their own character and significance. R&D is generally important for both production, and sales and marketing. This is because the car should be designed to be easily produced, while the products must appeal to the customers. Because of the size of the industry, the transport equipment sector spends most on R&D among all industries. For example, the UK Department of Trade and Industry (DTI) (1999) reports that the automotive sector spent £26 billion sterling, and accounted for 17.0 per cent of the world's top 300 companies in 1998. But the share of R&D to turnover was 4.3 per cent, which was less than the entire industry average of 4.9 per cent.

R&D is divided further into two stages: that is, the basic model development and the adjustment process to market requirements. The former includes basic research for new technology, which has become increasingly important due to the restraints of environmental and other regulations, and is one of the reasons for the consolidation in the auto industry from the late 1990s. It also includes the development of new cars, which cannot be changed easily once they are on the market.

On the other hand, the basic model of a car can and should be partly modified in order to fill the requirements of the market where it is introduced. Such modification would also be conducted in R&D, but it is really part of the second stage, the adjustment process. Obviously the basic development process is significant, but the difference between the home and foreign markets also makes the adjustment process crucially important. Production abroad could not reduce the load for the adjustment. Since not all the parts and components can be produced in the factory of the assembler, some of them have to be purchased locally. However, there is no guarantee that the company would be able to procure parts and components to the same standards as those in the home market. The difficulty of procurement in the host economy is partly caused by the incapability of the suppliers (MILAN, 1992; NEDO, 1993; Foley et al., 1996). Therefore, the production itself should be modified to local conditions. So the second stage of R&D is also needed from the manufacturing side.

Industry analysis does not always pay special attention to sales-related operations, but these do have some unique features. One of these is the high cost structure. One report suggests that the post-factory cost, including the margin, is 31 per cent of the showroom price, which is almost the same as the cost of the components (30 per cent) and much higher than the labour cost in the manufacturing process (20 per cent) (Mullineux, 1995, p. 11). This can vary from one company to another, but suggests the importance of the sales-related operation. Another feature is the diversification of the market conditions between countries, which is caused by different regulations and the different taste and preferences of customers. Because a car is one of the most expensive items that ordinary people will buy, the requirements of consumers are quite high. Some of these can be satisfied through the product itself, but others are services provided during and after the sale. The latter could heavily influence any future purchase decision.

4.2.2   Pharmaceutical Sector[2]

Because of the nature of the products, the pharmaceutical industry is the most R&D-intensive sector of all industries. The competitiveness of drug companies depends on the capacity to provide medicines with more efficacy and/or fewer side effects than existing products on the market. Without such drugs, no pharmaceutical company can enter the market by itself or survive over the medium and long terms (US Department of Commerce, 1986). At the same time, since the use of drugs is directly related to human health and life, safety is the highest requirement for marketing.

The R&D intensity of the pharmaceutical industry can easily be recognised from R&D expenditure. According to the 1999 ranking by the DTI (1999), the total R&D expenditure of 35 international pharmaceutical companies was £ 19.9 billion sterling, the third biggest among the 21 sectors of the DTI classification after information technology hardware and transport equipment.

The intensity ratio of R&D expenditures to sales shows the importance of R&D for the pharmaceutical industry, whose ratio is 13.5 per cent, the highest among all sectors. Thus, it can be said that drug companies allocate their own resources to R&D the most, and give priority to R&D above all else.

The R&D of the pharmaceutical industry can be divided into two parts: pre-clinical research and clinical tests. The former is the process before tests with human subjects are begun. Basic research involves a wide range of activities, from identifying the mechanism of a disease to synthesising thousands of potential chemical entities for a new medicine to conducting animal tests. It is expected that genome science will facilitate the discovery of appropriate chemical agents from fundamental disease mechanisms in the future, but basic research is still a complicated and time-consuming process. It takes two to three years for the chemical synthesising and screening, while the pre-clinical tests require three to five years. It is said that only five chemical entities from 5,000 to 10,000 candidates will pass through the above process and enter clinical tests (JPMA, 2003, p. 75).

Clinical research is also a significant time-consuming and costly process, which is subject to a number of clinical tests. In Phase I, the potential chemical agent for a new drug is tested by a small number of healthy people to judge whether it is safe for human beings. Phase II tests the drug on actual patients of the disease in question. The purpose at this stage is to check safety and efficacy, and to decide the dosage. The chemical agents that pass these two steps can enter Phase III, in which large sample tests are conducted with a wide variety of patients. During the tests, the pharmaceutical company concerned collects and collates the data, which is used for the application to. the central authority for marketing approval. The potential drug is compared with the existing drugs in the market for efficacy and side-effects. This takes between three and seven years, and the survival ratio in the clinical tests is one fifth. As a result, only one from the potential 5,000 to 10,000 chemical entities at the beginning of the R&D process will be approved by the central authority (ibid.). In addition, data concerning the medicine in question must be collected after the start of the sales. This is Phase IIIb or Phase IV, and requires the company to confirm the efficacy and safety with the actual treatment for the patients.

There are three further issues concerning the R&D of the pharmaceutical industry. First, due to the nature of the products, the applicability of one R&D result is quite low in the R&D for another new drug. Each chemical entity has to be checked at each stage, and a great deal of data is accumulated. Since the data are closely connected with each chemical entity, one data set for a particular chemical entity cannot be used for another. The mutual relationships between the R&D projects are much weaker than in other industries. In contrast, the auto industry shows an example of high R&D interchangeability in the common platform production system. A platform developed for a certain model can and should be the basis for another model, and that assumes close relationships between new car development projects. This is clearly quite different from the R&D for a new medicine. As a result, R&D in the pharmaceutical industry has an all-or-nothing nature, especially in the downstream process.

Another issue concerns patent protection for a new medicine. Because of its highly scientific chemical nature, a pharmaceutical product can easily be copied at little cost, and it is impossible to differentiate the original from the copy. Such a commodity has to be protected by patent. The patent becomes effective from the date of filing, however, not from the date of marketing the new medicine. This means that the R&D period, which has uncertainties, must be included in the patent protection period, even though the R&D in the pharmaceutical industry is very time consuming. A one-day delay in R&D may well result in a huge loss of sales of the particular drug. Thus, R&D is also a race against time (US Department of Commerce, 1986).

The final point to be added in the context of R&D in the pharmaceutical industry is the contract research organisation (CRO). A CRO is an independent party that conducts research for others under conditions based on a contract agreed beforehand. CROs are the result of the context of the development of outsourcing the R&D (Ringe, 1992; Howells, 1997). The CROs in the pharmaceutical industry mainly carry out the clinical tests on behalf of the research-based drug companies. Outsourcing the clinical tests to the CRO became popular from the early 1970s in the US and Europe (Spilker, 1994).[3] On the other hand, the CRO is quite a recent phenomenon in Japan, although expanding very rapidly (Jihou, 2003).

The production process of medicines is relatively less important than R&D, but has some unique features (Howells and Neary, 1995). The process is roughly divided into two stages. The first stage is to produce the chemical entity for a medicine, while the second stage is to formulate the chemical entity into the final form. The former, which is referred to as bulk production, is a more complicated process, and technologically more demanding than the latter. There are typically three types of bulk production: fermentation, synthetic organic chemicals and manufacturing from natural sources such as animals and/or vegetables. The selection of the production method depends on the medicine itself, and that has already been determined by the R&D. In the auto sector, it is possible for the production department to ask the R&D department to take into account the ease of manufacturing. However, in the pharmaceutical industry, it would be unimaginable to make such a request. On the other hand, the second stage of the production process requires less technology intensity due to the relatively simple process. There are different requirements for packaging among countries, but that has also already been decided through the marketing application to the central authority. Thus, while the production process in the pharmaceutical industry is important, nevertheless it is fair to give it less significance than the R&D.

Sales and marketing presents its own unique features in the pharmaceutical industry: the division among final consumers, the individuals who make the purchasing decision, and the bearers of the costs. The final consumers of a drug are the patients who generally are without any special knowledge about the goods they consume, and they do not decide which medicine should be taken. Rather, doctors and physicians prescribe drugs based on medical judgement. The crucial issues are the efficacy, the possible side-effects and the ease of the dosage. Since doctors and physicians are not always familiar with the information concerning all drugs, the situation needs to be reviewed constantly. Pharmaceutical companies conduct sales and marketing activities through a sales force specialised in promoting the company's own medicine to doctors and physicians, and comparing the medicines with others that are available. Because of the division between the final consumers and the decision makers of the purchase, these medical representatives (MRs) direct their sales activities towards the latter (Corstjens, 1991).

The second unique characteristic in the pharmaceutical industry is the price setting and the division between the final consumers and the payers. Unlike other industries, the price of a prescription drug is set in advance by the governments in Europe and Japan, at the time when the pharmaceutical company introduces the medicine. Once it is decided, there is little room for negotiation over the price at any stage, though there is a downward pressure of the price due to the national budget constraints in developed countries except for the US. The price of the same medicine can be different from one country to another, however, due to differences in the healthcare systems. At the same time, consumers do not pay for the drug, but the cost is borne by the national healthcare system or the insurance companies.

From the above summary of the general character of the auto and pharmaceutical industries, it can be seen that the production process is quite important for the car manufacturers, while R&D is crucial for the prescription drug companies. The sales-related operation in each industry has its own unique character. Such industry-specific features certainly affect the strategy of MNEs, and the different importance assigned to the business activities of the two industries leads to different strategies. Furthermore, the close relationships among these activities justify the FDI in non-manufacturing facilities by manufacturing MNEs, and this further provides the rationale for our perspective to investigate the non-manufacturing business of Japanese car and pharmaceutical companies.

4.3   EU MARKET OF THE AUTOMOBILE AND PHARMACEUTICAL SECTORS

Along with the industry-specific factors, the locational conditions cannot be ignored in addressing the main research themes. This section demonstrates the locational factors in Europe that influence the auto and pharmaceutical industries, bearing in mind the conditions that are changing or remaining the same because of – or instead of – European integration under the EU.

4.3.1   Automobile Sector[4]

First, attention should be drawn to the size of the market and the market structure in Western Europe, which is the biggest market in the world along with that in North America. New car registrations in 2000 were reported at 17 million in Western European countries, while those of the US, Canada and Mexico combined were 20 million. These two regions have captured 29.5 per cent, and 35.4 per cent of the world market, respectively (JAMA, 2002). In the Western European market, four European manufacturers (Volkswagen, Renault, Fiat and PSA), two American manufacturers (GM and Ford), and one Euro-American producer (DaimlerChrysler) are the main players with more than 1 million sales. Japanese car manufacturers commanded 11.4 per cent of the passenger car market in 2002, even including some companies that received foreign capital injections such as Nissan, Mazda and so on (SMMT, 2003). Thus, Western Europe is not only the biggest, but also one of the most competitive markets among the big producers in the world.

The European market has already matured and shows a cyclical pattern, rather than continuous growth. Four big European countries, Italy, Germany, France and the UK, had more than 500 cars per 1,000 persons in 1997. This is much less than in the US due to the geographic and social conditions of car use, but almost the same as in Japan (JAMA, 2000). This means that most families in Western Europe have already had at least one car. A new car purchase is not always the customer's first car. Therefore, the demand for new cars is affected very much by economic conditions, as people generally tend to use their existing car, and to postpone the purchase of a new one in a recession. For example, the differences in sales between the peak and the bottom in the first half of the 1990s was 23.2 per cent in Germany, 31 per cent in the UK, 25 per cent in France and 26 per cent in Italy (Figure 4.1). Even if the neighbour markets such as Eastern Europe and Turkey have the potential to grow, the manufacturers much adjust themselves to the mature market character in Western Europe.

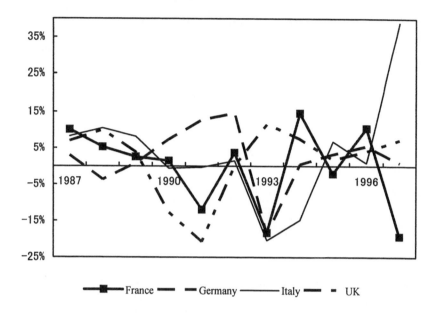

Source: calculated from JAMA (1999).

Figure 4.1   Trend of car demand in European countries (growth rate against the previous year)

The uniqueness of the European market is not found in the integration of national markets under the EU, but in the combination of integration and disintegration. The integrated aspects of the EU market had already been proceeding since the 1960s, and further advanced from the late 1980s. The first phase is the establishment of a customs union, and the final phase is the SEM. Table 4.1 reports the tariff reductions of the main EU countries following the establishment of the customs union in the 1960s. The internal tariffs between the founding members of the EU became zero by 1968, while the common external tariff was also reduced to 11 per cent by 1972. In spite of the fact that the UK was not a founding member, its tariff went down along with the common external tariff of the EU. Whereas a customs tariff of 11 per cent was imposed on trade between the UK and the EU countries until 1972, it was abolished when Britain joined the EU. The later EU enlargement also widened the customs union for the automotive industry.

In spite of the customs union, the automotive sector was heavily restricted by the NTBs. The Cecchini Report (Cecchini, 1988) points out the highest rank of the technical trade barriers imposed on the auto industry. In order to

Table 4.1   Tariffs on imported cars, 1956–1978 (per cent)

	Germany		France		Italy		UK	
	Ext.	Int.	Ext.	Int.	Ext.	Int.	Ext.	Int.
1956	17	30	35—45	30	–	–	–	–
1962	19	10	28	15	38	27	28	–
1965	20	3	25	9	31	14	26	–
1970	15	0	15	0	15	0	15	–
1972	11	0	11	0	11	0	11	–
1978	11	0	11	0	11	0	11	0

Note: 'Ext': external customs tariff against the non-member countries. 'Int': internal customs tariff among member states of the EU.

Source: Owen (1983, p. 56).

tackle the problem, the EU has drawn up lengthy measures under the SEM programme to harmonise technical regulation, to mutually recognise vehicle approval of a certain car from one member state to another, and so on. These measures have the aim of enabling the car companies to trade with other national markets more freely than before. Some NTBs were intentionally imposed against foreign cars to protect the national champion(s), especially under adverse economic conditions, since they could delay new model introductions. The removal of the NTBs can make competition in the industry fiercer than before, so consumers will be better off through price declines, an increase in the number of available models, and quality improvements. The manufacturers also benefit through harmonisation and mutual recognition, since the different regulations, standards and administrative procedures had duplicated development costs. More general SEM measures also assist the motor vehicle market. A typical example is the elimination of the customs procedure at the borders within the EU. This not only reduces the distribution time for cars, but also enables manufacturers to procure parts and components around Europe more easily and confidently (European Commission, 1997b). Thus, the customs union and the SEM have contributed to the integration of the EU car markets. In other words, European integration improves the locational conditions for attracting FDI, and enables car MNEs to operate from a regional perspective, rather than a national one (Hu, 1973; Maxcy, 1981; Rhys, 1989).

At the same time, the EU does not completely integrate the West European market, due to both its own imperfect integration programme and 'natural' barriers. Three main elements of the EU itself hinder integration of the internal market: the imported Japanese cars under the 'Consensus' between the EU and the Japanese Ministry of Trade and Industry (MITI), the block exemption, and safety and environmental incentives (Mason, 1994b; Mattoo and Mavroidis, 1995; Monti, 2000). From the late 1970s, Japan intensively exported cars to Europe as well as to the US which forced some national governments to take protectionist measures against Japanese cars. For example, France restricted the market share of Japanese cars to 3 per cent, while Italy permitted only 2,000 units of Japanese cars to be imported per year. The UK succeeded in making a gentleman's agreement with Japan over a voluntary export restriction. The situation was not compatible with the logic of the SEM, and these measures should be under the control of the EU. The result was the 'Consensus' between the European Commission and the MITI in 1991, under which the national restrictions would be gradually removed, and Japan was expected to be able to increase its share in previously protected markets such as southern Europe to between 7 and 26.9 per cent by 1999. The 'Consensus' was terminated by the end of 1999, but its effectiveness was being questioned due to the fact that Japanese manufacturers could not fill the given quota. However, it is true that Japanese car companies delayed the cultivation of southern European markets, and that the EU demonstrated the imperfection of market integration.

Another feature of disintegration is the block exemption of motor vehicle distribution and servicing from the EU competition policy (*Commission Regulation 123/85*). This allows manufacturers to select distributors, and to prohibit dealers from selling different makes in the same showroom. It is generally legitimised by the institution both of quality control for pre- and post-sales services, and of incentives for the manufacturers of promotional services. While the dealers could be protected from competition with the same brand in an exclusive territory, they must still face competitive pressure from other makes, which is also the basis for legitimacy. Indeed, the regulation permits a price differential between areas based on the exemption, but the current situation, especially across borders, exceeds the limits. The regulation was modified in 1995 to give dealers greater independence from manufacturers, but it still requires dealers to sell other makes separately (*Commission Regulation, 1475/95*). Although the regulation was again modified in 2002, allowing greater independence for the dealer (*Commission Regulation, 1400/2002*), it has often been said that the block exemption permitted the price differential of cars in the EU for far too long (Mullineux, 1995; Rhys et al., 1995).[5] For example, the biggest price difference of a same model between the cheapest and most expensive cars within the euro zone in 2000 was 29.1 per cent for the small car segment, 32.9 per cent for the medium-size segment and 29.9 per cent for the large vehicle segment (European Commission, 2001).

The third point allowing for national differences within the EU is environmental regulations. The EU has worked towards protecting the environment against pollution caused by auto exhaust fumes, scrapping cars and so on. The results of the European Commission's efforts were to set a common standard, but member states can impose stricter standards through domestic regulations. Stricter environmental protection is generally required in the countries in northern Europe, including the biggest market, Germany. At the same time, national governments can encourage customers to buy new environment-friendly cars. Such encouragement takes a different form from one country to another, for example, tax breaks or direct subsidies. The difference in the new car registration cycle among member states shown in Figure 4.1 is partly caused by such environmental incentives.[6]

There are some 'natural' barriers between European countries to becoming a single market from the group of national markets. Geographically, Europe shows some differences between the north and the south, which makes the requirements for automobile equipment and accessories different. For example, air conditioners are essential in the south, but can be an option in the north. The preferred size of a car also varies among countries. German customers generally tend to buy a big car, while Latin European countries prefer small cars. Because of driving on different sides of the road, right-hand drive cars are generally used in the UK and Ireland, and left-hand drive ones on the Continent. The average life expectancy of cars varies from one country to another. According to one report (Rhys et al., 1995, p. 165), in the Netherlands, people scrapped a car after 10.5 years of use, and Germany, France and the UK show a similar trend with an 11-year cycle. On the other hand, a car is driven for 15 years in Italy and Spain. Even if most of these differences are influenced by the auto industry's regulatory framework, it is easy to see the difficulty of integrating them into the pan-European factors, even with the development of the EU.

4.3.2 Pharmaceutical Sector[7]

As with the motor industry, Europe as a combined unit is the largest market for medicine in the world along with the US, although each country is relatively small to medium in size. The European market expended a total of £ 61 billion sterling on pharmaceutical products in 2001. The amounts for the US and Japan in the same year were £ 115 billion sterling, and £ 32 billion sterling, respectively. The share of each in the global market totalling £ 247 billion sterling was 24.7 per cent, 46.6 per cent and 13.0 per cent, respectively (JPMA, 2003). On the other hand, the pharmaceutical market structure is much less concentrated than that of the auto industry, whose top maker in Europe, Volkswagen group, held an 18.9 per cent share in 2001. According to the available data, the number of drug companies in the EU is

2,662, among which 15 firms raise more than 1 million ecus (European Commission, 1997a, p. 103). No Japanese pharmaceutical company is included in the list of leading companies in Europe.

The future of the European market needs to be viewed with some reservation, due to the limits of healthcare services (Howells and Neary, 1995; Wada, 1997). Generally, Europe's health services are based on a healthcare insurance system, though there are some differences between countries. Expenditure for medical services and prescription drugs are partly or fully covered by the healthcare insurance system. Some factors, however, such as new therapeutic methods and medicines, lead the increase in expenditures for health care, and sometimes exceed revenue. So governments introduce various ways to restrict and reduce expenditures, and drug price is one of the main targets. This is because the cost of drugs constitutes a large part of expenditures. Moreover, the ongoing ageing of society is creating anxiety about the healthcare system's sustainability in the future. Most European countries will experience an increase in the dependency ratio of the population aged 65 and over to those aged between 15 and 64, and the Organisation for Economic Co-operation and Development (OECD) estimates that the ratio will be about 30 per cent by 2020 (OECD, 1998, p. 29). Thus, there are many constraints on the healthcare system and on payments for medicines.

What was true of the auto sector can also be said for the pharmaceutical industry. The combination of the integrated and non-integrated aspects of the EU, rather than integration alone, produces the unique characteristics of the market. Since any prescription drug has to be approved before it is launched on the market, the most important issue concerns marketing authorisation. Two main methods of new drug approval have developed for the integration of the pharmaceutical sector under the SEM: the centralised approval procedure through the European Medicines Evaluation Agency (EMEA), and mutual recognition of drug approvals (European Commission, 1997a, 2000b; Wilson and Matthews, 1997). The centralised procedure is mandatory for biotechnology products, but optional for other high-technology medicines and those containing a new active substance. The EMEA is a relatively new organisation, created for the purpose of conducting the centralised procedure, and is located in London. EMEA operations began in 1995, and since then it has accumulated considerable experience. When a pharmaceutical company offers a potential medicine for approval through the centralised system, the EMEA judges whether that medicine is appropriate to market. Once marketing approval has been given by the centralised system, it is binding on all member states of the EU, and the pharmaceutical company can then sell the medicine in all EU countries.

Alternatively, a pharmaceutical company can choose the decentralised procedure for marketing authorisation. Non-biotechnological products are not always required to be submitted to the EMEA, but can be taken to market through the mutual recognition system, another route for gaining approval for European markets. The pharmaceutical company chooses a member state of the EU for starting the application procedure, and conducts the procedure with the national authority, rather than with the EMEA. Under mutual recognition, once one national authority approves the marketing of a medicine, the approval should be taken into account in the application procedure for other countries. The other countries have to grant marketing approval within 120 days, unless they have a reasonable objection.

Both of these procedures give a special advantage to pharmaceutical companies, which are not required to duplicate the clinical tests for the application. In the central procedure, the data for the EMEA are sufficient to gain marketing authorisation in 15 countries. After the approval in the first country, additional data are requested under mutual recognition, only if other countries have any serious scientific objections. Thus, the pharmaceutical companies need clinical data for only one application, and can reduce the costs for clinical tests. This is especially advantageous for new entrants such as Japanese pharmaceutical MNEs, since new firms entering the European market have to bear other costs such as establishing new facilities.

The availability of the clinical data is further widened to the global context under the International Conference on Harmonisation (ICH).[8] The ICH began in 1991 in order to harmonise the registration procedure for medical products among the three pillars, the US, Japan and the EU. The EU took the initiative in the light of its experience of integration from the late 1980s (European Commission, 1998). Since the development of the ICH, as well as EU integration, clinical tests in the EU have become increasingly important. This is because they reduce R&D costs and time for new drug introduction, both in the EU and in the other two big markets, the US and Japan. Thus, the ICH makes the locational condition for the pharmaceutical industry in the EU more advantageous.

In spite of the SEM and the ICH, there remain non-integrated aspects of the EU market, because of both national governments' commitments and 'natural' barriers. National governments are not only concerned with marketing approval, but also decide the details of the healthcare system. Even if a medicine is approved for sale within Europe, its price can vary from one country to another. The SEM does not require harmonisation of prices between countries (de Wolf, 1994; European Commission, 1997a). The retail price difference of medicines among member states ranged between 63.4 in France and 148.4 in the Netherlands in 1993, with the EU average at 100, and no convergence of prices was seen between 1988 and 1993. Even the same drug shows a large divergence in prices between countries (European

Commission, 1997a, p. 71). Thus, integration of the marketing procedure does not guarantee price convergence, and this means that MNEs must conduct sales operations at the national market level, as well as with a European perspective (Chaudhry et al., 1994).

The pharmaceutical market is more restricted by natural barriers than is the auto market, due to its own peculiar scientific features. The availability of the clinical data for marketing approval in the EU does not mean that the pharmaceutical companies may collect and process the necessary data for the application in a single country or a small number of countries. The health of the people is heavily affected by climate, life style and so forth. As a result, some diseases affect people in one country more than in another. For example, more than 300 per 100,000 people die of heart disease in the UK and Germany, while the ratio in France is nearly half that (Table 4.2). At the same time, the efficacy of a drug is different between groups of patients due to factors such as sex, weight, age and so forth. It is also claimed that there is a

Table 4.2   Death rate by major causes (unit: per 100,000 population)

Cause of death		USA	UK	Germany	France
Malignant	Male	220.8	293.1	269.6	309.3
neoplasm	Female	188.2	256.6	251.2	188.9
Diabetes	Male	17.4	10.8	18.8	9.5
	Female	21.7	12.6	35.8	13.2
Hypertensive	Male	11.7	5.5	11.0	8.0
disease	Female	15.4	6.4	22.5	13.1
Heart disease	Male	278.9	361.4	312.9	180.0
	Female	282.5	326.6	371.6	189.6
Cerebrovascular	Male	45.5	92.4	92.6	67.2
disease	Female	66.7	151.3	160.7	90.9
Pneumonia	Male	28.2	81.8	19.8	27.1
	Female	30.3	126.7	24.8	29.4
Total*	Male	901.6	1,116.1	1,028.8	981.8
	Female	806.5	1,146.4	1,135.8	867.6

Note:
USA: 1992; UK: 1993; Germany: 1994; France: 1993.
*: Total includes the death not caused by disease, such as traffic accidents.

Source: JPMA (1997, p. 3–7).

difference in efficacy between ethnic groups,[9] which are not evenly dispersed among European countries. In addition, doctors and physicians tend to prefer the data collected in their own country to that of other countries. Therefore, clinical tests should not be concentrated in a single country, even under the harmonisation of registration, and this certainly affects the strategy of MNEs.

This section has analysed the features of the European auto and pharmaceutical markets. Europe is the biggest market in the world for both industries, but the market structure for each industry is quite different. At the same time, special attention was paid to the parallel existence of integrated and non-integrated aspects of the European market seen in both sectors. Japanese MNEs cannot ignore Europe, because of its size and qualitative importance. At the same time, European integration makes the locational conditions more favourable. European integration itself creates unique difficulties for European operations, however, especially for Japanese MNEs, which have much less experience in Europe than the indigenous and US companies.

4.4   JAPANESE AUTOMOBILE AND PHARMACEUTICAL MNES

The previous sections summed up the industry-specific features, and the locational conditions within Europe. While both of these affect strategy setting by MNEs, the character of the companies themselves are also important. Each company has its own history, performance, preference and so on, and when a company adopts a strategy towards European business, such factors are significant. Therefore, this section will analyse seven sample Japanese MNEs, paying particular attention to their profiles, origins and foreign operations, especially in the US.

4.4.1   Three Automobile MNEs[10]

The general profile of three Japanese car MNEs is given in Table 4.3. Toyota is the largest company not only in the auto industry, but also in Japan as a whole. Nissan was originally the biggest car company in Japan, but has been in second place since 1962. However, in the 1990s, it was almost chronically in deficit, and had to receive a capital injection from the French car company, Renault, in 1999. Honda had always struggled in third position, but saw big success in the 1990s. Now, its domestic sales of cars are almost the same as Nissan's, and its consolidated profit is two-thirds that of Toyota, despite of the fact that its consolidated sales are less than half of Toyota's.

Table 4.3   Company profile of Japanese automobile MNEs

	Honda	Nissan	Toyota
Establishment	October 1946	December 1933	September 1933
Location of headquarters	Hamamatsu, (~1952), Tokyo (1952~)	Yokohama (~1944), Tokyo (1944~)	Toyota
Number of employees	28,500	31,128	65,551
Capital	86	605	397
Turnover	3,322	3,419	8,739
Consolidated turnover	7,971	6,828	16,054
Consolidated foreign turnover	6,222	4,523	10,457
Profit	242	293	892
Consolidated profit	609	710	1,414

Note: Financial data (billion ¥) is at the end of March 2003.

Sources: Annual reports and company histories.

The origins of the three companies show clear differences. Both Nissan and Toyota were established before the Second World War. On the other hand, Honda originally started as a motorcycle manufacturer, and did not start automobile production until 1963. Nissan was formed by the three companies Nippon Sangyo, Tobata Imono and Datsun in Yokohama in 1933, with the purpose of manufacturing cars under the mass production system (Nissan, 1983). Before manufacturing its own cars, the Osaka plant of the car division in Tobata Imono produced Datsun cars and components for Ford Japan and GM Japan. The main factory was constructed in Yokohama along with the Osaka factory, and rolled out its first car in April 1935.

Toyota is also a pioneer of the Japanese car industry, and started as one of the Toyoda family's businesses (Toyota, 1987). In 1937, Kiichiro Toyoda established Toyota Motor in Nagoya, and became independent from his father's company, Toyoda Automatic Loom Works. The main factory was

sited in Koromo village, the present Toyota city, Aichi in 1938. Because of
the government's military agenda, Toyota's first vehicle was a truck, but its
original aim was to produce passenger cars. Unlike Nissan, Toyota had no
direct relationship with Ford and GM, even if it closely analysed the products
and production systems of both companies. Thus, Toyota had to develop
production technology independently, while Nissan learned from its
relationship with foreign manufacturers or the success of merged companies.

Honda shows a quite different origin from Nissan and Toyota, since it
started out as a motorcycle producer after the Second World War (Honda,
1975, 2000). Soichiro Honda, the founder of the company, initially started
Honda Engineering Laboratory to develop motorcycles in Hamamatsu,
Shizuoka in 1946, and turned it into a corporation in 1949. Honda entered the
auto industry from the late 1950s, and the transformation was accelerated by
the government's industrial policy. The auto industry was one of the targets
of Japanese industrial policy, whose purpose was to restructure the economy
from light industries such as textiles to heavy industry (Komiya et al., 1988).
In order to make Japanese car companies more competitive in the world
market, the government planned to concentrate them into three groups
(Mutou, 1988). Even though this concentration policy was not realised, it
caused Honda to accelerate its entry into car manufacturing. Furthermore,
Honda recognised that it could not rely on the government.

The dependence of Japanese car companies on foreign markets is shown in
Tables 4.4 and 4.5, although the latter includes foreign production as well as
exports. The domestic performance and origin may well have had an
influence on the differences among the three. As the most successful
company in Japan, Toyota had exported a smaller share of its domestic
production than the industrial average until the mid-1990s. On the other hand,
Honda has been more oriented towards exports than the average, although
recent figures suggest that it is replacing exports with local production.
Nissan falls between these two (Table 4.4). At the same time, there is a
similar tendency among the three to bias their foreign sales towards North
America, although Nissan has a relatively higher share in Europe than the
other two (Table 4.5). This fact indicates that Europe is not only a difficult
market, but also offers growth potential for Japanese MNEs in the future.

The geographic distribution of foreign markets of each MNE can be an
important factor for setting their strategies. All three MNEs' foreign sales in
the North American market are much larger than the US share in the world
economy. They initially captured the North American market through exports,
but shifted to local production under the pressure of protectionism from the
late 1970s. The FDI into North America, however, showed the different
preferences among the three. Honda took the most aggressive approach to
locate in the US by itself. It originally started motorcycle production in Ohio

Table 4.4   Export share of car production in Japan (per cent)

	Total	Honda	Nissan	Toyota
1975	41.3	56.2	42.3	35.7
1980	57.4	77.0	53.6	49.9
1985	59.1	69.1	55.4	46.7
1990	49.2	58.4	39.6	36.3
1995	43.1	53.5	34.7	34.4
2000	45.4	40.9	45.8	48.3
2002	46.6	35.8	46.2	50.0

Source: JAMA, various issues.

*Table 4.5   Geographic breakdown of turnover of automobile MNEs
(billion ¥, March 2003)*

	Total	Japan	Foreign total	N. America	Europe	Others
Honda	7,971	1,748	6,223	4,968	662	993
	100.0%	21.9%	78.1%	57.3%	8.3%	12.5%
Nissan	6,829	2,305	4,524	2,785	975	763
	100.0%	33.8%	66.2%	40.8%	14.3%	11.1%
Toyota	16,054	5,596	10,458	6,244	1,547	2,667
	100.0%	34.9%	65.1%	38.9%	9.6%	16.6%

Source: Annual reports.

in 1979, and in 1982 this plant became the first Japanese car-producing plant. Now, Honda possesses two plants in Ohio, one in Alliston, Canada, from 1984, and one in El Salto, Mexico from 1995. Nissan set up its first plant for knockdown production in Mexico in 1966. Engine production and full-line assembly started in 1978. In 1980, a US plant for small trucks was planned, and production started from 1983 in Smyrna, Tennessee. Now, this plant also produces passenger cars. Toyota's entry into American production was the most cautious, and was initially based on a joint venture with GM in California from 1984. A fully-owned plant was established in Kentucky in 1986, which now has a production capacity of 500,000 cars per year. At the same time, Toyota set up its own plant in Ontario, Canada in 1986, and further extended to Indiana in the US in 1996. The 2001 production of these three MNEs in the North American Free Trade Agreement area (NAFTA) is shown in Table 4.6.

Table 4.6 Japanese passenger car and truck production in NAFTA, 2001 (units)

	Honda	Nissan	Toyota
Canada	370,994	–	166,131
USA	694,660	326,225	968,082
Mexico	23,825	327,923	–
Total	1,089,479	654,148	1,134,213

Source: JAMA (2003).

4.4.2 Four Pharmaceutical MNEs[11]

The basic features of the four pharmaceutical MNEs are given in Table 4.7. Many pharmaceutical companies in Japan were originally established not to invent and develop new chemical entities, but to operate as wholesalers. For example, Takeda started its operation more than two hundred years ago, in 1781, as a wholesaler of medicine in Osaka. After the Meiji Revolution in 1867, Japan opened its market to the rest of the world, and pharmaceutical companies could import drugs made by modern pharmacology. Because of insufficient scientific knowledge, it was natural for Japan to rely on foreign-origin drugs, and new drug companies to import foreign medicines were established. The other three companies investigated, Fujisawa, Sankyo and Yamanouchi, are included in this category, and they tend to concentrate in Osaka. The only exception among the four is Sankyo, which initially set up its headquarters in Yokohama near to Tokyo.

Unlike other industries, the pharmaceutical industry was not covered by the MITI's industrial policy, but is supervised by the MHW. The chief objective of the government for the pharmaceutical industry is to guarantee the highest level of efficacy and safety of medicines under the national healthcare system, rather than the development of the industry itself. The growing domestic market for 'me-too' drugs or those licensed-in from US and European companies, however, had long given Japanese firms favourable conditions for staying in the home market. Few incentives for exports and FDI made them pursue the licensing-out policy of Japanese-origin medicines. Since the late 1970s, however, the Japanese government has tended to restrict the price of medicines, and allows 'me-too' drugs to be approved for sales much less than before. Such a change in the domestic market has led Japanese pharmaceutical companies to cultivate foreign markets through FDI (Reich, 1990).

Table 4.7   Company profile of Japanese pharmaceutical MNEs

	Fujisawa	Sankyo	Takeda	Yamanouchi
Establishment	January 1894	March 1899	June 1781	April 1923
Location of headquarters	Osaka	Yokohama (~1913), Tokyo (1913~)	Osaka	Osaka (~1942), Tokyo (~1942)
Number of employees	4,640	6,033	7,888	4,072
Capital	38	68	63	99
Turnover	257	402	759	346
Consolidated turnover	382	569	1,046	506
Consolidated foreign turnover	178	158	409	194
Profit	41	80	269	98
Consolidated profit	61	80	405	103

Note: Financial data (billion ¥) is at the end of March 2003.

Source: Annual reports, company histories.

It is crucial for pharmaceutical firms to possess new drugs with a competitive edge in the world market. Some analysis suggests an improvement in the new drug invention capability in Japan from the 1970s, but it was not yet sufficient for international competition (Reis-Arnd, 1987; Thomas, 2001). Table 4.8 shows the strategic medicines of the four drug MNEs, all of which were first introduced in the Japanese market, and led the growth of foreign sales including licensing-out. The introduction dates confirm that they strengthened their capabilities from the 1970s, since it is a time-consuming process for pharmaceutical companies to launch a new medicine from the discovery of a new chemical entity.

Table 4.8   Main international drugs of Japanese pharmaceutical MNEs

		Sankyo		Yamanouchi	
		Mevalotin	Noscal	Gaster	Harnar
1)	Therapeutic area	Lipemia	Diabetes	Peptic ulcer	Dysuria
2)	Launch year	1989	1997	1985	1993
3)	Export (1998, bn. ¥)	57.6	21.2*	5.2	3.6
4)	Ranking in Japan, 1998	1	4	13	17
5)	Marketer in the US	Bristol Myers Squibb	Warner Lambert	Merck	Boehringer Ingelheim

	Fujisawa	Takeda			
	Prograf	Leuplin	Takepron	Blopres	Actos
1)	Immuno-suppressant	Cancer	Peptic ulcer	Hyper tension	Diabetes
2)	1993	1985	1992	1997	1999
3)	6.9	29.0	45.5	9.0	n.a.
4)	11	3	2	7	—
5)	FHI	TAP	TAP	TAP	TPA

Notes:
FHI: Fujisawa Healthcare Inc. (100 per cent ownership); TAP: 50–50 joint venture with Abbott; TPA: Takeda Pharmaceutical America (100 per cent ownership).
*: Sales terminated in 2000 due to side-effects.

Source: Annual reports, company brochures, Jihou (2000)

At the same time, because of the different therapeutic areas and methods of serving foreign markets, exports can be different from one market to another. Some medicines are for more widespread illnesses than others, and exports can be bigger. The difference between Fujisawa's Prograf, on the one hand, and drugs like Sankyo's Mevalotin and Takeda's Takepron, on the other, is a typical example. The former is for patients who have received a liver transplant operation, while the latter are for lipemia and stomach aches caused by peptic ulcers, respectively, both of which are more widespread illnesses. On the other hand, the small amount of exports by Yamanouchi is largely explained by the fact that Yamanouchi's Irish plant rather than its

Japanese plant is the main supply source of the bulk of Gaster to Merck, which is licensed to sell Gaster around the world other than in Japan and some Asian countries.

Foreign turnover, which includes not only the main products mentioned above, but also other medicines and other products such as healthcare supplements, shows the geographic differences in each MNE (Table 4.9). Such differences, however, show the same pattern as the automobile sector. The difference between the two sectors is the shift in market entry mode, from licensing-out to self-marketing in the pharmaceutical sector, and from exports to local production in the auto sector. The features of each MNE in the US, where their turnover exceeds that of any other region will now be clarified.

*Table 4.9   Geographic breakdown of turnover of pharmaceutical MNEs
(billion ¥, March 2003)*

	Total	Japan	Foreign total	N. America	Europe	Others
Fujisawa	382	203	178	110	51	17
	100.0%	53.3%	46.7%	28.8%	13.4%	4.5%
Sankyo	569	411	158	82	63	13
	100.0%	72.2%	27.8%	14.4%	11.1%	2.3%
Takeda	1,046	636	409	262	129	17
	100.0%	60.8%	39.2%	25.1%	12.4%	1.7%
Yamanouchi	506	311	194	115	70	9
	100.0%	61.5%	38.5%	22.8%	13.9%	1.8%

Source: Annual reports.

Fujisawa conducts the self-marketing of its own novel drug, Prograf, through Fujisawa Healthcare Inc., which developed from an acquired company, Lyphomed. Fujisawa Healthcare Inc. started in 1985 with a capital participation in Lyphomed of 22.5 per cent of the capital, and the full acquisition was completed in 1989. The following year, both prescription and generic drugs were consolidated under the name Fujisawa USA Inc. From 1991 to 1992, however, Fujisawa experienced some problems with the acquired company, such as the camouflaging of clinical data and underfilling of medicine capsules. The resultant loss was reported to be $7.2 million (¥6.5 billion) (Jihou, 1994, p. 71). Nevertheless, Prograf was introduced in the US in 1994. Fujisawa USA Inc. sold the generic division, and restarted as a prescription drug company, Fujisawa Healthcare Inc., from 1998.

Sankyo licenses out its own drugs to foreign companies, and exports the bulk from Japan. The first novel drug by Sankyo, Mevalotin, is licensed out to Bristol Myers Squibb, and the second one, Noscal, to Warner Lambert in the US. At the same time, a joint venture with Warner was set up in 1996 as Sankyo Parke Davis, which intends to conduct the marketing of Noscal in parallel with Warner Lambert. With Noscal's unexpected side-effects which caused damage to the liver, Sankyo and Warner Lambert had to terminate the sales of Noscal in 2000. Sankyo Parke Davis is still committed to the marketing of Sankyo-origin medicines in the future (Sankyo, 2000), although the original plan for the North American business had to be significantly modified .

The main US business of Takeda started with a joint venture with Abbot, Takeda Abbot Pharmaceuticals (TAP). The co-operation with Abbot dates from 1977, when the introduction of Leuplin initiated the joint venture. TAP's original plan was to sell Takeda's antibiotics in the US, but the vice-president of TAP insisted on changing the business plan to introduce Leuplin (Nikkei Business, 1997). Takepron, TAP's next medicine, also enjoyed great success, and sales in North American totalled ¥262 billion in 2003. Such success caused concern to Takeda, however, because the joint-venture partner, Abbot, had never agreed on the full acquisition of TAP by Takeda. Takeda therefore expanded its marketing capacity by establishing a fully-owned subsidiary, Takeda Pharmaceutical America, along with TAP, in the US.

Yamanouchi shows the largest foreign sales along with Takeda among the four. This, however, needs to be treated with caution, since the main drugs of Yamanouchi were licensed out, and part of the US sales includes healthcare supplements, rather than prescription medicines. Yamanouchi had formerly had a co-operative agreement with Eli Lilly, including negotiations to establish a joint venture in the US in 1983. However, the agreement ended when the partnership was dissociated due to disagreement over the details of the future project (Takahashi, 1988). The US entry by Yamanouchi itself was heralded by the acquisition of the local healthcare supplement company, Shaklee, in 1993 (Takahashi, 1988; Azuma, 1991). Indeed, Yamanouchi recognises the importance of the US prescription drug market, but the delay of its US operation is attributed to its inability to find an appropriate candidate for acquisition in the US. This led Yamanouchi to license out its main products. The US business was reorganised, and in 1999 the production division and the R&D of the formulation technology division became independent from Shaklee, the acquired company, under the name Yamanouchi Pharma Technology (Yamanouchi, 1999).

This chapter has analysed the industry-specific factors, integration and disintegration of the European car and pharmaceutical markets under the EU, and the company characteristics of seven MNEs. Both the differences and the similarities were investigated, and these are likely to affect the European strategy and management of the automobile and drug MNEs.

NOTES

1. The description in this section is based on the following literature: General Policy Review Staff (1975), Jones and Prais (1978), Maxcy (1981), Altshuler et al. (1984), Bloomfield (1981, 1991), Rhys (1989), Womack et al. (1990), Law (1991), Dicken (1992b, Ch. 9), Jones (1994), Freyssenet et al. (1998), Fujimoto (1999) and Whisler (1999).
2. The summary of the industry-specific features in the pharmaceutical sector is based on the following literature: Burstall et al. (1981), US Department of Commerce (1986), Reis-Arnd (1987), Prentis et al. (1988), Grabowski and Vernon (1990), Corstjens (1991), Ballance et al. (1992), Taggart (1993), Spilker (1994), de Wolf (1994) and Howells, and Neary (1995).
3. However, note that the pharmaceutical companies were always very much related to outside co-operators for R&D in the early twentieth century. See Liebenau (1984).
4. The basic features of the car market and industry in Europe is derived from the following sources: Owen (1983, ch. 4), Bhaskar (1989, 1990), Rhys (1989), Smith and Venables (1990), Salvadori (1991) Dicken (1992a), Laux (1992), Morris (1992), Forum on the European Automobile Industry (1994), Mattoo and Mavroidis (1995), Mullineux (1995), Rhys et al. (1995), Bordenave and Lung (1996), European Commission (1997b), Deutsch (1999), Economist Intelligence Unit (1999), Hirst and Thompson (1999) and Johnson and Turner (2000).
5. On the demise of the block exemption, see *Financial Times*, 10 January 2002.
6. For example, *Financial Times*, 17 November 1998 reported there the slowdown of Italy's registration was caused by the ending of government incentives.
7. The character of the pharmaceutical market and industry within Europe is derived from the following literature: Burstall and Senior (1985), Burstall (1990), Macarthur (1991), Howells (1992), Chaudhry et al. (1994), de Wolf (1994), Kanavos (1996), Chaudhry and Dacin (1997), European Commission (1997a, 2000a, 2000b), Wilson and Matthews (1997) and Methe and Penner-Hahn (1999).
8. Concerning the ICH, see the home page of the International Federation of Pharmaceutical Manufacturers Associations (IFPMA), www.ifpma.org.
9. The different efficacy of a medicine among patients is confirmed through various interviews including those held at the R&D facility of Japanese MNEs in Europe, the JPMA, and the MHW.
10. The company-specific characteristics of the car MNEs in this section are based on the publications of each company, such as annual reports, company histories and brochures as well as research on the individual companies. See Cusmano (1989), Keller (1993), Mair (1994), Dymock (1995) and Fujimoto (1999).
11. This section on the company-specific features of pharmaceutical MNEs is derived from the publications of each company, such as annual reports, company histories and brochures and so on, as well as research on them, which is not as extensive as that on the auto companies. See, for example, Takahashi (1988), Azuma (1991), Howells and Neary (1995), Nippon Yaku-shi Gakkai (1995) and Giga et al. (1996).

5. Locational Pattern of European Subsidiaries

5.1 INTRODUCTION

Having recognised the uniqueness of the European economy under continuing European integration, the next step is to start analysing the location of Japanese MNEs in Europe. The unique nature of the European economy is not only social and cultural, but also has an institutional and dynamic character due to the EU. This means that, since the locational conditions are continually changing, the adjustment and adaptation to such changes is crucial for companies within Europe, irrespective of their nationality. As the outsiders and relative newcomers, Japanese MNEs face the serious question of *which European country* they should choose when establishing their subsidiaries in Europe. Once a subsidiary has been set up in one country, it is not easy to move to another without creating friction with local and national governments, the trade union and so on. For example, Ford and GM decided not to produce cars in the UK from 2000, but still continue to manufacture components such as engines. This fact suggests the difficulty of complete divestment. Thus, location is the first theme to be examined.

Here, we shall review the detailed questions to be examined concerning the location of Japanese MNEs. Since previous work tends to deal with US cases, the first task is to confirm the locational pattern of Japanese FDI into Europe. Then, the next important point is to examine both the manufacturing sites and the non-manufacturing facilities. This approach can be justified by the fact that, although manufacturing MNEs include non-manufacturing activities from R&D and sales-related business to regional management within their own activities, few investigations have been conducted on these activities as a comprehensive unit. Such fact-finding is the basis for further analysis on MNEs' decision making concerning location. The supply-side conditions will be considered as factors influencing the division of labour within Europe and industrial agglomeration. Moreover, the factors highlighted by Porter's Diamond are also of interest concerning the locational decision.

This chapter takes the following structure, in order to investigate the location theme. First, consideration will be given to the locational pattern and the actual activities of Japanese auto and pharmaceutical enterprises, as well as the factors determining the location (5.2). Then, the implication of the findings for the previous literature will be considered (5.3). The concluding remarks will be given in the final section (5.4).

5.2 LOCATION OF JAPANESE AUTOMOBILE AND PHARMACEUTICAL MNES

The analysis on Japanese auto and pharmaceutical MNEs starts by confirming their locational pattern in Europe. Four different facilities will be investigated, that is, R&D, production, sales-related operations and the EHQ, since the summary of the previous literature highlighted the shortcomings especially in respect of activities other than production. Indeed, none of the companies examined here possesses all four kinds of facilities, nor do the same facilities have the same importance even within the same company. Nevertheless, the investigation both of manufacturing and non-manufacturing facilities will extend our understanding.

5.2.1 Production Facilities

This subsection examines the production facilities of both the auto and pharmaceutical MNEs. The production process can be the benchmark for the manufacturing industry, even if its importance varies from one industrial sector to another. Chapter 4 showed that the automobile industry is a typical sector, whose competitiveness relies a great deal on the production process. On the other hand, the pharmaceutical industry is at the opposite extreme from the car industry. With this in mind, the locational pattern of the factories of the car and drug MNEs can be analysed.

Figure 5.1 shows where three motor and four pharmaceutical MNEs set up their plants in Europe. Some manufacturing facilities such as Toyota's Portuguese and Czech plants, are not fully owned, but are joint ventures. In both industries, each company possesses more than one factory within Europe, but the competence allocated in each factory is slightly different for each, even within one company. For example, all of the car MNEs' UK plants are full-line assembly, while some of the continental factories supply the parts for the UK and other plants. The novel medicines of the Japanese MNEs examined here are produced or packaged mainly in Irish plants except in the case of Sankyo, but the continental plants tend to be obtained through acquisition. This shows a tendency for concentration of the main plants in a certain country in each industry: the UK for autos, and Ireland for the pharmaceutical industry. The diversification of Toyota's plants, however, becomes clearer from the late 1990s. Therefore, in seeking the determinant

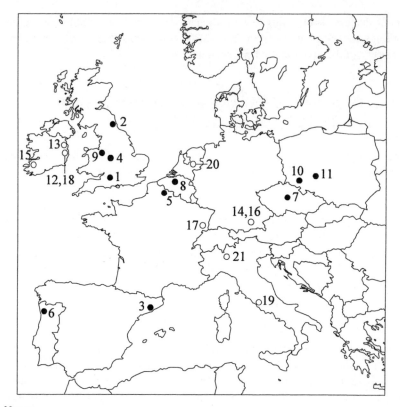

Notes :

Auto plants : ●	Assembly	Components
Honda	1	8
Nissan	2 - 3	—
Toyota	4 - 7	9 - 10

Pharmaceutical plants : ○	Bulk	Packaging
Fujisawa	—	14 - 15
Sankyo	—	16 - 17
Takeda	12	18 - 19
Yamanouchi	13	20 - 21

Figure 5.1 Auto and pharmaceutical plants of Japanese MNEs in Europe

factors for plant location, it is essential to assess both the tendency to concentrate plants at the beginning, and also the later dimension towards diversification, especially in the case of automotive MNEs.

First, it should be emphasised that the low-wage factor cannot fully explain the situation mentioned above, as Table 5.1 suggests. The primary motive for Japanese car MNEs to invest in the EU is to avoid trade friction and national import barriers through European production (Hudson, 1995; Sachwald, 1995a).[1] Note that the main Japanese factories for passenger cars tend to be concentrated in England, but Toyota shows a new direction in expanding its facilities to the Continent. The UK has not always been a cheap labour country among the European car-producing countries. The wage differential with, for example, France or Italy is not so wide, while Spain provides a cheaper level than the UK. Furthermore, the UK-based car industry lost its competitive edge in the 1970s as production halved.[2] This fact may cause the Kojima model to be rejected. At the same time, Toyota's diversification to France indicates the limitations of both the product life-cycle model and the agglomeration hypothesis, while the establishment of plants in Eastern Europe is likely to justify the product life-cycle model.

Table 5.1 Indices of hourly compensation costs for production workers in manufacturing (index: US=100)

	1985	1990	1995	1999
UK	48	85	80	86
W. Germany	74	148	184	140
France	58	107	116	94
Italy	59	117	94	86
Netherlands	67	121	142	125
Belgium	69	129	155	119
Portugal	12	25	31	—
Spain	36	76	75	63
Greece	28	45	53	—
Ireland	46	78	79	71
Japan	49	86	139	109
USA	100	100	100	100

Source: US Department of Labor, Bureau of Labor Statistics, September 2000.

On the other hand, Ireland is the preferred country of Japanese pharmaceutical MNEs for establishing plants. The establishment of Irish plants seems to support both the agglomeration model and the Vernon-

Kojima model. The compensation costs in Ireland, however, are higher than those of the Iberian countries or Greece (Table 5.1). Furthermore, since the production of medicine is not labour intensive, the attractiveness of cheap labour is limited. In addition, the Japanese drug industry has never been troubled with trade friction, unlike the case of the auto industry. Moreover, transport costs are minimal because the size and weight of medicines are very small compared with their price. Thus, it might not be necessary to establish a production site in Europe, but rather to export from Japan. In fact, Howells (1992) suggests that the production and the supply of medicine should be considered from a global rather than from a European perspective. Others such as Spilker (1994), however, insist on the merit of multi-production sites for pharmaceutical companies. This is mainly explained by risk management considerations. According to this view, it is natural for a company to establish its factory abroad for the purpose of avoiding risk, rather than simply for a cheap labour site.

Consequently, the location of Japanese auto and pharmaceutical plants in Europe should be seen from a wider perspective than the cheap labour factor. The location of car factories is determined by a combination of the Porter's Diamond factors, while the government factor is the most important for pharmaceutical production sites. The analysis starts with a detailed investigation of the automobile MNEs, followed by an examination of the pharmaceutical MNEs.

Even if a simple discussion regarding cheap labour is not appropriate, the factor concerning the workforce should not be ignored, but rather assessed more carefully. The workforce can be a resource factor of Porter's Diamond, and should be considered with respect to the transferability of the flexible production system. This system requires certain conditions, and the UK offered favourable ones such as language, industrial relations and the availability of middle managers. The flexible production system that was developed in Japan requires all concerned parties, from the employees to the suppliers, to co-operate with one another and contribute to raising productivity and improving quality (Womack et al., 1990). The working practices in Japanese plants, however, were previously unfamiliar in other countries. The transfer of the flexible production system was crucial, and close communication was necessary both in the factory and with suppliers, in order to understand and carry out the working practices of Japanese MNEs, which had little experience themselves of full-line assembly abroad. Thus, three Japanese auto MNEs in the UK have their own supporting programme for the British suppliers, in order to satisfy the requirements of the assembler (MILAN, 1992, 1996; NEDO, 1993; Foley et al., 1996).[3] Some trade unionists at different Japanese car plants confirmed the close communication with the company through frequent discussion. In addition, a Japanese MNE executive commented: 'since we had had some experience of the car production business in the USA, it is convenient to communicate in English'. Thus, one of the attractive factors of the UK was its use of English, the first foreign language of the Japanese, which was a necessary condition to transfer the flexible production system to abroad.

Industrial relations is one of the key factors for the success of car manufacturing, but it has had its problems. Car manufacturing in the UK had deteriorated before the arrival of Japanese MNEs, and industrial relations were a contributory factor (Church, 1994).[4] If Japanese car MNEs had passively accepted the traditional industrial relations in the UK, they would certainly have failed in their British venture. In fact, they actively pursued the establishment of co-operative relations between the company and the workers (Wickens, 1987; Eastwood and Hunt, 1993; Ando, 1997). The single union agreement with the Amalgamated Engineering Union, arbitration procedures, and frequent talks between managers and employees through the company council are used to construct the basis for co-operation. Most of these practices are common among the three Japanese automobile MNEs. The only exception is that Honda does not recognise the trade union at all. Thus, industrial relations played a significant role, but were not a given condition. Indeed, Japanese car MNEs are not the front runners in changing industrial relations in the UK, but rather the followers after those in the electric and electronics equipment industry (Dunning, 1986). Nevertheless, it is fair to say that Japanese auto MNEs had to construct a new style of industrial relations independently, and they succeeded.

Another factor is the availability of middle managers with some experience in the car industry. According to interviews with some trade unionists in the UK, the auto companies in general hesitate to employ workers at the shop-floor level with experience in other car companies. This is mainly because of the different working practices among the car companies. Middle managers, however, need some experience to operate the subsidiary and the factory. In this respect, the UK had relatively abundant resources with favourable terms for Japanese companies. The UK car industry had been performing badly long before the arrival of the Japanese MNEs, and a restructuring process was already under way. Some managers were not satisfied with the management of the companies in Britain,[5] and the job opportunities offered by Japanese companies presented a good challenge to try a new management style. Indeed, an interviewee at a Japanese plant in the UK expressed appreciation for the work by a British manager:

> The managing director has been playing an extraordinary role in developing the corporate culture in this plant. He and his British colleague have tried hard to eliminate the old British tradition of industrial relations, that is, 'them and us'.

On the other hand, it was more difficult to find experienced managers on the Continent, since the situation was not as bad as that of their British counterparts in the middle to late 1980s, when Japanese MNEs invested in Europe. Thus, Japanese MNEs found it easier to employ resourceful management staff in the UK than on the Continent.

The second factor of Porter's Diamond, the existence of supporting industries, is somewhat ambivalent in the UK, especially in the context of European integration. Indeed, the UK's parts and components industry has been relatively competitive compared to the assemblers (Bhaskar, 1979). However, the freer internal market of the EU enables assemblers to be less dependent on British suppliers, and procure inputs from a pan-European perspective (Amin and Smith, 1991). The local content requirement is not restricted to British suppliers, but to those in the EU. In fact, the UK suppliers for Japanese car plants in the UK account for between 50 per cent and 74 per cent of all European suppliers (Table 5.2). This fact suggests that Japanese MNEs do not always have to rely solely on UK suppliers, but actively attempt to improve the supply capacity through their own supporting schemes.

Table 5.2   Number of UK and European suppliers for Japanese car plants in the UK

	UK	Rest of Europe	UK Share (%)
Nissan	131	71	64.9
Honda	148	53	73.6
Toyota	105	105	50.0

Source: Derbyshire County Council (1996, p. 13).

The third factor concerns demand, which has not only quantitative but also qualitative features. The UK market was the second largest European market for Japanese cars after Germany, due to the relatively free market access compared with southern European countries. In addition, a large share of the UK market was the fleet market, whose customers are not individuals but private companies, public organisations and business users. Here, customers tend to prefer cars that are domestically made, or cars made by companies that have UK production facilities (Rhys et al., 1995). Therefore, establishing a UK plant can positively influence the UK market by appealing to the 'Made in Britain' sentiment.

Furthermore, the UK government provides favourable conditions for Japanese FDI. The government attitude towards foreign business has long been relatively liberal (Strange, 1993). Although it regulated local content above 80 per cent of the factory price, once this was achieved, the British government not only approved Japanese cars made in England as 'UK cars', it also actively persuaded other EU member states to accept them without national limits. This was quite different from the attitude of the French government in the 1980s. When Fuji Heavy Industry (Subaru), another Japanese car manufacturer, planned to set up a car plant in France in 1988, the French government was not supportive of the project (Mason, 1994b).[6] Thus, government support made Britain more attractive than France or Italy for Japanese car MNEs at that time (Lehmann, 1992), although the political environment in those countries changed since the late 1990s, as we shall see below.

On the other hand, the concentration of the main plants in the pharmaceutical sector is mainly explained by the government factor of Porter's Diamond, that is, the generous tax system of Ireland. Note that Irish labour costs were not as cheap as in the Iberian countries or Greece until the late 1980s, even if it was expected in the early 1970s that Ireland would attract Japanese FDI because of the cheap labour (Sekiguchi, 1979; Darby, 1997). Along with this, the less labour-intensive nature of drug production is not so dependent on low wages. Needless to say, the demand factor of Ireland itself does not play a significant role, due to the small size of the Irish economy. In spite of the concentration of pharmaceutical FDI in Ireland, no interviewee at any Japanese drug MNE mentioned the importance of suppliers or related industries. This might well be because of the technological conditions for drug production. Therefore, the Irish factories are based rather on the generous tax incentives offered by Ireland. The maximum corporate tax is just 10 per cent until 2010, while capital grants and other assistance can be provided (O'Donnell, 1991; Ernst & Young, 1992; Raines and Brown, 1999). This contributed to Ireland absorbing more than 120 drug companies. Japanese MNEs are no exception here, and an interviewee summarised the importance of the corporate tax as follows:

> We have a plan not to return the profit in Ireland back to the parent in Japan, but rather to reinvest in Europe for the expansion. Thus, the low level of the corporate tax is quite attractive to fully utilise the earnings in Europe.

Thus, the government factor played a crucial role in attracting Japanese pharmaceutical plants to Ireland, rather than other factors such as resources or demand.

In addition to these common factors among MNEs in each industry, other elements can be specific to the location decision of each MNE. The financial aid of £100 million, which contributed roughly 8 per cent of the total investment cost of £1.2 billion, attracted Nissan's investment in northern

England, an area approved for economic aid by the EU based on considerations of supporting a less-developed area (Aaron, 1999; Nissan Motor Manufacturing (UK) Ltd., 1999; Loewendahl, 2001). Before Nissan decided to invest in the UK, the objections from the trade union in Japan were based not only on the fear of job losses, but also on the possibility of the failure of the British project and the subsequent burden of the loss on the domestic business (Cusmano, 1989). Government aid still plays an important role in Nissan's decision to continue small car production in the UK.[7] Honda and Toyota did not rate government aid as highly as Nissan, when they decided to make investments in the UK. Rather, Honda preferred a location based on the proximity to the plants of the Rover group, with which Honda had enjoyed partnership relations since 1979 (Edwardes, 1983). Under this partnership, Honda supplied engines to Rover, while the latter provided some components such as body panels from its Longbridge and Cowley plants. This, rather than government aid, could contribute to cost efficiency for Honda.

Along with the common preference for locating pharmaceutical factories in Ireland, there were also some differences among the three drug MNEs when making the locational decision. Yamanouchi set up its Irish plant as the springboard for its own internationalisation in the future, and as the supply base for the bulk of the American and European markets. In addition, it expected to diversify the risks caused by stoppages in the plant in Japan. The establishment of Fujisawa's plant in Ireland was influenced by the consideration of utilising the resources of Klinge, the acquired German company, which already had an Irish plant. Chapter 4 showed that Fujisawa suffered badly from its US operation in the early 1990s, and this made Fujisawa more cost conscious. Its relatively small company size from a global standpoint also led Fujisawa to utilise the acquired company's resources. On the other hand, Takeda's choice of an Irish plant was partly a passive result of its own group operation. Greran Pharmaceutical, one of the Takeda's group companies and a generic medicine firm, originally started to build a factory for packaging new medicines for the Japanese market in 1995, but marketing approval was not readily obtained and the Irish plant had not operated at all. A forceful request from Greran persuaded Takeda to buy the facility in Ireland, which packages products made by Takeda (Jihou, 1998, pp. 90–91).

The determinant factors for concentrating the auto and pharmaceutical plants in the UK and Ireland, respectively, have been described above. But, Japanese car and pharmaceutical MNEs also possess continental factories, and the reasons for such a situation should be elucidated. In the motor vehicle sector, Toyota has aggressively pursued a continental orientation from the late 1990s, but the other two MNEs are not as active as Toyota. Thus, the case of

Toyota will be examined and compared with the others. The pharmaceutical firms' decisions are much more likely to be based on considerations over the relationship with national governments than those concerning production costs.

Toyota changed its European strategy around the mid-1990s, and its French factory was expected to play a strategic role. Toyota had long been satisfied with its status as a niche maker in Europe with a 2 to 3 per cent market share. After gaining high status in the US through local production and exports, as well as because of more severe competition on a global scale, the European market became more important for Toyota in the mid-1990s. This changed Toyota's European strategy, which now aimed at being a main player in the European market with a market share of at least 5 per cent (Toyota, 1998).

Establishing a second plant in France was the result of several factors. Toyota was not satisfied with the performance of the UK plant according to its own standards, and wanted to have the sister plants in the UK and France compete with each other. From the experience of the Kentucky factory, which has a 500,000-unit capacity, the expansion of the UK plant was judged to exceed efficient management. At the same time, the concentration of production in a single location means the concentration of risks, including exchange rate volatility, especially in the context of the uncertainty of the UK's membership in the EMU. From the viewpoint of marketing, establishing a factory in France could positively influence sales in southern Europe, where the presence of Toyota is weak. Even if the fleet market is not as important in southern Europe as in the UK, market presence positively affects people's mindset. Toyota itself expects that psychological factor to work. The objection against Japan from the French elite including politicians had become much weaker, while French rural areas such as Valenciennes warmly welcomed Toyota (DATAR, 1997). Furthermore, through its tour of the potential sites and discussions with the local people, Toyota came to recognise that France has its own flexibility of labour management.[8] In addition, transplanting the flexible production system could be achieved with assistance not only from Japan, but also from the British plant.[9] The Valenciennes location was desirable because of the good transportation links through the Eurotunnel for conveying the engines produced at the Shotton plant in the UK, which is currently the only source of Toyota's engines in Europe.

Along with the enlargement of the EU, and the growth potential, the diversification of Toyota's continental plants points towards Poland and Czech Republic. This seems to follow the Vernon-Kojima model, with the difference that Toyota owns the UK and French plants, and has expanded its capacity in Europe, rather than relocating plants from high- to low-wage countries. Toyota's aggressive strategy of diversifying European plants follows the example of US automobile MNEs (Maxcy, 1981; Dassbach, 1989).

At first glance, Toyota seems to offer an exceptional case for diversification, but an in-depth analysis of Nissan and Honda clarifies the reason for the difference. The answer is the less favourable performance of the last two, both in the parent company and in the European market. Nissan's European operation has not been as favourable as that in the UK, due to the poor performance of the Spanish subsidiary for the 15 years since 1980, when Nissan started to participate in its management (Keller, 1993; Shirai, 1994). Furthermore, in the 1990s Nissan as a whole had the worst performance of its own history since 1933. As a result, Nissan received a capital injection from Renault, the French car assembler, in March 1999, and started restructuring its entire business from October, a process known as the 'Nissan Revival Plan' (Nippon Keizai Shinbunsha, 2000). Indeed, after exhaustive investigations and negotiations with the British government, the trade union and Renault, Nissan decided to continue its three-line production in the UK with 500,000-unit capacity. This decision was reportedly based on government aid, promises from the trade union to raise productivity including instituting a night shift, and higher procurement from the Continent.[10] In addition, the capital participation by Renault changed the possibility of plant diversification in Europe, and an interviewee explained this point as follows:

> Now, we are consolidating the European operation based on profitability, and have enough capacity to fulfil the demand for Nissan cars. There is no need to expand the plants at the moment. If we can increase the sales both in Western and Eastern Europe in the future, then we will be able to use the facilities of Renault around Europe.

Honda does much better than Nissan in the US and domestic markets, but sales in Europe, with some 2 per cent of the market share, restricted its strategic choices. Honda's sales in Europe reached 180,000 units in 2002, a figure that was much smaller than those of Nissan with 353,000 units, and of Toyota with 627,000 units (SMMT, 2003). The sales figure is also less than the full capacity of the Swindon plant, some 250,000 units per year. Therefore, Honda has been exporting some cars made in the UK to the US, so that the Swindon plant can maintain its capacity utilisation level. Its present performance does not permit a diversification strategy, but Honda needs to raise its sales in Europe. If sales in Europe increased, there may well be a possibility that Honda could establish a second factory. In that case, one of the possibilities is a continental plant, as well as the expansion of capacity in the UK. Thus, the continental orientation in Europe can be a strategic alternative for Japanese car MNEs to plant concentration in the UK, but each company's situation may well affect how it makes the choice.

On the other hand, the continental orientation by Japanese pharmaceutical MNEs was based on other considerations. The plants other than the Irish ones for Sankyo, Fujisawa and Yamanouchi were the consequence of the acquisition of Luitpold, Klinge and the pharmaceutical division of Royal Giest Brocades, Brocades Pharma, respectively. From a purely economic point of view the concentration of the production facilities could achieve economies of scale, but maintaining plants on the Continent is likely to be based on political considerations. Despite the integration of new drug approval at the European level, the prescription drug price in each country is still set by the national government. It is said that the existence of any facility of the company concerned tends to ensure a preferable price decision (Chaudhry and Dacin, 1997; European Commission, 1997a). Thus, it was necessary for the three MNEs to retain the facilities, so that they can maintain good relationships with the national governments. Since Sankyo did not possess its own marketing subsidiary in France until 2002, it is appropriate to exclude the French plant from this consideration, because the French market is the second largest in Europe.

This subsection has described the concentration of car plants in the UK and pharmaceutical plants in Ireland, and suggests a continental orientation. This leads to some interesting points. First, the choice of the UK is not based on a simple low-wage consideration but on more complicated factors. Second, diversification is not an irrational choice even within an integrated Europe. Here, both the government factor and the change of government attitude towards the inward FDI play a significant part. Third, company-specific factors such as the performance of the company, the strategy towards Europe and internationalisation, and the relationship with the internal and external partners are crucial for the location of the manufacturing facilities.

5.2.2 Sales-related Facilities

Products manufactured in the plants have to be distributed to customers. Because of the products' characteristics, the post-factory business is quite important for both the auto and the drug industries. Since this is also true for foreign operations, Japanese MNEs became deeply involved in the post-factory process.[11] This subsection will examine this aspect with regard to both the car and pharmaceutical MNEs.

Figure 5.2a summarises the location of the sales-related business of Japanese auto MNEs in Europe,[12] while the location of the pharmaceutical subsidiaries is shown in Figure 5.2b. The actual businesses of these subsidiaries differ slightly between the industries. The car MNEs established national distributors, as well as warehouses. The former exclusively import the cars concerned, set up the dealer network for the cars of the contracted assembler, organise the training for the services provided by the dealers and garages, and so on. The latter is the logistic centre for cars, parts and components for the national distributors or the dealers and garages. The subsidiaries of the pharmaceutical companies deal with the marketing activities, which have a unique importance as mentioned in Chapter 4. The very small transportation cost of medicines, however, makes logistic facilities unnecessary. At the same time, a common tendency can be recognised, that is, the diversified locations at each company level among the four different facilities examined. This seems unreasonable in the context of European integration, which has been promoting market integration. At the same time, a precise investigation makes clear the differences in the diversification among the companies. For example, Takeda owns the least subsidiaries, whereas Honda and Yamanouchi extended their sales-related facilities considerably. Nevertheless, the establishment of warehouses is common among the car MNEs, while Nissan and Toyota have made rapid progress, Honda does not have widespread facilities. Thus, the diversification tendency in the context of European integration should be examined, while the differences among MNEs should also be considered.

The wide spread of fully or partly controlled sales-related subsidiaries in Europe suggests that the integration level of the European market is not the same as a national market such as that found in the US, and that some industry-specific factors also have an influence. Because of the operational content of national car distributors, it is natural for the location to be affected by demand factors. Note that there could be two different aspects of demand factors, that is, the quantitative and qualitative aspects. The fact that all Japanese car MNEs established national distributors in the big countries in the EU such as Germany or France indicates the significance of the domestic market even in the context of the development of the SEM.[13] The demand size of the national market is more significant in the pharmaceutical industry, since the EU is responsible for the integration of the new drug approval procedure, but not the national healthcare system. Thus, all four pharmaceutical MNEs own sales-related subsidiaries in large countries.

At the same time, the qualitative aspect of demand had a more significant impact on the diversified location of Japanese MNEs. In spite of European integration, the car and pharmaceutical markets in the EU are still segmented by regulatory and natural obstacles, as we saw in Chapter 4. In the car industry, the regulatory factor consists of the import quota on Japanese cars agreed upon between the European Commission and MITI, the block exemption of car dealerships, the approval of the national assistance scheme for environmental purposes, and so on (Deutsch, 1999; Mason, 1994b; Mattoo and Mavroidis, 1995). The national healthcare system can be different

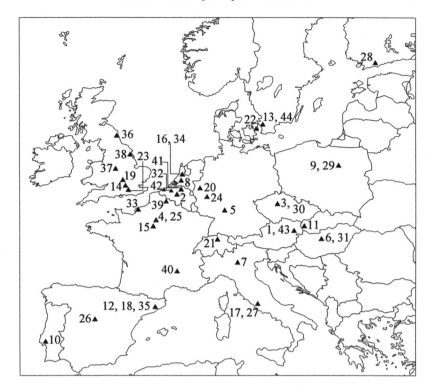

Notes:

Auto sales-related subsidiaries : ▲	Marketing subsidiaries	Car & components warehouse
Honda	1 - 14	32
Nissan	15 - 21	33 - 36
Toyota	22 - 31	37 - 44

Figure 5.2a   Auto sales-related subsidiaries of Japanese MNEs in Europe

from one country to another in Europe, and close contact with the central authority is important for drug firms (Corstjens, 1991; Chaudhry et al., 1994). The natural obstacles in the motor vehicle market include the difference in national preferences for car size, accessory specifications, customers' purchasing behaviour and so on (Mullineux, 1995; Rhys et al. 1995). Some of these were constructed in the process of motorisation in the country concerned, while others are influenced by natural and environmental factors. The prevalent illnesses, the preferred information concerning drugs, the

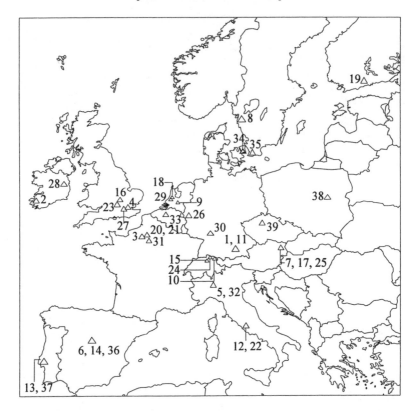

Notes:

Pharmaceutical marketing subsidiaries : △	
Fujisawa	1 - 10
Sankyo	11 - 20
Takeda	21 - 26
Yamanouchi	27 - 39

*Figure 5.2b Pharmaceutical sales-related subsidiaries of Japanese MNEs
          in Europe*

ethnic groups, competing medicines and so forth are different among
European countries, as seen in Chapter 4. The detailed communication with
concerned parties such as doctors and physicians is crucial for the sales of
medicine in each country. Moreover, such qualitative features of national
markets can change, and MNEs have to adapt to them as quickly as possible.

In order to maintain and establish a company presence in each market, the establishment of their own sales network becomes more and more crucial. Mullineux (1995, p.11) comments that the national car distributor was 'the public face of the manufacturer'. On the other hand, Chaudhry and Dacin (1997, p. 688) reported the response from the managers as 'a reactive response to the changing pharmaceutical marketplace', and this may justify the diversification of the sales-related subsidiaries.

This diversification at each company does not mean that all MNEs follow the same pattern. Some cover a wide spread of countries, others are relatively concentrated in a small number of big countries. Despite the tendency to prefer big markets, there are some differences among the three car MNEs, especially with regard to warehouse establishment. The marketing subsidiaries of the four pharmaceutical MNEs are allocated differently from one MNE to another.

The difference found in the location of sales-related subsidiaries including the logistic centre can be explained by a combination of factors: the existing resources, sales in Europe and the European strategy. The widest coverage of Honda's own national distributors was based on the existing facilities for the motorcycle sales subsidiaries, which were set up much earlier than those of the car distributors. At the same time, the location of the logistic centre represented an upgrading from the existing facilities for distribution or as the site for the production facilities. The former can be typically found in Nissan and Honda on the Continent, the latter are those in the UK and Nissan's Barcelona logistic centre, where the commercial vehicle plant is located. All of these were located at a place that had good infrastructure for transportation, and this suggests that the business contents influence the location. At the same time, under the SEM the logistic centre can cover markets across national borders, thus reducing considerably the delay in distribution attributable to customs. An interviewee emphasised this point as follows:

> The transportation of cars and components crossing national borders within the EU is very smooth. This enables us to depend on the components procured from abroad for the UK plant, and to deliver the cars very efficiently.

On the other hand, the sales volume and the company strategy towards Europe also affected the locational pattern. Honda's car sales in Europe are the smallest among the three auto MNEs, and that limited Honda to establishing only one logistic facility as was the case for its manufacturing sites. The opposite can be said in the case of Nissan, which sells some half a million cars a year, and aims to improve its competitive edge through the logistic centres. At first, Toyota dragged its feet on this issue, despite having a similar volume of sales as Nissan. Until 2000, it possessed only one car warehouse in the UK, and a components warehouse in Belgium. This is mainly because Toyota had not considered the European market to be as significant as Japan and the US, and had hesitated to make a full commitment. However, the establishment of the French plant indicates a change in Toyota's European strategy, and the European sales-related operation has become more important. Thus, it now has more warehouses on the Continent, and adopts the same strategy as Nissan.

Wider coverage by the sales-related subsidiaries can be seen in the pharmaceutical sector, and this was influenced by the entry mode and the strategy towards the European market. Under the different national healthcare systems, the pharmaceutical companies can set up sales-related subsidiaries in the country they are targeting within Europe or license out to the local marketers. The self-marketing has a double effect on European business. That is, it can earn a higher margin than licensing out, while the costs for maintaining the subsidiaries may also be high. The latter consideration would be especially serious under a situation where the introduction of a new drug may not proceed smoothly, or the sales of a drug may be lower than predicted. Therefore, the degree of diversification of the marketing subsidiaries within Europe reflected the marketing strategy of Japanese drug MNEs. The large market orientation can be found in Takeda, while the other three pursued widespread operations. In view of the combined size of big countries, Takeda is satisfied with its concentration strategy. One interviewee commented:

> The share of the four countries [Germany, France, Italy and the UK] for Takeda is between 60 and 70 per cent of its sales in Europe. The extension of its own subsidiaries to other countries could only contribute to a marginal growth of sales. The only exception is Spain, in which Takeda will establish its own stake in the future.

Widespread orientation was possible through the acquisition of local firms by the other three drug MNEs. The acquisition of Brocades Pharma by Yamanouchi in 1991 brought it extensive subsidiaries in Europe, since Brocades Pharma already had a wide marketing network. Sankyo also adopted the same strategy to establish a marketing network in Europe, through acquisition of the German company, Luitpold. There was a notable lack of marketing by Sankyo in France until 2002, mainly due to the problem of side-effects from its own drug, Noscal. Sales of Noscal were halted in 1997, and Sankyo modified the extension of its sales facility. On the other hand, in spite of its relatively small turnover among the four, Fujisawa also adopted the same strategy as Yamanouchi and Sankyo. The acquisition of the German firm, Klinge, enabled Fujisawa to set up a base in German-speaking countries, but the character of Fujisawa's own novel drug Prograf, an immunosuppressant, can explain the expansion of the marketing network.

Because of its unique and special usage for patients who have received a transplant, the marketing activities are limited to a few medical facilities in a country, such as big hospitals that can conduct a transplant operation and treat such patients. The more subsidiaries a company possesses, the larger is its turnover. This is the consideration of the above three companies, and the acquisition of a local firm with a sales network in Europe is the method to realise such a strategy. The success and character of novel medicines, however, heavily influenced the strategy of each company.

This subsection has recognised the diversification of the sales-related subsidiaries in Europe, and analysed the determinant factors. The common features between the two industries suggest the limits of European integration, the importance of national market size and the qualitative differences among European countries. In other words, the demand factor of Porter's Diamond can be confirmed on both quantitative and qualitative aspects. At the same time, some differences indicate other influential factors. The car MNEs aimed to reap the benefit of the SEM through their warehouses. The difference between Takeda and the other three MNEs in the pharmaceutical sector, on the other hand, points to the entry mode and company strategy as the significant factors.[14] In addition, company-specific factors can be identified here, and play an important role in explaining the differences between MNEs.

5.2.3 R&D Facilities

R&D is crucial to determine the competitiveness of a company. A great deal of research identifies the internationalisation of R&D, which leads to the widespread locational pattern (Howells, 1990; Odagiri and Yasuda, 1997; Pearce, 1997). At the same time, R&D includes a broad category of activities such as basic research, the adjustment of basic products to local requirements, scanning local technology and information, and so forth (Pearce, 1992). Needless to say, the R&D facility is the most concerned with 'knowledge-seeking' investment. This subsection will investigate the pattern and determinant factors for Japanese car and pharmaceutical R&D sites in Europe. Figure 5.3 shows the locational pattern and the activities of the R&D facilities of both Japanese car and pharmaceutical MNEs.[15] As with the manufacturing and sales-related facilities, there are similarities and differences between the two industries and among the MNEs. As a general tendency, the MNEs examined here preferred big countries like Germany and the UK for the R&D location with some exceptions, such as those of Toyota and Nissan in Belgium and that of Yamanouchi in the Netherlands. The present R&D activities of Japanese car MNEs are categorised into three main fields: the adjustment of the basic model and the verification of parts and components procured locally; the collection of data and information

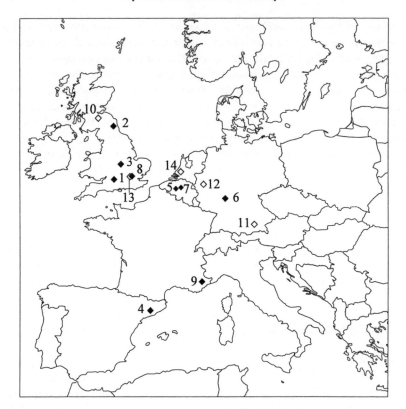

Notes:

Auto R&D : ◆	Development centre	Information collection	Design centre
Honda	1	6	6
Nissan	2 - 4	7	8
Toyota	5	5	9

Pharmaceutical R&D : ◇	Basic research	Clinical development
Fujisawa	10	11
Sankyo	—	12
Takeda	—	13
Yamanouchi	—	14

*Figure 5.3 Auto and pharmaceutical R&D centres of Japanese MNEs
         in Europe*

concerning technical regulations, legal requirements and so forth; and the designing of new models in Europe. On the other hand, medical R&D is roughly divided into three main parts: basic research, pre-clinical testing and clinical testing, although Japanese drug MNEs conduct their European R&D activities in the first and third areas. Pre-clinical testing such as animal tests is excluded from European R&D, due to its scientific and experimental nature. Basic research is crucial for inventing new drugs, but only Fujisawa among the four conduct it in the UK. Indeed, Yamanouchi was the first Japanese pharmaceutical MNE to site a basic research laboratory in Europe in 1990, but this facility was closed down in 2002. At the same time, the clinical development facilities are concentrated in one or two countries at each company level. From the above comments the question to be asked is what kind of 'knowledge', as well as other influencing factors, attracted Japanese car and drug R&D facilities?

The description of the locational pattern of Japanese R&D sites in Europe should be explained along with their actual activities, since the different activities naturally require different 'knowledge', and other factors (Cantwell et al., 2001). In spite of the difference between the two industries, talented human resources are an important factor for attracting the R&D that will decide the competitiveness of Japanese companies in Europe. This can be confirmed in the design studio for the motor vehicle MNEs, and in the basic research laboratory in the pharmaceutical sector.

Even if the size of the car design studio is small, its strategic importance is crucial. Because automobiles sometimes reflect the status or lifestyle of the owner in Europe, the appearance of a car is one of the most important factors in the customer's decision-making. In addition, since customers' tastes in Europe are different from those in Japan, the design of the basic model developed in Japan is not always acceptable in Europe. Further, Europeans do not clearly distinguish one Japanese car company from another, and they often do not refer to a model as a 'Honda car', for example, but as a 'Japanese car'. This is quite disadvantageous for non-price competition (Gibson, 1999; Harada, 2000). A managing director commented:

> It is often said in Europe that Japanese cars are very reliable and relatively cheap. This assessment may well be quite favourable for our cars. But some say that Japanese cars are 'pensioners' cars', and this means that our cars lack something other than the reliability and the price. Cars designed to appeal to European customers may be the answer to this question.

In order to improve the competitive edge in car design, Japanese MNEs have to adapt the basic models to European taste. A design studio is established to acquire talented designers, and to obtain 'knowledge' about suitable designs. Nissan and Honda looked to Germany to provide such creative resources, although Nissan relocated its design centre from Munich to London in 2003.[16] On the other hand, Toyota recognised southern France as the appropriate site (Nikkei Business, 2000b). In addition, the market each company targets positively influenced the locational decision. Germany is the largest market in Europe, while France is one of the most important markets for Japanese car companies that has not been fully cultivated due to protectionism, especially in the 1980s. In order to collaborate with the R&D centre in Cranfield, UK, and to avoid the duplication with Renault, Nissan chose London for its design studio relocated from Munich. The different emphasis on these big markets at each auto MNE explains the different location of the design studio among the three.

Like car companies, some of Japanese pharmaceutical MNEs also established R&D facilities in Europe to supplement their own weaknesses. The basic research laboratory contributes to this aim, though with differences among the four. Yamanouchi and Fujisawa selected the UK for the basic research location, although the former closed its basic research laboratory in Oxford in 2002. On the other hand, Takeda and Sankyo did not establish such a facility at all. This situation makes clear their strategy for technology sourcing. That is, Yamanouchi and Fujisawa actively seek to gain medical scientific 'knowledge' independently, while Sankyo and Takeda hesitate to fully commit in Europe.

Japanese pharmaceutical MNEs aim to supplement their capacity with the introduction of 'knowledge' from abroad. Basic research to investigate novel drugs is still lower in Japan than in Europe and the US, as the small number of Japanese-origin medicines in the world market ranking suggests.[17] Both Yamanouchi and Fujisawa have been trying to fill the gap in their own research capacity in Japan through establishing basic research sites in the UK. Since the UK is one of the most advanced countries in blockbuster drug invention in the world from the standard of sales per drug, with a relatively smaller number of new chemical entities introduced than in the US or continental European countries (Howells and Neary, 1995; Turner et al., 1997), it was natural to choose the UK for basic research.

The actual locations of Yamanouchi and Fujisawa were far apart, but they shared a common factor: that is, the proximity to a university. In spite of the closure, it is worthwhile examining why Yamanouchi established a basic research laboratory.[18] The laboratory was located in Oxford, and it was based on the profit raised from its Irish plant. Oxford was selected from several candidate places by the director himself, based on the availability of the land, preparation of the existing building, proximity to the colleges in Oxford and so forth. The close communication and exchange of information with the university laboratories contribute to improving the research capacity.

Fujisawa's facility for basic research, Fujisawa Institute of Neuroscience in

Edinburgh (FINE), the sponsored laboratory at Edinburgh University, was established in 1992. Edinburgh University was selected for its accumulation of research in the area of neuroscience, the area that Fujisawa wished to develop. In order to strengthen its research basis financially and scientifically, the university was also keen to secure a contract with Fujisawa. The chairman of the institute commented:

> When Fujisawa's feasibility study team visited Scotland, I met them and put the case for Edinburgh University. I had already visited Japan, and have met some Japanese scientists at the top universities in Japan. Fujisawa seemed to appreciate not only the plan I presented, but also our network with other scientists including Japanese ones.

Fujisawa has good access to academics, since the facility is on the university campus. Thus, the interests of both sides were in tune, although we cannot ignore the university's active approach.[19]

On the other hand, Takeda and Sankyo did not establish a basic research facility in Europe, but preferred co-operation with foreign partners over the short or medium term. For example, Takeda secured a research agreement with SmithKline Beecham, the UK drug company,[20] while Sankyo allied with the Medical Research Council, a public research institute in London (Sankyo, 2000). This was based on their strategy to concentrate basic research in Japan. The strong capacity in basic research at Takeda justified this approach. Takeda filed 1,139 patents between 1980 and 1996 in Japan, and was the only Japanese pharmaceutical company to file more than 1,000 patents (JPMA, 1997, p. 1–45). Sankyo introduced a series of blockbuster drugs from the late 1980s, such as Mevalotin, the medicine for lipemia, which were developed by its research laboratory in Japan and contributed to the sales growth. The strong capacity of Takeda and Sankyo in Japan might well make them hesitate to establish their own facilities, and they rely on co-operation with foreign partners to source the scientific medical 'knowledge' abroad.

The other R&D facilities are mainly concerned with collecting the 'knowledge' necessary for introducing products to the European market. Some of these are required as regulatory matters, others for the purpose of efficiency. The regulatory knowledge in the auto industry includes technical standards, environmental regulation, government support for the industry and so on. Along with the development of the EU, it was justified for Toyota and Nissan to possess facilities for such a purpose. One interviewee at Honda considered that 'since the regulations, technical standards and so on in Germany are the highest in Europe, the cars satisfying German requirements can easily be accepted in other European countries'. As a result, Honda sited its information collecting facility in Germany. The different weight on knowledge influenced the locational pattern of this type of R&D facility, and the knowledge here is closely concerned with the governmental factor.

At the same time, the efficient supply of cars needs another kind of knowledge. The R&D sites of Honda and Nissan in the UK, that of Nissan in Spain, and that of Toyota in Belgium are allocated this kind of role. The flexible production system relies not only on the flexible and high level of working practice in the plant, but also on the supply of high quality parts and components. The initial selection of the suppliers is crucial for smooth production on the assembly line, while the continuous improvement of suppliers is another requirement of Japanese companies. In order to maintain close communication with the manufacturing process, the R&D facilities should be located near the factory. Toyota formerly possessed the parts and components evaluation facility at the UK Burnaston plant. Along with plant diversification, however, Toyota relocated to Brussels. This facility evaluates all parts and components for European plants, and adjusts the basic model of cars, if necessary. In other words, the determinant factor in this case was not a host-country-specific one, but rather the proximity to the facility or the contents of the development operation.

Because the products closely concern human health and life itself, the knowledge necessary for legally approved marketing is more important for the pharmaceutical MNEs than for any other industry. All four MNEs possess their own development facilities, so that they can collect the necessary clinical test data for new drug approval in Europe. There are two important findings regarding the location issue in the context of European integration. The first is that, despite the different conditions for clinical tests in Europe shown in Chapter 4, two favourable factors, that is, the SEM and the CRO, enabled Japanese pharmaceutical MNEs to concentrate their clinical research sites in one location. The second is that the establishment of the EMEA in London significantly influenced the location. These points will be examined in turn.

The SEM integrated the new drug approval system, and pharmaceutical companies can choose the central system or the mutual recognition system (Thompson, 1994; Abraham and Lewis, 2003). The great advance is that clinical data, which are collected and used for filing for marketing authorisation in one country, can also be used in another. Before the SEM, Takeda and Sankyo oriented towards big countries like Germany for clinical research mainly because of the demand size factor. Takeda originally started R&D in Hamburg (Takeda, 1983), and established an R&D centre in Frankfurt in 1988. However, the centre was moved to London in 1998. Sankyo's clinical research site was established in 1985, also before the start of the SEM (Sankyo, 2000). The SEM, however, enabled the development and authorisation of new drugs for the European market in a small country like the Netherlands, where Yamanouchi possesses a large R&D facility inherited from the acquired company, by mutual recognition. Therefore, it was rational for Yamanouchi to utilise and expand the resources of the acquired company in the Netherlands. Fujisawa's clinical centre in Germany was based on the same consideration as Yamanouchi's utilisation of the acquired company's resources, though Fujisawa did not fully integrate the acquired company until 2002. The knowledge for new drug development can and should be gathered and utilised from a pan-European perspective rather than from national market considerations. Since the SEM improved the knowledge utility and influenced the location of the clinical test facility, the entry timing also played a crucial role in the decision.[21]

At the same time, each Japanese pharmaceutical MNE concentrates clinical research in one facility, despite the diversified conditions in Europe. The natural disintegration of clinical test conditions in Europe, as we saw in Chapter 4, did not lead drug development subsidiaries to adopt a pattern similar to that found for sales-related activities. This can be explained by the availability of CROs, and closely concerns Porter's supporting industry factor. Using CROs enables locational concentration of drug MNEs' R&D sites. Since CROs actually conduct the clinical tests for the pharmaceutical companies, the latter do not have to conduct tests themselves. Moreover, the coverage of the CRO is not restricted within the country of origin, and some provide cross-border coverage. Even if one CRO does not cover all the target countries, the drug company merely arranges contracts with two or more CROs to carry out clinical tests in the main markets. Therefore, Japanese pharmaceutical MNEs can concentrate their own R&D facilities in one country, and put together the appropriate portfolio of contracts with CROs. Thus, Japanese MNEs can make huge savings on the investment costs of the R&D facility and staff. A top director of a Japanese R&D centre in Europe commented: 'because of the availability of CROs, the number of staff is one twelfth for the same amount of clinical tests in Europe than in Japan'. Thus, the CRO is the main reason for Japanese MNEs to invest and concentrate R&D facilities in Europe.

Following the establishment of the EMEA, a consequence of European integration in the pharmaceutical industry, London attracted the interest of Japanese pharmaceutical MNEs. Filing a new drug application is not the end of the procedure, but the beginning of a lengthy examination taking from six months to two or three years. In this process, a pharmaceutical company would often be required by the central authority to supplement the data on efficacy, side-effects and so on. In addition, since the EMEA is a relatively new body, its ability to smoothly approve new chemical agents as new medicines is not fully appreciated. Thus, the pharmaceutical companies need to be in close proximity to the body itself, in addition to responding to requests from the EMEA. Takeda is a step ahead, having moved its R&D centre from Frankfurt to London in 1998. Sankyo also established an information collecting office in London, though its limited competence can be explained by the failure of Noscal in Europe. Fujisawa and Yamanouchi do not appear to have taken any concrete action in response to the EMEA, because both of them already possessed subsidiaries in or near London, and also because both companies prefer the mutual recognition procedure rather than the central one under the EMEA. Further, Yamanouchi has little difficulty with the distance from the Netherlands, since it takes only about two hours to travel between London and Leiderdorp, where its R&D centre is located. Thus, as with the auto MNEs, the pharmaceutical firms also intend to follow the development of European integration.

The FDI for the R&D facilities in Europe was an important knowledge-seeking investment for both industries and was divided into two main parts: FDI to supplement companies' own weaknesses, and FDI to gain the knowledge necessary to appropriately and/or efficiently supply the European market. Indeed, the national conditions for R&D are different among European countries, as are the national markets, but the concentration and allocation of R&D sites as a part of the company strategy can be recognised. Thus, European integration as well as entry timing have some impact on the decision making by Japanese MNEs.

5.2.4   European Headquarters

One of the well-known development patterns of MNEs is to manage their operations regionally (Stopford and Wells, 1972). The establishment of a regional headquarters typically fits this pattern. Along with increasing the commitment in Europe, all of the Japanese companies examined with the exception of Takeda followed this path in Europe. The location of the European headquarters (EHQ), however, is completely different for each company. This subsection looks at the EHQ location and the reasons for site selection.[22]

In spite of the fact that all Japanese car MNEs have their own EHQs, the locations are completely different among the three, while the EHQs of the pharmaceutical MNEs are in Germany or the UK (Figure 5.4). On the other hand, Takeda does not have an EHQ at all. It is quite natural for the EHQ of each MNE to be sited in only one place, because of the competence given from the parent in Japan to manage the European operation. The figure shows some features of the locational pattern, such as the diversification among the six establishing an EHQ, the general tendency towards the continent, which differs from the production facilities, the division of the preference between large and small countries in Europe, and so on. Chapter 7 will detail how the

EHQs supervise the operation not from a national, but from a European perspective. Each MNE decided the location of its EHQ to effectively conduct this central role. The next step here is to investigate the determinant factors for the location.

The managerial importance of the EHQ requires two factors irrespective of the industry: good infrastructure, and the availability of high-quality local staff. For the purpose of supervising the European operation, the EHQ has to communicate closely with the national subsidiaries. The progress of information technology can improve the communication between the EHQ and the subsidiaries, but face-to-face contact is still important for co-operation and co-ordination. In fact, one interview was conducted on the occasion of the interviewee's visit from the EHQ to the plant for a business meeting, not at the EHQ office. According to the interviewee, 'this kind of plant or other subsidiary visit from the EHQ was not an exceptional case, but quite normal business practice'. De Meyer (1989) reported the case of Ford, which operated its own planes for twice daily flights between the UK and Germany in order to keep in close touch with its two main subsidiaries in Europe. This confirms that the importance of face-to-face communication is true not only for Japanese MNEs, but also for other MNEs. As a natural consequence of this consideration, all six EHQs are located in or near a national capital (London, Paris and Brussels) or a big city (Munich), and can enjoy good infrastructure such as a large international airport and highway access.

The local staff are also an important consideration for the locational decision. Here, all of the MNEs selected the site for the EHQ to utilise existing resources. The three auto companies had already had, to some extent, business experience in the EHQ location. For example, Nissan had formerly operated a logistics business in Amsterdam, in which Nissan first set up its own EHQ, although it subsequently moved the EHQ to the present location near Paris in 2003. Toyota ran a branch office in Brussels from 1969 which accumulated know-how and information on European markets (Toyota, 1987, p. 472). It is quite usual for MNEs with little experience in international business, such as Japanese pharmaceutical MNEs, to depend on local staff with much more experience in Europe than their Japanese counterparts. Note that the human resources employed to conduct the EHQ operation were often taken over from the acquired company, and this dictated to the location of the EHQ. For example, Fujisawa could not fully integrate the acquired company until 2002, but it still succeeded in transferring some local staff to establish an EHQ in Munich. In this sense, the location of the EHQ in the pharmaceutical sector was also heavily influenced by the entry mode. On the other hand, Yamanouchi formerly conducted its strategic decision making EHQ operation in Leiderdorp, where the acquired company was located, but

Notes:

Auto EHQ : ★	
Honda	1
Nissan	2
Toyota	3

Pharmaceutical EHQ : ☆	
Fujisawa	4
Sankyo	5
Takeda	—
Yamanouchi	6

Figure 5.4 Auto and pharmaceutical EHQs of Japanese MNEs in Europe

later relocated to London, whose attractiveness lies in the availability of external resources such as management consultants.

At the same time, the different preferences of large and small countries should be considered. This is an especially serious question in the automobile industry, since the division among the pharmaceutical companies can be partly explained by the different locations of the acquired company. Nissan and Toyota prefer a small country location, while Honda prefers a large country. Since Nissan was aware of a big difference between Britain and the Continent, it wanted to avoid the bias of the appreciation of the European economy and the development of European integration. Further, the larger continental countries were thought to hold some prejudice concerning the relationship between their own domestic market and the European market as a whole. Thus, Nissan opted for the Netherlands. Later, Nissan relocated its EHQ near Paris, but this can be explained by its need to maintain close communication with Renault, which possesses a 44.5 per cent share in Nissan. On the other hand, Honda made a different assessment of the relationship between the manufacturing site and the EHQ: the proximity of the plant and market was the most important factor for Honda to locate its EHQ in the UK. This can be confirmed by the other business divisions, that is, motorcycles and power equipment products. The motorcycle division in the EHQ was shifted from the UK to Italy, while that of power equipment products was relocated to France. Italy and France are the main markets for Honda's motorcycles and power equipment, respectively.

This investigation suggests that in spite of the different locations, the EHQ was established on the basis of its role in Europe, which is supervising the national subsidiaries and European operation as a whole. Good infrastructure and the possibility of fully utilising its own human resources were the main factors common to both industries. Further examination, however, made clear the significance of the entry mode for the pharmaceutical MNEs, while the assessment of the relationship between the production and market affected the decision of car MNEs.

5.3   IMPLICATIONS FOR THE PREVIOUS LITERATURE

The previous section looked at the location of Japanese car and pharmaceutical MNEs in Europe, and the reasons for their locational pattern, with respect to both the factory and the non-manufacturing facilities. Furthermore, the investigation was done at the company level, and examined the actual operation of European subsidiaries. From this analysis, some interesting patterns emerge. First, the production and R&D facilities are similar within each industry. Second, the sales-related facilities are slightly different among MNEs in the same industry, but there is a similar general tendency between the two industries, that is, a geographical divergence in spite of European integration, and the large national market preference. Finally, the most differentiated pattern is the location of the EHQ. Based on these findings, the determinant factors of the location in comparison with the previous research were reconsidered. Some of the observations support the earlier work, while others reject it or require some of the models and the predictions to be modified. Hence, it is worth summing up the agreements and the disagreements between the previous research and the findings in this chapter.

First, both car and drug plants are located in countries with relatively cheap labour costs within the EU, although not cheaper than in the Iberian countries or Greece. This picture seems to support both the models offered by Vernon (1966, 1979) and Kojima (1978), since they predict FDI flow from high- to low-wage countries. The sequence of the investment in the EU by Japanese companies, however, sounds a cautionary note concerning their predictions. Nissan had already invested in Spain, though for the production of commercial vehicles, before establishing its British plant, while Toyota built a second factory in France. Their movements are in the direction of shifting plants from relatively low- to high-wage countries in the EU, which is completely contrary to Vernon and Kojima. Concerning the pharmaceutical facilities, there is no co-relationship between technology level and location. Yamanouchi invested first in Ireland with a higher technology facility, that is, bulk production, while the latecomers Fujisawa and Takeda set up lower-level facilities, that is, packaging factories. Other facilities on the Continent were the result of the entry mode by Japanese drug MNEs, rather than the precise calculation of locational conditions, as well as political considerations concerning relations with the national government. Thus, since the simple wage factor cannot fully explain the location within an integrated Europe, but an approach combining Dunning (1988, 1993) and Porter (1990) may well be more appropriate.

Second, the industrial agglomeration approach (Krugman, 1990; Baldwin, 1994) has to be modified, though not rejected. The precise investigation of the determinant factors indicates that the facts are more complicated than that the model predicts. The auto plants were concentrated in the UK, and they were based on the transferability of the flexible production system, rather than the external economy. The language and the availability of middle management were the main concerns for the companies with regard to the labour force. In addition, the external economies had little influence on the selection of the UK. The British car industry was declining before the arrival of the Japanese MNEs, and the UK could not be seen as an attractive site without a drastic change in the locational conditions. Japanese car MNEs played a leading role in realising such change. This means that MNEs were not passive actors, but active ones with regard to locational conditions. Moreover, since workers with experience in other companies generally tend to be excluded from recruitment in the auto industry, one of the main factors of the external economies is rejected. Concerning the pharmaceutical case, the attraction of Ireland was mainly the generous incentives provided by the government, such as low corporate taxes, rather than the external economies. No interviewee mentioned the external economies as the determinant factor for Ireland. The agglomeration was not based on the external economies, but rather on the government factor. Furthermore, the entry mode certainly influenced the location, as the case of Fujisawa suggests.

The third significant conclusion is that R&D facilities show two kinds of knowledge-seeking investment. The first is to complement a company's own weakness in the European or global market. These are concentrated in the design studio for car MNEs, and in the basic research laboratory for the pharmaceutical MNEs. While the auto companies saw the importance of the external economies in the case of the establishment of the design studio in the UK, Germany or France, the pharmaceutical firms preferred to locate their basic research facilities near or in a university, to benefit from an exchange of academic and scientific information. On the other hand, appropriate and efficient operation requires another type of R&D. The proximity between the factory and the development and verification facilities in the car industry is crucial due to the sharing of knowledge for efficient manufacturing. In the pharmaceutical sector, the clinical development facilities collect the knowledge necessary for marketing authorisation, and the entry timing and mode heavily influenced the location for such knowledge collection. In addition, the concentration of the clinical research facility at each pharmaceutical company is based on the supporting industry factor of Porter's Diamond, in this case the utility of the CROs.

The fourth point is that European integration had some effect on the location. European integration encouraged Japanese MNEs to restructure their European operations, including the establishment of the EHQ, to follow the development of European integration through the data- and information-collecting facility in or near Brussels, the establishment of a warehouse covering areas that extend across national borders and so on. The decision to establish an EHQ, however, does not a priori lead to a particular locale or country. Rather, there are some variations among the companies, who choose a location according to their own history in Europe, the company strategy, the judgement on the situation in Europe, the entry mode and so forth. Although the EMEA is the most advanced product of European integration in the pharmaceutical industry, it failed to attract all of the four companies to London; however, the future is not clear. On the other hand, both natural and political obstacles forced Japanese MNEs to set up sales-related facilities, at least, in the big markets within the EU. With the development of European integration, the ensuing benefits can vary from one time to another. Therefore, the timing of the entry by Japanese MNEs affected the locational pattern in the context of European integration.

Finally, the significance of company-specific factors on the locational pattern was recognised. These include the firm's performance, the history of European operations, the entry mode, the assessment of European markets and so on. For example, diversification within the EU seems to be co-related with the performance of the company in question. The most successful company among the three car MNEs, Toyota, is diversifying its plants, while the other two MNEs were unable to follow suit in spite of their intention to do so. The expansion of Japanese drug firms in Europe was based on their novel drugs, which are highly competitive in the world market. The success of the new drugs led them not only to establish factories in Europe, but also to set up research facilities. The diversification or expansion of a better-performing company within the EU, however, proceeds not in all activities but only in selected ones. Here, the selection is dependent on the nature of the industry as well as the company strategy.

The above summary on the implications of the findings in comparison with the previous research evidences the utility of Porter's Diamond in the context of considering the locational advantages of the eclectic paradigm. At the same time, the MNEs made their decision to invest abroad not always passively, but actively, according to locational conditions. The assessment, adaptation and cultivation of the locational conditions may well vary from one company to another, and between the industries. Therefore, the company-specific factors were no less important than the locational conditions, and these points were made clear through the precise investigation at each company level.

5.4   CONCLUSION

In this chapter, the location of Japanese MNEs in Europe was examined through a precise inquiry at the level of each company. The approach taken enables us to understand the situation and the determinant factors of the location more deeply than the aggregated data suggests. Some of the findings support the previous literature, but others do not. The re-examination of the previous research through these findings has thrown light on the themes to be developed further in the following chapters.

These themes are twofold: the timing and the mode of entry into the EU, and management at the European level. The location of some facilities, especially in the case of the pharmaceutical MNEs, was greatly influenced by the entry mode. The timing of the entry was crucial for the selection of the site, due to the change of the locational conditions in a dynamic time series, which is also affected by European integration. This theme will be addressed in the next chapter.

The managerial aspect will be reviewed further in Chapter 7. Japanese MNEs established various subsidiaries in various European countries. Each subsidiary cannot concentrate on its own business in isolation, or be independent from the whole business of the particular MNE. Rather, the subsidiaries must closely co-ordinate their operations with one another. Thus, the management of national subsidiaries in Europe should be controlled from a pan-European perspective, to maximise the benefit of the locational advantage and the network of European subsidiaries. This makes the management aspect of Japanese MNEs within Europe in the context of European integration an appropriate theme to be addressed.

NOTES

1. Concerning protectionism in Europe itself, see Mason (1994b) and Deutsch (1999).
2. The UK produced 1.9 million cars in 1972, its peak of production, but production declined to 0.9 million in 1984, when Nissan decided to set up the plant. The data is from SMMT. See also, Whisler (1999).
3. See also, House of Commons, 'Competitiveness of UK Manufacturing Industry', Memorandum submitted by Nissan Motor Manufacturing (UK) Ltd. (MC22), Memorandum submitted by Toyota Motor Manufacturing (UK) Ltd. (MC37).
4. On the other hand, Whisler (1999) maintains that the rigidity of the British car corporations and the national socio-economic institutions are the fundamental reasons for the decline.
5. Concerning this issue, Peter Wickens, the first personnel manager of Nissan Motor Manufacturing UK, told the Employment Committee, 'there will be some organisations that take that short-sighted view; in my view it is the wrong long-term view for British industry' (Minutes of Evidence taken before the Employment Committee, 17 March 1993, p. 120, 537).
6. See also *Nippon Keizai Shinbun* (Japan Economic Journal), 10 September 1988, 15 November 1988, and 5 June 1989.
7. *Financial Times*, 25 and 26 January 2001.
8. An interviewee at Toyota pointed out examples such as using part-time workers, and changing the working shift between two and three along with the demand cycle in a year. Concerning the difference of the managerial practice in Europe, see Lane (1989).
9. *Financial Times*, 30 June 2000.
10. *Financial Times*, 31 July 2000, 28 August 2000, 29 September 2000, 17 October 2000 and 26and 26 January 2001.
11. All activities concerning post-factory business activities including distribution are referred to here as sales-related operations.
12. Some of the facilities in the figure are not independent subsidiaries specialising in sales-related operations, but are involved in other subsidiaries. For example, the warehouses in the UK tend to be part of the manufacturing subsidiary.
13. The different timing of establishing the national distributors even among the big countries in Europe should be considered along with the entry mode, and this will be done in Chapter 6.
14. The entry mode and the effect of the timing will be discussed in Chapter 6.
15. Toyota owns the R&D centre for the Formula One Race in Germany. However, it was established for completely different reasons and strategy from its other European operations,

and it was excluded from the research.

16. The relocation of Nissan's design centre will be considered in Chapter 6 in the context of the internationalisation process.
17. In the best 20 products in 1996, only Mevalotin of Sankyo and Gaster of Yamanouchi are ranked in at sixth and eleventh, respectively (Scrip, 1999, p.129).
18. The reason for the closure will be examined in Chapter 6.
19. There is another similar case, Eisai, a Japanese pharmaceutical company, has a basic research facility on the University College London campus. The proximity to the university laboratory could be the reason for the locational decision.
20. The information is from Takeda's company brochure.
21. The implication of the entry timing will be looked at in depth in Chapter 6.
22. Because of its uniqueness and importance, the operation of the EHQ will be examined in Chapter 7.

6. Entry Mode into Europe

6.1 INTRODUCTION

This chapter will analyse the entry mode of Japanese MNEs into Europe. It was suggested at the end of the last chapter that the location of Japanese MNEs in Europe is closely related with the entry mode and timing, and it is logical for the research to advance the examination on this theme. The entry mode reflects the regional and global strategy of the MNE concerned. Since there are some advantages and disadvantages to each entry mode, the choice is based on the capacity and preference of the MNE. At the same time, the locational conditions also influence the entry mode, because the environmental factors outside the company may provide favourable conditions for one entry mode, and unfavourable ones for another. This applies more so in Europe, where the locational conditions have been changing along with European integration. Furthermore, every entry can be different in the process of its own internationalisation, due to the development of the company itself.

Chapter 2 listed the issues to be raised concerning the entry mode in the process of internationalisation, but it is convenient to summarise them here. As in the case of the location theme, the existing research focuses on the FDI into or by the US, and fact-finding on Japanese cases will be the starting point. Then, both the manufacturing and non-manufacturing facilities in Europe will be examined. The determinant factors will be further analysed, in particular the change of the entry modes and the determinant factors in the developmental context of the MNEs concerned.

The analysis in this chapter takes the following structure. First, the actual entry mode and the sequential development of the seven companies in Europe are summarised (6.2). In the following section, the determinant factors for selecting the entry mode will be considered, paying attention to the significance of the internationalisation process (6.3). Then, the implications of the findings will be compared with previous work (6.4). The concluding section provides a summary, and clarifies the relationship with the other two main themes (6.5).

6.2   ENTRY OF JAPANESE MNES IN A TIME SERIES

In order to fill the gap in the previous research, this section will look at the entry modes of Japanese auto and pharmaceutical MNEs into the EU in the light of the mutual relationships that have developed between the MNEs and the EU. Three stages will be discussed in the following analysis, based on the development of international business: the initial stage of exports or licensing, the main stage of investing in principal business activities and further developments. Each of these stages has its own requirements, and retains and accumulates knowledge appropriate for the business. The following subsections will discuss each stage in turn.

6.2.1   The Initial Stage

The analysis in this subsection will address the differences and similarities of the entry mode and the type of business between the two industries, and the incremental commitment of Japanese MNEs in the EU. Along with the gradual development of the Japanese car industry, the entry by auto MNEs aimed to cultivate the European market mainly through exports from Japan. Because of the relatively weak position of the Japanese drug industry in the world market, the aim of the pharmaceutical companies was originally more modest, namely to license-in European drugs for the domestic market.

The auto companies began exporting in the late 1950s, but expansion had to wait until the 1970s. Total car exports from Japan were just 7,000 units in 1960, then 1.3 million units in 1971, and reached a peak in 1986 with 4.6 million units (JAMA, various issues). The establishment of a European foothold by Japanese auto MNEs followed the growth of exports, although the initial commitment was modest. Usually, the automobile companies signed contracts with local companies on the national distribution of cars exported from the home country (Mullineux, 1995), thus following the industry norm for the export of cars from Japan. This was a common feature of Toyota and Nissan at this stage, but Honda took a different path by establishing its own distributors. Toyota started exporting to Denmark and expanded its contracts with national distributors in the 1960s.[1] Nissan chose Finland as the first European country for its exports, and also increased its national distributor contracts with local firms.[2] On the other hand, Honda established its own distributors – not all of these were originally concerned with cars, but handled the motorcycle business.[3] It is not clear from the available information exactly when Honda's distributors turned mainly to automobiles, but they formed the basis of the car business at the later stage.

Another interesting feature at this stage of entry is that the car MNEs preferred to start their European business not from the main economies but from the peripheral ones, such as Denmark in the case of Toyota and Finland for Nissan. Japanese cars were less competitive in the early 1960s than they were from the late 1970s, which led the companies to avoid direct competition in the main car-producing countries in Europe such as Germany and France. The car industry was symbolic of a country's industrialisation, and the national champion policy favoured the national companies in the larger European countries (Lehmann, 1992). Thus, Japanese car MNEs avoided direct competition with European producers in their own home markets at the very early stage of entry.

Unlike the other cases of national distributors, both German and Belgium ones were based on the full ownership. German national distributors were originally local companies, but both Nissan and Toyota took over full ownership in 1973 and 1974, respectively, mainly because of the poor sales performance. The restructuring process was accelerated by the first oil shock in 1973 (Nissan, 1983, 1985; Toyota, 1987). It is not difficult to understand that Germany was too large a market to ignore completely. On the other hand, the importance of Brussels as the 'capital of the EU' was the main factor for the full ownership of subsidiaries in Belgium. Toyota moved its European representative office from Copenhagen to Brussels in 1969 (Toyota, 1987), while Nissan's Brussels representative office was founded in 1964 (Nissan, 1983, 1985). Honda made a full commitment in Belgium through its subsidiary, combining the marketing and motorcycle production facility in 1962 (Honda, 2000). Thus, in spite of full ownership, the German and Belgium entries differ considerably.

The last point is that some small production sites were set up at this initial stage. These were the Toyota plants in Portugal and Ireland (Toyota, 1987). The Portuguese plant was established in 1968 as a joint venture on a minority share basis with a local company, and proceeded with the knockdown production of Toyota cars. This was mainly because Portugal's trade policy restricted the imports of cars. Another case was the knockdown production licensed to an Irish company from 1973 to 1983. This is also explained by the import restriction on cars imposed by the Irish government. The uniqueness of the Irish policy was that, if the company gained more than 5 per cent of the market share through knockdown production, it could be approved for imports from the home country. This system helped Toyota to increase its market share in Ireland both through knockdowns and exports. Ireland's membership in the EU, however, liberalised trade policy, and Toyota ended knockdown production in 1983. These two cases suggest both the importance of national government policy and EU membership for entry, and this will be examined in a later section.

With regard to the Japanese pharmaceutical companies, the initial European operation was more modest than that of the car MNEs. The motivation for drug firms was the import or the license-in of the drugs invented in Europe (Macarthur, 1991), in order to maintain and increase their domestic sales in Japan. Because medical science was less developed in Japan, most of the drugs sold there were originally invented in the US and Europe. The share of foreign-origin medicines reached 75 per cent of the domestic market at its peak (Seo, 1987, pp. 53–5). Thus, licensing-in had formerly been the most important international business for Japanese pharmaceutical companies. However, this had not always needed a permanent subsidiary specialised for that purpose. As long as licensing-in was conducted on an irregular basis, it would be sufficient for those concerned in the parent company to make business trips abroad.

During the long period between the mid-1960s and the mid-1980s, the engagement of Japanese pharmaceutical MNEs in Europe was basically a limited one, such as setting up representative offices or making business trips to secure license-in contracts. In 1964, Takeda established a medical division in its German subsidiary (Takeda, 1983), which conducted a bulk trade in vitamins, while in 1955 Sankyo set up a representative office in Basel, Switzerland based on its close relationship with Sandoz (Sankyo, 1979). Both of these were new ventures, aimed at collecting medical knowledge and information in Europe. The status of their affiliates clearly indicates that their European business was still marginal and not established on a permanent basis. This also enabled them to use their own financial resources, due to the very small size of the European facilities.

Following the improvements in the Japanese pharmaceutical industry (Reis-Arnd, 1987; Reich, 1990), the European business gradually became more sophisticated. It changed in nature from that of a passive actor collecting information and potential drugs for the Japanese market to that of an active one cultivating the European market through licensing-out their own drugs. Then, Japanese drug MNEs increased the number of representative offices to conduct both the license-out and the license-in business. Takeda's German subsidiary in Hamburg extended the role of the drug division to support the licensee in Europe from 1971 (Takeda, 1983, pp. 665, 879). When Takeda introduced its original drugs through license-out, first in Italy and then in other European countries from the early 1970s, it recognised the need to back up the licensee. Thus, the German subsidiary strengthened the medical division and its activities covered cross-border areas. The other two firms, Fujisawa and Yamanouchi, also set up representative offices in Europe: Fujisawa first located in London, in 1979, and then in Milan, in 1986,[4] while Yamanouchi opened the representative offices in London, Frankfurt and Paris in 1980, 1987 and 1989, respectively.[5] In contrast, Sankyo continued to operate its European business for licensing-in and -out through the Basel representative office until 1985.

With regard to setting up a European business before investing in the main operation, certain features typify the entry mode as the initial stage of Japanese MNEs. First, both industries undertook modest engagement in Europe. Despite the expansion of exports, auto MNEs tended to depend on local companies as the national distributors. The pharmaceutical companies had only their representative offices or the pharmaceutical division in a subsidiary. Second, there are some divergent entry modes in the auto sector, for example, joint ventures in the knockdown production of cars, and acquisitions of German distributors. Full ownership preference was demonstrated by the Belgium office or subsidiary. Third, drug companies show a preference for full ownership over a subsidiary or representative office, since all of them are relatively small concerns. In summary, the entry strategy of Japanese MNEs at the initial stage was generally cautious and passive.

6.2.2 The Main Stage

By concentrating on the business operated within Europe, it is noticeable that Japanese companies have upgraded their operations from merely exports or license-in and -out to a commitment to main activities such as full-line production in the car industry, and self-development and self-marketing by the drug firms. This is the main stage of their internationalisation, since these activities constitute the primary operations, as described in Chapter 4. The entry mode also differs from the initial stage, and this subsection will elaborate on the entry modes of car and pharmaceutical MNEs at this main stage.

The principal feature of the second step taken by Japanese car MNEs to commit to the European market was the establishment of full-line assembly plants. The FDI in the car plants indicates a change in the European strategy from mainly exports to local production. Therefore, it is essential to trace the choice of the entry mode for the production facilities. The Japanese automobile industry faced a tide of protectionism from the late 1970s, not only in the US but also in European countries (Noelk and Taylor, 1981; Tsoukalis and White, 1982). In order to solve the difficult political situation, Japanese companies shifted their supply base from the domestic plants to those abroad. European business followed this general direction, and Japanese car companies set up plants one after another from the mid-1980s (Thomsen and Nicolaides 1991; Sachwald, 1995a). This entry mode preference became common among the three MNEs, and greenfield investment was chosen over any other mode for the full-line assembly plant. It will be shown, however, that auto MNEs at first hesitated to make a full commitment to European production, and their first steps towards car manufacturing demonstrates the differences among them. This passive and cautious entry strategy is consistent with a fairly large 'psychic distance' (Johanson and Wiedersheim-Paul, 1975; Johanson and Vahlne, 1977).

All three MNEs established UK plants in the 1980s through greenfield investment, as a result of trial and error. Nissan was the first among the three to start up European production, and tried all three entry modes. Honda collaborated with British Leyland (later the Rover group) well before its own full-line production was established. In spite of some minor joint ventures or knockdown production, Toyota was the last of the three to manufacture cars in its own plant in Europe, and in the interim kept a watching brief on its rivals and European conditions in general. Because of its importance, it is worthwhile looking at each MNE's entry into the manufacturing field.

In 1980, Nissan launched two projects to produce cars in Europe, but neither of them was satisfactory. The first, in January 1980, was an involvement in Motor Iberica in Spain through a minority shareholding (Nissan, 1983; Pallares-Barbera, 1996). The Spanish company had formerly produced agricultural machines and trucks before the capital participation by Nissan, which provided the production technology for commercial vehicles. Later, Nissan's stake exceeded 50 per cent in 1982, and Nissan became the major shareholder. Through full ownership and a change of name to Nissan Motor Iberica, widening the product line to include recreational vehicles, and restructuring the business, including a reduction in the payroll, it nevertheless took the Spanish subsidiary nearly 15 years to turn its operation from chronic loss to break-even (Shirai, 1994). Nissan adopted the acquisition method to establish a presence through production in Spain, but it is questionable whether the result was favourable.

At the same time, a joint-venture project between Nissan and Alfa Romeo, an Italian car producer, was attempted in Italy (Nissan, 1983). At the request of Alfa Romeo, negotiations started in March 1979, and the 50–50 company, Alfa Romeo e Nissan Autoveicoli (ARNA), was set up in December 1980. The plant was located in Avellino in southern Italy. The planned capacity was 60,000 passenger cars with 1,500 jobs, but this target was never reached during operations between 1983 and 1987. Finally ARNA was sold to Fiat, another Italian carmaker, when that company bought Alfa Romeo itself in 1987. Thus, entry through joint venture was a great disappointment for Nissan (Darby, 1996). As Eriksson and Majkgard (1998) suggest, 'experiential knowledge' at the first step heavily influences later decision making. It was predictable that Nissan would turn to greenfield investment in the UK.

The failure of the projects in Spain and Italy could be explained by labour matters. Nissan had to modernise the Spanish facility. The models produced there were limited to light commercial vehicles, but they were not competitive in Europe. The most serious problem, however, was the excess labour force, but strict labour legislation made it difficult for Nissan to reduce the number of employees. Even in 1994–95, Nissan Motor Iberica needed to reduce the workforce from 7,000 to 6,000 (Shirai, 1994, p. 6). In 2000, the number of workers in the UK plant was some 5,000, indicating the seriousness of the delay in restructuring Spanish subsidiary, though the problem cannot be attributed to the entry mode alone. The ARNA joint venture also faced labour management problems (Darby, 1996). Nissan could not introduce the flexible production system as it wanted to, because of opposition from Italian workers who were unfamiliar with Japanese-style management and knew only the mass production system. In addition, the quality of the cars produced by ARNA was always lower than expected, a factor that finally led Nissan to give up the venture.

Honda undertook a collaborative venture with a local firm, British Leyland, for the first step of local production, and then became independent. Starting from the licensing of medium-sized car production technology from Honda to British Leyland in 1979 (Edwardes, 1983), the collaboration proceeded relatively smoothly to the joint development of a new executive car in 1983 (Dymock, 1995). Furthermore, to demonstrate their constructive relationship, Honda UK Manufacturing Ltd and Rover exchanged 20 per cent of their shares with each other in 1990. A possibility for their relationship to evolve into a 50–50 joint venture in the UK arose in the mid-1990s, but this vanished with the acquisition of Rover group by BMW, a German car company. Prior to this, according to one interviewee:

> We [Honda] were consulted about the possibility of the full acquisition of Rover by British Aerospace. Then, we were prepared to buy up to 50 per cent of the share, but not 100 per cent. Full acquisition was rejected because of the low brand image of Rover on the continent.

Because BMW intended to buy all the shares, British Aerospace, which held the Rover group share, sold Rover to BMW. After the acquisition, Honda bought back Honda UK Manufacturing Ltd. from BMW, and sold the 20 per cent Rover share held by Honda to BMW. The relationship became increasingly arm's-length, rather than mutually co-operative, and now Honda is an independent player in Europe. Independence is one of Honda's most important company philosophies (Porter and Takeuchi, 2000), and the departure from the co-operative relationship with Rover is unlikely to seriously damage its European operation.

After their experiences concerning car manufacturing in Europe, all the Japanese auto MNEs chose greenfield investment in full-line plants in the UK. Nissan decided to establish a manufacturing site in Sunderland, northern England in 1984, and commenced production there from 1986. The British plant is reported to be one of the highest productivity plants in Europe.[6] Honda's UK subsidiary for manufacturing was set up in 1985, but the original operation was to conduct the pre-delivery inspection of the Honda badged cars made by Rover between 1985 and 1989 at the Swindon plant. The same plant introduced engine production for the Rover group, and further extended the manufacturing of Honda cars from 1992 with the supply of main components such as body panels and diesel engines from Rover.[7] Toyota decided to produce cars in Europe in 1989. It adopted the same method, greenfield investment, for its assembly plant in Burnaston, central England, and the engine plant in Shotton, North Wales. The first car was rolled off the line at the end of 1992. Toyota had formerly had some small manufacturing stakes in Europe, as seen in the previous subsection, but none of them had feedback effects for the British project. Thus, Toyota independently had to build up production capacity from scratch. Chapter 5 showed that Toyota now owns the second assembly plant in France to produce the smaller cars. Even though the British and French plants were established in different years, in 1992 and 2001 respectively, both of them were greenfield ventures, as was the component plant in Poland, which started production in 2002.[8]

The literature survey suggested that there is no clear industry-specific preference for the car manufacturing sites. However, some interesting characteristics emerge at this stage for Japanese car MNEs. The first is the cautious approach to establishing UK plants, the convergence to greenfield investment, and the time constraint of 1992. Nissan and Honda had tried entry modes other than greenfield investment, while Toyota observed the others' projects closely before finally entering full-line assembly in the UK. The second feature is that after initial caution, the preference of all three MNEs was a wholly-owned new project, that is, greenfield investment, rather than joint venture or acquisition. The last point is that Honda and Toyota were influenced by EU integration when they established their UK plants. Both companies started production in their UK plants before the end of 1992, when the SEM would be completed. One interviewee commented:

> We were afraid that the SEM would become a 'Fortress Europe' against Japanese cars including ours at the end of the 1980s. Thus, the establishment of a UK plant and the commencement of production had to be before the end of 1992, so that we could obtain the status of 'European producer'.

The fear of a 'Fortress Europe' was not realised, but nevertheless the SEM had a big influence on the decision making and the timing of a plant's establishment.

Unlike the auto case, which showed convergence of the entry mode to greenfield investment, the main stage of the pharmaceutical MNEs to commit to their European business demonstrated different preferences by each company. The pharmaceutical MNEs took a major leap and established their own European subsidiaries for the main business, that is, development through the clinical research and marketing their own medicine, as well as through production, although these were variations in the order and timing. The entry modes of the pharmaceutical MNEs can roughly be classified into two categories: a preference for joint ventures, and a preference for acquisitions. Both of these were supplemented by greenfield investments. The various European strategies followed by the different MNEs will be outlined below.

The first type of entry preference for joint venture can be seen at Takeda, which was the first pharmaceutical MNE to enter the European business, albeit with a degree of caution (Takeda, 1983). After years of supporting licensees from the drug division of its German subsidiaries, Takeda set up a joint venture with Roussel Uclaf in France in 1978. The French venture started with a minority shareholding (5 per cent), but the contract included an agreement to increase Takeda's share to 50 per cent as sales increased, and in 1983 the relationship between Takeda and Roussel Uclaf became a 50–50 joint-venture partnership. Other moves were the establishment of joint ventures in Germany and Italy in 1981 and 1982, respectively. The German venture was originally for an equal 50 per cent share with Grünental, while Takeda initially owned the minority share in the Italian joint venture with Cyanamid (38.46 per cent). All these were mainly committed to the development and marketing authorisation of Takeda's own drugs and domestic sales in each country, with support from the drug division of Takeda's German subsidiary in Hamburg.

The other three pharmaceutical MNEs, on the other hand, basically intended to enter the European business through acquisitions. In 1983, Fujisawa agreed a 28 per cent capital participation with the German firm, Klinge, but the contract included the possibility of majority ownership in the future. Fujisawa increased its share in Klinge to 74 per cent in 1988, and took over control of the German firm. The acquisition of Klinge brought Fujisawa some resources and facilities outside Germany, which enabled Fujisawa to expand its presence in Europe. A typical example is the Irish plant, which was constructed on the site of Klinge's Irish subsidiary in 1990 and included the land and human resources of the acquired company. The factory might therefore be regarded not as a greenfield investment but as a hybrid of greenfield investment and acquisition. On the other hand, some of the marketing network in Europe, such as the Austrian subsidiary, was also developed from Klinge's subsidiaries. Sankyo took a big step towards developing its European business through the acquisition in 1990 of Luitpold, a German pharmaceutical company (Sankyo, 2000, ch. 7). Luitpold had a sales network within Europe but not in France, and some countries outside Europe, as well as production facilities in Germany and France. Therefore, the acquisition of Luitpold provided Sankyo with a quick and extensive means of entry into Europe. In order to establish its own marketing network, Yamanouchi bought a Dutch firm. In 1991, Yamanouchi reached an agreement with Royal Gist Brocades, the chemical company in the Netherlands, concerning the purchase of the pharmaceutical division, Brocades Pharma. Through the acquisition, Yamanouchi could immediately establish a development facility and pan-European network for marketing.

At this stage, all four drug MNEs combined greenfield investment with joint ventures or acquisitions. Takeda and Sankyo set up new drug development facilities in Germany in 1988 and 1985, respectively, through greenfield investment. Takeda's R&D centre employing some 40 staff was separated from the subsidiary in Hamburg and relocated in Frankfurt, in order to benefit from the personnel and experience of the European business. For example, the chief manager of development in Europe endorsed the development process for Takeda's first drug in Europe, and has been working for more than two decades in both the Hamburg subsidiary and the Frankfurt R&D centre. Sankyo Europe in Düsseldorf was a completely new venture specialising in clinical tests, although in 1999 it was still operating with a small staff of 20, including three Japanese.[9]

Fujisawa and Yamanouchi, on the other hand, differed slightly from Takeda and Sankyo in the scale of their use of greenfield investment. Fujisawa extended its European subsidiaries to countries other than those that Klinge had formerly covered. The representative office set up in London in 1979 was given the competence for phase I clinical tests, and became the Clinical Research Centre in 1985. Preparing for the introduction of Fujisawa's own new novel drug Prograf, the immunosuppressant, the company actively established marketing facilities in the UK, Italy and France in 1993 and in Spain in 1994.[10] The French and Spanish subsidiaries were set up through greenfield investment, while the existing representative offices were upgraded in the case of the UK and Italy. Before expanding the marketing network in Europe, Fujisawa founded its European headquarters in Munich, Germany, in 1991 through greenfield investment along with Klinge, which is mainly allocated the Prograf business.

Yamanouchi had already undertaken greenfield investment before the acquisition of Brocades Pharma.[11] Bulk production in Ireland was the starting point for Yamanouchi's full international commitment, and the plant commenced production in 1988 as a fully-owned new venture. Yamanouchi's first novel drug, Guster, was produced in the Irish plant largely for Merck, which contracted to market Guster through its own network in the world market other than Japan and some Asian countries. The second step was to set up a basic research institute in the UK, and the Yamanouchi Research Institute (YRI), was established in Oxford in 1990.[12] Starting with the appointment of the top director, YRI was also constructed from scratch. YRI conducted basic research on cell biology, which was not formerly a strong area for Japanese medical science or Yamanouchi. Although the director is an English scientist, the institute is fully owned, controlled and financed by Yamanouchi.

In summary, the second stage in the pharmaceutical MNEs entry into Europe shows variation among the four. Sankyo gained a production facility through acquisition, while Yamanouchi undertook a new venture for a more sophisticated facility than the others. Fujisawa fully utilised the acquired company's resources, but the Irish plant was a new one. With regard to R&D, clinical development facilities show the greatest difference among the four: joint venture and later greenfield investment by Takeda, greenfield investment from the start at Sankyo, an acquisition by Yamanouchi, and the hybrid case of Fujisawa. On the other hand, acquisition of a local company was preferred for the marketing network, except for Takeda whose preference was for a joint venture.

This summary shows some interesting features, which are not common to the two industries. First, the auto MNEs tended to prefer greenfield investment, despite some trial and error at the beginning of full-line production in Europe. This is particularly relevant in view of the uncertainties caused by the SEM's completion by 1992. Second, the pharmaceutical preference indicated a tendency for acquisitions, although greenfield investments were also chosen in some cases. Takeda shares the common tendency not to prefer new ventures, but is also exceptional with regard to its joint venture preference. Third, there is no consistent order among the drug MNEs for entering into development, production and marketing at each company.

6.2.3 Further Developments

Japanese MNEs did not stop once they had set up facilities in Europe, either manufacturing plants as in the auto industry or development and marketing subsidiaries as in the pharmaceutical sector. Rather, all of them proceeded to secure their business by establishing supplementary facilities. Here, there is a clear tendency towards full ownership, although some facilities were established through greenfield investments and others were acquisitions.

After establishing UK plants, all three car MNEs showed an inclination to support the European business more fundamentally than before. Along with establishing production facilities, the auto MNEs extended their activities to non-manufacturing activities such as R&D and regional management by setting up their R&D centres and EHQ, principally through full ownership. However, some of these methods involved greenfield investment, while others necessitated an upgrade of existing affiliates or representative offices by increasing their competence. Nissan and Honda established new EHQs in 1989 in the Netherlands and the UK, respectively, while Toyota upgraded its Brussels representative office to EHQ status in 1990. On the other hand, the R&D facilities were also the result of a greenfield investment in the case of Honda in Germany in 1988 and in the UK in 1992. Nissan chose both greenfield investment and the upgrade method for its R&D. The former was used for the R&D centre in the UK and the design centre in Germany established in 1988 and 1992, respectively, and the latter for its Spanish and Belgium facilities in 1989. Further, the design centre was moved to London, in 2003. Toyota's Belgian R&D facility set up in 1989 was a greenfield investment, but the part of designing new cars in this R&D centre was relocated to southern France in 2000. The development and verification sites in Germany in 1987 and the UK in 1992 were also new ventures, and the latter relocated to Belgium in 2000.

Moreover, although seeking full ownership, the auto MNEs adopted a different approach for the national car distributors – these tended to be acquired or under majority ownership. Since Honda already had its own European sales force for motorcycles and power equipment from the 1960s, the necessary facilities for car sales were not to set up new subsidiaries, but to upgrade the existing ones. Acquisitions of national distributors were made by Nissan in France, Italy and the Netherlands from the mid-1980s (Nissan, 1996). On the other hand, negotiations concerning the acquisition of the UK distributor faced serious disagreement over conditions. Nissan, therefore, had to relinquish the acquisition of Datsun UK, the former local stake for distributing its cars, and establish its own national distributor from scratch.[13] At the same time, in the 1980s Nissan established a warehouse for cars and parts in the Netherlands, and then extended its affiliates to Spain, France and the UK. Most of Toyota's national distributors were established around the time when the UK factory started production, except for the German national distributor (Toyota, 1997). Toyota's distributors were established through acquisitions or minority ownership, which could be increased to a majority. Originally, only the UK had warehouse facility, but as sales increased, Toyota set up warehouses on the Continent around 2000.

From the early 2000s, adaptations were made in response to the changing external and internal conditions in Europe in the auto MNEs, though they did not always involve expansion. Honda expanded its capacity at the Swindon plant, reorganised the sales and marketing network in Europe, and relocated its EHQ from Reading to Langley, near London. Nissan, whose total performance was so bad that it needed a capital injection from Renault in

1999, also restructured its European business, so as to maximise the synergy effects with Renault. For example, the sales and marketing network including the dealer outlets were consolidated, while the EHQ was moved from Amsterdam to Trappes, near Paris, where the headquarters of Renault is located. Toyota is the most aggressive in expanding its facilities in Europe. It decided to establish its own transmission and engine plant, and a joint-venture plant for diesel engines with Toyota Industries Corporation in Poland; it is also constructing a small car assembly plant based on a joint venture with Peugeot-Citroen in the Czech Republic, which is due to start production in 2005. Here, both a greenfield investment and a joint venture have been undertaken to enter Eastern Europe, and the reasons for this will be considered below.

Further developments in the pharmaceutical MNEs in Europe showed a similar pattern to that of the car MNEs: complementing the results of the main stage, and further developing their presence with full ownership of the subsidiaries and affiliates. First, companies upgraded their existing facilities. Takeda extended its own R&D operation by setting up a London branch of the German centre in 1995. In 1998 the German centre was closed, and the main activities were moved to London, in order to closely monitor and maintain contact with the EMEA. Sankyo and Yamanouchi restructured their acquired companies into EHQs, enabling them to supervise their European operations. Luitpold was renamed Sankyo Pharma GmbH in 1997, while Brocades Pharma was renamed Yamanouchi Europe in 1994. Along with these changes, Yamanouchi rebuilt the R&D facility in Yamanouchi Europe, and reconstructed the plants in the Netherlands and Italy.

The late 1990s witnessed the additional but different development of Takeda in Europe. The marketing subsidiary in the UK was reformed through a greenfield investment in 1997. In the same year, the drug plant was acquired in Ireland from Greran Pharmaceutical, a Japanese company, which has a close relationship with Takeda. The factory processes the bulk drugs imported from Japan to package them in final form. In addition to this processing factory, a bulk production plant was established in Ireland through a greenfield investment in 2002. In 1998, Takeda bought its partners' shares of the joint ventures in France and Italy and took over full control. Further, a stake in the German joint venture was also acquired with the aim of obtaining full ownership in 2002. Thus, there was a shift in preference as Takeda moved from joint ventures to full ownership.

The expansion of facilities through greenfield investment can be seen in Sankyo and Yamanouchi. Since Luitpold did not always cover small countries in Europe, Sankyo extended sales subsidiaries.[14] The subsidiaries that were established in Austria (1994), the Netherlands (1996), Finland (1996) and Belgium (1997) were extensions. In 1997, a small representative office with a staff of three was set up in London as a new venture. The purpose of this office is to collect medical information, including that concerning the new drug approval system conducted by the EMEA. The follow-up development after Yamanouchi's acquisition of Brocades Pharma was to extend the subsidiaries and affiliates for marketing purposes into countries where Brocades Pharma had never previously had any stakes. As a result, Yamanouchi covered most European countries, including some in Eastern Europe such as Poland (Yamanouchi, 1999). In 2003, Yamanouchi separated the strategic decision making from the clinical development in the EHQ in the Netherlands, and moved the former to a new UK subsidiary in London. This new subsidiary became Yamanouchi's new EHQ, and consolidated the national sales business in the UK. As a result, the Dutch subsidiary concentrates on the clinical development. At the same time, the basic research laboratory in Oxford was closed down in 2002, and activities were concentrated to the Tsukuba laboratory in Japan.

Uniquely, Fujisawa entered into basic research in Europe, not through its own facility but on the basis of a contract.[15] In 1992, Edinburgh University agreed to conduct basic research for Fujisawa for five years at the Fujisawa Institute of Neuroscience in Edinburgh (FINE). The contract can be renewed every five years. According to this contract, FINE receives new chemical entities and neuroscience researchers from Fujisawa. As a result, Fujisawa has a basic research capacity in Europe that is contractual, rather than based on full ownership.

Fujisawa merged Klinge and Fujisawa GmbH, the EHQ, and reorganised the operation in 2002. Fujisawa GmbH continues to be the EHQ, while Klinge was renamed Fujisawa Deutschland and supervises the German operation. With the change of office and other aspects, Fujisawa consolidated its operational structure, thus simplifying the former double structure involving Klinge and Fujisawa GmbH. This confirms that Fujisawa has also followed the pattern to full ownership.

In sum, the further developments of Japanese MNEs after they established their main business operation show some interesting features. First, the full ownership preference has become more pronounced. Second, in the auto sector, greenfield investment tended to be chosen for upstream operations, while acquisitions were preferred for the sales-related subsidiaries. Third, the drug MNEs opted for more greenfield investment, although they tended to be relatively small concerns. The final point is that all of the MNEs examined here actively restructured their operation in Europe through upgrading their existing facilities or their acquired companies, or through consolidating their facilities. In some cases, such as Toyota and Takeda, the purpose of the restructuring process was to expand capacity.

This section has analysed the three-stage entry mode of Japanese MNEs.

From the historical point of view, Japanese car MNEs started their European business by exporting through a local agent, and have not always preferred full ownership (Table 6.1). The main car assembly business in Europe, however, was developed from scratch with full ownership, though the process of trial and error shows some difference among the three auto MNEs. The follow-up development after committing to production was roughly divided between the acquisition of national distributors, and supplementing the European business through the establishment of R&D facilities and an EHQ by way of greenfield investments. Research confirmed the entry mode variations between the businesses before and after production.

With regard to the pharmaceutical cases, the pattern of Japanese drug MNEs showed a kind of cyclical shift, which started from the common strategy, greenfield investment, through the divergent ones, and generally returned to greenfield investment (Table 6.2). All the companies started with a similar strategy of making small investments, such as setting up representative offices. At the next stage of establishing main business subsidiaries in Europe, there were divergences in corporate strategies. Yamanouchi preferred a new venture for production, while the others chose acquisitions for manufacturing. Acquisitions were undertaken for all sales-related subsidiaries except those of Takeda. Fujisawa's approach, however, can be classified as a hybrid case between acquisition and greenfield investment. Indeed, of the four MNEs, only Fujisawa and Yamanouchi established a basic research laboratory in Europe, and they adopted completely opposite approaches to establishing their facilities, as Penner-Hahn (1998) discovered with regard to cases in the United States. Convergence complemented the shortcomings of the acquisitions or joint ventures, and this was the preference for full ownership.

This section has investigated the entry mode of Japanese automobile and pharmaceutical MNEs into Europe, and its changing pattern in the process of the development of their European business. Unlike the previous literature, the findings are not merely limited to manufacturing facilities, but also include non-manufacturing sites. The differences between the MNEs in an industry, between the two industries, and between one point of time and another even within an MNE are addressed. The next section will discuss the reasons for the choice among the three entry modes, especially bearing in mind the internationalisation process.

Table 6.1   Classification of entry mode by Japanese automobile MNEs

		First stage	Second stage	Third stage
Honda	JV		Collaboration with Rover National distributor in Portugal	
	AQ	National distributor in Sweden		
	GFI		UK plant R&D in Germany ←————— National distributor	EHQ R&D in UK —————→
Nissan	JV		Manufacturing with Alfa Romeo	
	AQ	National distributor in France, Germany	Motor Iberica including marketing facility	National distributor in the UK
	GFI	National distributor in the Netherlands	UK plant	Warehouses R&D EHQ
Toyota	JV	Portuguese plant		Polish and Czech plants
	AQ	National distributor in Germany		National distributor in Finland, France, Italy, Spain, Sweden, the UK
	GFI		UK plant	French and Polish plants R&D EHQ Warehouses

Note: JV: joint venture; AQ: acquisition; GFI: greenfield investment.

Table 6.2   Classification of entry mode by Japanese pharmaceutical MNEs

		First stage	Second stage	Third stage
Fujisawa	JV			FINE
	AQ		Klinge	
	GFI	Representative offices in the UK, and Italy	Irish packaging plant Marketing in France, Italy, Spain, and the UK R&D in UK EHQ	
Sankyo	JV			
	AQ		Luitpold ➡	Upgrade to EHQ
	GFI	Representative office in Switzerland	R&D in Germany	Marketing in Austria, the Netherlands, Finland and Belgium Representative office in the UK
Takeda	JV		Marketing in Germany, France and Italy	
	AQ			Marketing in France and Italy Irish packaging plant
	GFI	Representative office in Germany	R&D in Germany	R&D in the UK Marketing in the UK Irish bulk plant
Yamanouchi	JV			
	AQ		Brocades Pharma ➡	Upgrade to EHQ
	GFI	Representative office in the UK, Germany, and France	Irish bulk plants R&D in the UK	Marketing in Spain

Note: JV: joint venture; AQ: acquisition; GFI: greenfield investment

6.3   DETERMINANT FACTORS FOR ENTRY

The last section confirmed the entry modes of Japanese car and drug MNEs into Europe in light of the sequential pattern of expanding their European business. Firms do not always adopt the same entry mode, while each of the three modes is selected in each industry. At the same time, there are differences and similarities among the MNEs within the same industrial sector, as well as between the two industries. This section will examine what factors influence the MNEs in their selection of entry modes, based on the literature survey in Chapter 2. Special attention will be paid to the locational conditions, which have been changing under European integration. The internationalisation process model suggests a change in the capacity of a firm through the accumulation of knowledge in a time series, and the importance of this is not ignored. In a time series, however, not only does the company's capacity change, but also the environmental factors. The locational conditions are an important factor, but they are dealt with less explicitly. Thus, in this section, the influence of European integration on the entry mode will be examined.

6.3.1   Joint Ventures

On the basis of a relatively broad definition,[16] cases such as a co-operative agreement, like the partnership between Honda and Rover, or a minority Japanese shareholding, such as Takeda in France, can be included in the joint-venture category. It is noteworthy that joint ventures do not always take an ideal form, that is, 50–50 ownership between the partners. In spite of different forms, however, there are some similarities that point to the common determinant factors of the selection.

First, joint ventures were preferred by Japanese MNEs in the relatively early stage of European entry. Such a preference can largely be explained by two factors: the financial costs and the costs concerning uncertainties and risks. The financial costs may well be more important in the early stage than the later. The relatively small size of a company limits the investment capacity, and leads to the option with less cost. The necessity of investing in regions other than Europe, especially in North America, limited the allocation of the resources for Europe. In addition, the small market also led the MNE to choose a joint venture, due to the difficulty of raising enough revenue for the investment.

The joint ventures by the automobile MNEs are typical cases of exploiting their smaller financial cost advantage, but the same factor also influenced the pharmaceutical companies. Honda's partnership with Rover started and developed at the same time as Honda's plant in the US in 1982. The US market was more important for the company than that in Europe, and thus the latter was based on the partnership with Rover. In addition, Honda had always been the smallest among the three MNEs. When Nissan chose a strategy to produce cars abroad from the late 1970s, it used various methods in various countries. These included the plants in North America, capital participation in the Spanish company, Motor Iberica, from 1980 and investment in the UK in 1982. This situation might well have required Nissan to reduce its investment cost in Italy through the joint venture with Alfa Romeo. Toyota's minority joint venture in Portugal is mainly restricted by the size of the Portuguese market (Takahashi, 1997). On the other hand, when Takeda stepped up its own business in Europe from the late 1970s, a joint venture was chosen due to cost restrictions. This was mainly because at that time the clinical tests for new drug approval had to be duplicated, since there was less integration within the EU. The fact that the joint ventures were limited to the three main countries of Germany, France and Italy also affected Takeda's financial cost considerations.

The second point concerns the uncertainties and risks due to the lack of experience in foreign business in the early stage (Kogut and Singh, 1988; Agarwal and Ramaswami, 1992). The unfamiliarity with European auto manufacturing operations may well have affected the choices made by Honda and Nissan, since no Japanese car company had ever set up a full-line assembly in Europe. Honda was the first company to establish a factory in Europe in 1963, but it was for motorcycle production. That operation was not without its problems (Honda, 2000), and might well have made Honda more cautious about the risks involved in the initial stage of car production in Europe. On the other hand, the consideration of uncertainties and risks also applies to the pharmaceutical MNEs, because of the high rate of failure in the development process. The rate of failure may well be higher in foreign countries than in Japan due to the unfamiliarity, and a lack of experience also makes a company more cautious. Thus, Takeda preferred a joint venture for development and marketing in the main European markets at the early stage, while Fujisawa secured a contract agreement with Edinburgh University for basic research activities.

In addition, the accessibility to knowledge is also a favourable factor for joint ventures as well as acquisitions. Sales-related knowledge about the target countries is necessary, and the subsidiary in each country needs to acquire knowledge about the local environment. Both joint ventures and acquisitions can offer the necessary knowledge, but preference for one or the other reflects the strategy of the company. Takeda preferred joint ventures, while the other three pharmaceutical companies, especially Yamanouchi and Sankyo, favoured acquisitions. An interviewee at Takeda in Europe emphasised the difficulty of the foreign business, and commented:

We are not sure whether ownership guarantees control over the subsidiary abroad, but we are sure that experience is a more important factor than ownership. Therefore, a joint venture was more favourable than an acquisition, at least until we accumulated experience of international business to a certain level.[17]

There is a similar tendency to prefer joint ventures and acquisitions over greenfield investments in the case of the sales-related facilities at the auto MNEs, with the exception of Honda. This issue will be addressed in the following subsection on acquisitions.

Another interesting point is that Yamanouchi and Sankyo have not adopted a joint-venture strategy in Europe at all. This is explained by the disadvantage of joint ventures compared with other methods, namely that of having less control over the operation. From its past experience in the US, Yamanouchi excluded joint ventures from its European entry, while Sankyo intended to avoid the complications caused by the co-existence of joint ventures and licensing. In the 1980s, Yamanouchi entered into a partnership agreement with the US drug company Eli Lilly (Takahashi, 1988). The co-operation was not a success, and Yamanouchi was dissatisfied with the collaboration. According to one interviewee, the main reason for the failure was that it was quite difficult to reach a compromise on how to conduct their co-operative business. The co-operation agreement was finally dissolved, and Yamanouchi's American business was delayed. Sankyo, despite its capability of inventing novel drugs, had long hesitated to launch into international business by itself (Nikkei Business, 2000a). As a result, most of Sankyo's main drugs were licensed out to European or American MNEs; for example, Mevalotin was licensed out to Bristol Myers Squibb. This situation made adjustment between the license-out contracts and joint ventures more difficult. In addition, Sankyo judged that the longevity of the joint venture was also an obstacles.

The point to be addressed here in the context of internationalisation concerns the duration of joint venture. A joint venture is not permanent, but rather it tends to result in failure (Nissan and Alfa Romeo), termination (Honda and Rover), or acquisition of the partner's share (Takeda). A joint venture is likely not only to save on financial and uncertainty costs, but also to lead to the loss of full control. Nissan could not maintain its high standards in the ARNA joint venture auto plant, largely because the Italians did not accept Nissan's style of production control. Although the stated reason for ending the partnership was BMW's acquisition of Rover, Honda nevertheless experienced irritation at the differences between both sides. The development process for new models, for example, took longer under the partnership, due to the necessity for the engineers from both sides to agree on minute points. The following interview statement clearly shows the difficulty of control.

We were very happy with the collaboration with our partner, since we could reduce the initial investment costs and the uncertainty. However, it was also true that the discussions with our partner made it difficult to make a quick decision regarding strategy. There were some cases of disagreement concerning minor issues, which took longer than our own decision making.

The same situation as that in the auto industry can be found in the pharmaceutical sector, and the case of Takeda is typical. Takeda moved to acquire the shares of the joint-venture partner, in order to obtain full control of the subsidiary in question.[18] Takeda has been systematically developing activities in Europe through the introduction of a range of its own drugs. In this process, it has been accumulating experience and knowledge of European business. Thus, it has come to rely less on joint ventures, and more on expanding its presence based on its own judgement and analysis. As the internationalisation process model indicates (Johanson and Vahlne, 1977; Andersen, 1993; Eriksson et al., 1997), in conjunction with an accumulating business experience in MNEs, the knowledge gained from the local partner becomes less important. In other words, the limited duration of a joint venture may well also be brought about by its own success.

The last point regarding joint-venture entry concerns the timing in the context of European integration. It is noteworthy that the joint ventures were often undertaken in situations where the EU had not yet fully integrated the national markets. Takeda preferred joint ventures, before the new drug approval system under the EU had been realised. However, with European integration on the drug marketing approval system under the EMEA in London, Takeda reorganised its R&D operation and moved its R&D centre for clinical tests from Germany to the UK. This fact supports the contention that Takeda's early entry affected its mode of entry. An interview with a Takeda employee in Europe commented: 'In those days when Takeda shifted from license-out to self-marketing, the cross-border consideration for clinical tests and marketing was not as logical as nowadays'. It should be recalled that Toyota discontinued the licensing of knockdown car production in Ireland after Ireland's transition period of membership in the EU. On the other hand, minority share in a joint venture has been maintained in Portugal, a country included in the 'Consensus between the EU and Japan' on the restriction of car imports which lasted until 1999. The partnership between Honda and Rover and the joint venture between Nissan and Alfa Romeo occurred when protectionist pressure from the member states was strong, and the EU could not prevent it from a pan-European perspective. In so far as the auto industry concerns the national interests of the member state, a close relationship with a company in the target country may well advance business in Europe. The more the regulatory framework becomes set at the EU level, however, the more MNEs need to conduct their business from a European perspective. Thus, with the development of European integration, joint ventures become less attractive.

Here, Toyota's joint ventures into Poland and the Czech Republic will be examined. While Toyota produced the diesel engine through its joint venture with one group company, Toyota Industries Corporation, it will assemble small cars through its joint venture with Peugeot from 2005. The question is, why did Toyota choose to set up joint ventures in its latest investment in Europe? The answer lies in uncertainty and the learning effect from the partner. Needless to say, Poland and the Czech Republic are less familiar to Japanese companies, including Toyota, than West European countries. The transition of these countries from the planned economy to the market economy has experienced some difficulties, and they still cannot be treated the same as their Western counterparts. Thus, the uncertainty costs can be higher than in Western Europe, and may well be one reason why Toyota opted for joint ventures. At the same time, the collaboration with the joint-venture partner is expected to bring some advantages for Toyota's European operation. An interviewee emphasised this point as follows:

> In spite of a recent upturn of sales, Toyota is still a challenger in Europe. We appreciate Peugeot's operation, which has increased the market share and profits. From the joint venture with Peugeot we can learn about things such as procurement in Europe. On the other hand, since Toyota depends on the supply of diesel engines from Toyota Industries Corporation in Japan, it is quite natural to request co-operation in diesel engine production in Europe.

In other words, the new situation resulting from the opening-up of Eastern Europe, and the strategy of using external resources, to some extent justified Toyota's choice of joint ventures in Eastern Europe.

A joint venture provides a favourable option for entry into certain environments, even if it is not a permanent form of organisation. Here, it is worth emphasising that some of the advantages offered by a joint venture can also be obtained through acquisition. Thus, the next subsection considers acquisitions in comparison with joint ventures, as well as with another full ownership entry mode, that is, greenfield investment.

6.3.2 Acquisitions

Unlike a joint venture, the entry modes of acquisition and greenfield investment entail full ownership of subsidiaries. A clear contrast examined in the preference for one or the other between the car and drug MNEs, when they stepped up their business in Europe from mere exports or licensing-out. Acquisitions were preferred by the pharmaceutical companies for establishing their presence, while the auto companies chose greenfield investment. Thus, the main focus here will be on the determinant factors for acquisitions in the case of the pharmaceutical MNEs, and those for greenfield investment for the automotive companies. However, some exceptions were found. Therefore, the question whether or not common factors exist between the two industries will be examined, first with regard to acquisitions.

The preference for acquisition by the pharmaceutical firms is clear, and three out of four pharmaceutical MNEs – Fujisawa, Sankyo and Yamanouchi – chose this method for starting up their own main business in Europe. Indeed, the acquisition was not always realised by an initial outright purchase, but sometimes proceeded gradually. At a certain point in time, the situation could be misinterpreted as a joint venture or capital participation, rather than as an acquisition. Therefore, a consideration of the situation in the long-term context enables a more precise understanding. Furthermore, when the process to obtain ownership of the acquisition was gradual, an attempt was made to confirm the initial intention of MNEs at the interviews. Fujisawa's acquisition of Klinge, which took a number of years before it achieved majority ownership, is an example of this gradual process. Interviews confirmed that although the owners had agreed to the acquisition by Fujisawa from the beginning, it intended to sell its share of Klinge bit by bit, for legal and tax reasons. In contrast, Yamanouchi bought the pharmaceutical division of Royal Giest Brocades outright. Sankyo started with a capital participation in Luitpold in 1990, but soon fully acquired the company in 1991. Despite the different process, the preference for acquisitions shown by the pharmaceutical MNEs is quite clear.

The fact that the drug companies tended to choose acquisitions is explained first by the rapid and extensive entry into the complex and large European market. Most of the interviews confirm that this was necessary for several reasons. In general, as we saw in Chapter 4, the pharmaceutical industry needs a speedy introduction of new drugs. In addition, the Japanese national health insurance system and the competitive conditions in the Japanese market changed dramatically from the late 1970s (Nippon Yakushi Gakkai, 1995). The Ministry of Health and Welfare (MHW) began to regularly reduce the price of ethical drugs listed on the national health insurance system. The new drug approval system was also changed to give preference to novel drugs and less support for the me-too drugs on which Japanese pharmaceutical companies had long relied. In addition, foreign companies that had previously operated joint ventures with Japanese companies dissolved these joint ventures and became independent competitors of Japanese companies.[19] As a result of the fiercer domestic market, Japanese companies had to internationalise their operations if possible. Because of budget constraints, European drug markets are not growing as strongly as those in the US (Gambardella et al., 2000), but speedy entry for Japanese MNEs was still necessary. Vasconcellos and Kish (1998) maintain that the different economic performance between the home and the host country significantly affects the acquisition, and the findings in this book confirm that under pressure from the home market, acquisitions were preferred to ensure speedy entry conditions.

Access to the resources of the acquired company is no less important than speedy entry. In spite of the integration of the new drug approval system in the EU, there are still many differences from country to country, especially with regard to marketing. Prescriptions by doctors are influenced not only by their knowledge of drugs, but also by the medical culture, which varies from one country to another (Corstjens, 1991). Thus, the sales force of a pharmaceutical company needs to understand what information doctors require, how to stress the advantages of its own drug compared to others, and so on. It would require a great deal of time to establish a network of subsidiaries from scratch. Acquisition enables the acquiring company to obtain both the network of subsidiaries and the experienced staff. Bresman et al. (1999) maintain that the knowledge transfer from the acquiring to the acquired company is important, especially in the early stage of post-acquisition, but it is still true that full access to the knowledge of the acquired firm is preferable to partial access through a joint venture. An interviewee at the EHQ of a pharmaceutical MNE commented:

> As well as rapid and widespread entry, the merits of acquisition for us are to obtain the human capital, the business know-how, and the patents of the acquired company, which can be used to extend the patent of the existing medicines through a new drug delivery system.

Another aspect of the advantages brought by acquisitions is that the acquired company itself can support the start-up costs for introducing new drugs. Even if a pharmaceutical MNE has a novel drug that can be competitive in foreign markets, it needs to be approved by the authority for introduction into the market concerned. In order to gain approval, a company has to conduct clinical tests, but this yields neither sales nor profits during the development and filing period. Without the financial flow, a company cannot introduce a new drug by itself. The acquired company can provide the necessary financial resources for the costs of new drug introduction through sales of its existing assets such as medical products, even if they are not necessarily novel drugs. For example, 35 per cent of Yamanouchi Europe's sales in 1996 is from the drugs inherited from the acquired company, which is much larger than from Yamanouchi's own drug introduced in 1995.[20]

Finally, entry timing in the context of European integration is related to the preference for acquisitions. The period when Japanese drug companies began entering into the EU was the heyday of the 1992 SEM programme. Although there were no serious disputes between Japanese and European pharmaceutical industries, it was not clear whether the EU market would be open to outsiders. Generally, the best course for Japanese MNEs was to establish their status as inside players in the EU (Macarthur, 1991). However, a more important point is that the SEM provided the conditions for wide entry through acquisitions, since it accelerated the integration of the new drug approval system. This could reduce the costs caused by the duplication of clinical tests, and the wide entry would lead to more sales under the development of European integration. This shows a clear contrast with Takeda, which, as seen in the previous subsection, could not enjoy the benefits of European integration when it entered into Europe. Thus, acquisition is the favourable mode of entry for Japanese pharmaceutical MNEs.

With regard to the acquisition strategy in the automobile sector, some of the determinant factors in the pharmaceutical industry are also common to the car companies. Most of the acquisitions by the auto MNEs were conducted to obtain national distributors, although one was the case of Nissan's acquisition of Motor Iberica. Nissan tried all three entry modes in the early 1980s, and the acquisition of the Spanish commercial vehicle producer, Motor Iberica, was one of them. Here the speed of entry and the cheap price were reported to be motivations for the acquisition (Sato, 2000), though the business was not as successful as expected (Shirai, 1994). Acquisitions other than Nissan's were made by European MNEs, too. Some were successful and others failed. An example of the latter was the acquisition of Rover by BMW, while that of SEAT by Volkswagen was a success. Nevertheless, Nissan's experience does not merely confirm the advantage of speedy entry by acquisition, but also supports Woodcock et al.'s (1994) argument that acquisition does not produce as favourable a performance as greenfield investment.

Most acquisitions by Japanese car MNEs were of national distributors, which had always been the agencies for car imports from Japan. The main role of a national distributor is not restricted to imports of cars from the assembler for domestic dealer outlets. Rather, they maintain close contact with the dealers and collect information personally, in order to become fully conversant with demand conditions and trends that could not always be obtained from public sources. A reliable relationship with dealers is not established instantly, but has to be built up over a long period. Therefore, auto companies preferred to acquire national distributors. Nissan's UK distributor was set up from scratch, but this was because of a disagreement between the owner of the former local distributor and Nissan. Nissan originally intended to establish a marketing subsidiary in the UK through acquisition, but the conflict with the UK distributor forced Nissan to relinquish the acquisition. If the conditions had been fulfilled, Nissan would have chosen acquisition rather than greenfield investment. In other words, the intangible assets of a local firm concerning the marketing operation are as important for the auto industry as they are for the pharmaceutical industry.

Honda is unusual in that most of its subsidiaries were started by greenfield investment. This can be explained by its unique product line-up. Honda produces and sells products that are closely related to one another: from power equipment through motorcycles to passenger cars. Honda's entry into foreign markets generally starts with power equipment or motorcycles, and is then extended to cars. Honda is the world leader in the first two categories, which need relatively small investment compared with cars. Through the sales of power equipment and motorcycles, knowledge of and experience in the market concerned can be accumulated in the company. Honda internalises these, and utilises them for the motor vehicle business. Thus, most European subsidiaries for marketing Honda vehicles were not acquisitions, but greenfield investments with support from other business divisions of the company.[21]

From a consideration of the determinant factors for acquisitions, some important points can be recognised. The first is that fast and wide entry through acquisition appealed to Japanese pharmaceutical MNEs which, with the exception of Takeda, were the relative latecomers. The acquisition of a European company with some subsidiaries in Europe gives Japanese MNEs an advantage for establishing a European presence. Second, the resources brought by the acquired company are an incentive, especially for the marketing operations in both industries. The resources appealing to MNEs are both the financial flows and the intangible assets, such as marketing-related knowledge. The third point is the importance of the locational conditions especially those brought about by European integration. The previous subsection showed that less integration led the MNEs to opt for joint ventures, whereas here the opposite situation, namely the advance of European integration, provided favourable circumstances for full ownership, especially in the case of the pharmaceutical MNEs. At the same time, European integration does not necessarily unite the national markets into a single entity, and that justified the acquisition of national companies for the sales-related subsidiaries. The complicated locational conditions in Europe influenced the decision to choose an acquisition. The different preference for joint ventures and acquisitions shown by Takeda and the other three pharmaceutical MNEs typically illustrates this point. Last but not least is the fact that the acquisition choice was influenced a great deal by the existence and character of the acquired company, as the cases of Nissan and Fujisawa suggest. MNEs cannot make an acquisition unless there is an appropriate target, and the assets of the acquired firm are not always sufficient to tempt the acquiring company. Furthermore, the inherited resources cannot be fully and properly controlled and managed by the parent company.

6.3.3 Greenfield Investment

At a glance, greenfield investment seems less favourable an entry mode than the other two. It requires considerable financial resources to build a factory and offices. Establishing subsidiaries is a lengthy business, particularly with regard to construction and staff recruitment. The least amount of knowledge on the host economy is available, since the new subsidiary commences operations with no resources transferred from a local company, contrary to the situation regarding joint ventures and acquisitions. The lengthy start-up time plus less knowledge and experience can increase the uncertainties and risks. However, in spite of these disadvantages, greenfield investment was chosen the most by the car MNEs for European subsidiaries in all business areas other than sales-related ones. The case of the auto MNEs is in line with the general tendency of Japanese FDI, which Yamawaki (1994) confirms both in Europe and the US. The main reason for selecting greenfield investment is having control over the subsidiaries (Woodcock et al., 1994), and this is also true for Japanese auto MNEs. The determinant factors for greenfield investment will be investigated mainly through the auto industry, although the pharmaceutical companies will also be examined.

First, the introduction of a unique production method by Japanese auto companies led them to prefer greenfield investment. The competitiveness of Japanese cars depends on low cost and a low rate of defects, which are based not on mass production but on flexible production system (Womack et al., 1990). Even if flexible production system could be operated independently from the environment in Japan, it is much more difficult to replace the existing mass production system. This is because transforming mass production to flexible production system requires a great deal of restructuring of existing facilities and business methods (Starkey and McKinlay, 1993).[22] These include all aspects of car production not only within the plant, but also with respect to suppliers. In the process, the company often faces serious opposition from several sides, such as trade unions. Even when the 'decline' of the British car industry in the 1970s provided some plants for acquisition, no Japanese firm was interested. The legacy from the existing firms or plants was calculated to exceed the costs of a greenfield investment. This point was still true in the 1990s, when Honda rejected the full acquisition of Rover despite their collaboration.

Greenfield investment is the best way to introduce a company-specific production method. It enables a company to construct a plant that fulfils the strategy requirements of the company. Methods for recruiting, training and allocating the staff can be designed to suit the specific company (Wickens, 1987; Garrahan and Stewart, 1992; Foley et al., 1996). The relationship with the trade union is not necessarily influenced by the tradition of the industry. Nissan and Toyota concluded a single union agreement with the Amalgamated Engineering Union. A trade unionist commented as follows:

> A Japanese electric and electronics equipment company and Electrical and Electronic Telecommunication Plumbing Union [which merged with Amalgamated Engineering Union to form Amalgamated Engineering and Electrical Union] first negotiated a single union agreement including the arbitrage procedure, which was different from the previous custom of British trade unions with regard to problem solving with the company. When Amalgamated Engineering Union tried to be recognised as the single union by Japanese car MNEs, it followed this example, and was subsequently chosen as the single union at Japanese car plants.

However, it is possible for MNEs not to recognise the trade union, for example, Honda in the UK. The suppliers' relationship is another important issue (NEDO, 1993; Derbyshire County Council, 1996). On one hand, the available knowledge is relatively limited in the case of a greenfield investment, and finding and selecting suppliers is time consuming. There are some advantages, however, in establishing new supplier relationships different from those under the mass production system. For example, the new plant does not have to continue business with inferior suppliers, which are likely to be continued in the case of a joint venture or acquisition.

Second, it is important to have control over subsidiaries other than the manufacturing ones, in order to keep local production efficient and competitive. For this purpose, it is desirable to collect, select and process knowledge on the national economies from a pan-European perspective. Consequently, Japanese MNEs established their own EHQ, and because of its importance the EHQs were set up through greenfield investment or upgraded from their own existing facilities. The R&D facility also has the important role of maintaining the competitive edge in the foreign market. The design of Japanese cars had always been negatively evaluated, and Japanese companies needed to address this aspect. With respect to setting up a facility to design new cars to be sold in a local market, the important thing is to acquire not the facility, but the personnel resources with the suitable talent. Interviewees at three car MNEs commented on this point, for example:

> The design of cars needs special talented people, who emphasise the environment and atmosphere of the working place. The best facility can help to attract and recruit the designers, and help them to do a good job. However, the facility itself never designs cars.

In so far as design is one of the most important non-price competitive factors, it would be difficult to acquire the design studio from competitors in Europe. Furthermore, the R&D to adapt the basic model developed in Japan to European conditions also necessitated greenfield investment. Such adaptation requires adjustment of the components provided from local suppliers, whereas Japanese MNEs sometimes have to adapt the basic model to locally procured components, due to their weak bargaining power in Europe compared with local suppliers. The R&D facility should be established near the plant in order to support it. The uniqueness of the production system by Japanese car MNEs needs a high-level facility for this, and the consideration of control over the facility justifies greenfield investment.

Third, the other side of the same coin is that the limited availability of a suitable company for acquisition leads to greenfield investment. Finding a suitable target for the EHQ and R&D facility is the most difficult task. A regional headquarters such as the EHQ is a result of internationalisation and necessitates a change in company organisation (Stopford and Wells, 1972). As far as the main subsidiaries within a region are established by greenfield investment, it would not be a natural choice to acquire a company to supervise that region. If each acquired company had always operated in a geographically limited area such as the domestic economy or some neighbouring countries, it is not logical to add another company above them. If one company already covered the region, the MNE should acquire that firm rather than smaller firms limited within the domestic economy. Of course, it is possible to establish the EHQ through the transfer of the regional supervising competence to the acquired company, as in the case of Yamanouchi and Sankyo. Here, the acquired company already had some national subsidiaries. However, the entry and expansion of European business by auto MNEs is quite different from the pharmaceutical ones. The same point on the availability of a target can also be true for the R&D facilities.

Greenfield investment is also chosen by the pharmaceutical MNEs, largely for two reasons: to supplement other entry modes, and to obtain control over the subsidiaries. The entry by Japanese drug MNEs through joint ventures or acquisitions brought the weaknesses of such ventures as well as the benefits. The disadvantage of an acquisition or joint venture was that it did not cover all European countries. The companies acquired by Fujisawa, Sankyo and Yamanouchi lacked subsidiaries in some main markets in Europe, while Takeda has never set up a joint venture in the UK market. Large markets such as Spain, France and the UK, at least, should be included in the European business network, in order to increase turnover. Resources such as knowledge, experience, staff and so on from both acquisitions and joint ventures can be utilised to expand the marketing network during the third stage, even if greenfield investment were chosen. In addition, in some cases such as Takeda in the UK, an MNE could save on investment costs by using the MR contract staff.

There are a number of differences between the auto and the pharmaceutical sectors: the former tended to use acquisition for supplementing its European business after establishing plants in the UK, while the latter made greenfield, investments at the third stage. This can be explained by the different availability of targets. The motor MNEs had always had a business relationship with national distributors in Europe, and joint ventures or acquisitions at the expanding stage of the internationalisation process are a kind of extension of the previous business. Because of the enduring relationship, they already knew of the target companies. In addition, national distributors conduct their business mainly within their domestic market, and that may prevent any overlap of the business with the existing interests of Japanese car MNEs. On the other hand, most of these conditions were not fully satisfied in the pharmaceutical industry, except for Takeda, which acquired joint-venture partners for the same reason as the car MNEs. The overlap of the subsidiaries between a Japanese firm and a local company, especially in the big markets, might well require Japanese companies to restructure them, and that caused the pharmaceutical MNEs to hesitate before making any acquisitions. An interviewee in Europe commented, 'If a suitable firm for our business is available, we would go to acquire it. However, the best target is not always available in the real world'.

The second determinant factor, control over the subsidiaries, was the same as in the case of the auto sector, but among the MNEs the attitudes are not the same. It is worth reconsidering that Fujisawa set up its EHQ in Munich through greenfield investment along with the acquired company, Klinge. Despite majority ownership, Fujisawa did not always control Klinge, and the necessary restructuring did not proceed smoothly. The fact that Klinge had not agreed to change the name of the company is a typical example of the failure to establish control over the acquired company. Thus, Fujisawa needed to re-build the network in Europe to establish its own control, and greenfield investment was the most suitable means of doing this. Furthermore, the uniqueness of Prograf provides an ideal condition for greenfield investment for development and marketing, because it is a kind of niche market product, whose marketing target is big hospitals conducting transplant operations. As a result, the EHQ did not require a large financial input, or medical representatives. Thus, Fujisawa's greenfield investment was a rather passive choice.

In contrast, Yamanouchi's decision to a plant and basic research institute through greenfield investment is more similar to the case of the car MNEs – control was the dominating factor. Yamanouchi's Irish plant undertakes bulk production, while others merely package chemical entities imported from Japan. The necessary technology level is much higher in bulk production than in packaging, while the company needs to commit much more for designing and constructing the plant itself. The greenfield investment for Takeda's new Irish bulk plant was based on the same reason as Yamanouchi's, likewise the greenfield investment in the case of the auto sector, which showed a different preference over the entry mode between greenfield investment for full-line production and joint ventures for knockdown production. Yamanouchi's basic research institute was set up with the profit generated by the Irish plant. The activities of this facility were certainly important for Yamanouchi in two ways: to strengthen the capability of finding potential chemical entities for new drugs, and to utilise these for cross-licensing agreements with other companies. In order to retain the intellectual assets, Yamanouchi preferred full ownership of the basic research facility. The additional consideration is the same as for the design studios of car MNEs. Pharmaceutical MNEs needed to construct a suitable facility for research purposes, and greenfield investment was the best method to achieve this. In fact, Yamanouchi gave to the chairman of the basic research institute full responsibility, from selecting the site right through to management of the operation.

European integration also had an influence on greenfield investment. On one hand, European integration was likely to accelerate the rate of such investment in that the policy stance of the EU against the rest of the world was not clear, and Japan in particular feared a 'Fortress Europe' mentality. Under such circumstances, the selection of greenfield investment by Japanese car MNEs indicates how significant they considered the issue of control to be. On the other hand, the SEM created favourable conditions for greenfield investment for the purpose of extending the sales-related facilities in pharmaceutical MNEs; there were considerable savings in new drug development costs because of less duplication. At the same time, more favourable conditions under the SEM did not always lead to the same entry mode for the sales-related facilities between the two industries at the further development stage. This can be explained by their different experiences, which might well be affected by their different competitive position in the world market.

In sum, there are basically two determinant factors for greenfield investment: the control over subsidiaries, and the lack of available local firms for joint ventures or acquisitions. The control factor in the auto sector was decisive with regard to the difference between the flexible and mass production systems, and greenfield investment was chosen in setting up the UK plants. Even in the pharmaceutical sector, the more important the control factor on the business of the subsidiary, the more the MNE in question tended to choose greenfield investment. The Irish bulk plants of Yamanouchi and Takeda are the most typical examples, along with Fujisawa's establishment of its EHQ.

The absence of a suitable target for a joint venture or acquisition inevitably leads the MNE to choose greenfield investment or not to invest at all. The clear contrast between the auto and pharmaceutical sectors in supplementing the marketing subsidiaries in Europe is significant. This does not merely suggest the significance of the target, but also indicates that the previous operation and coverage of the main venture in Europe played a crucial role in determining the suitable character of the target and in finding it.

6.4   IMPLICATIONS FOR THE PREVIOUS LITERATURE

The previous sections examined the entry modes of Japanese car and drug MNEs into the EU in the sequential process of internationalisation, and considered the determinant factors of their selection. This section will compare these findings with the previous literature, and show that the uniqueness of the method used has given rise to a new understanding of the entry mode.

First, there is a difference in entry modes for production between the two industries, although there is a similarity in the determinant factor. The auto MNEs tended to choose greenfield investment, which was the result of convergence after some trial and error. Yamawaki (1994) reached the same conclusion on the preference for new ventures by Japanese MNEs. On the other hand, Japanese pharmaceutical MNEs showed great differences among themselves, and the modes chosen by them for their production sites ranged from greenfield investment by Yamanouchi to acquisitions by Sankyo and Takeda, and the hybrid case of Fujisawa. This is different from the general tendency of Japanese manufacturing FDI found by Yamawaki. However, such differences can be explained by the importance of control over the plant in both industries. Yamanouchi's plant is for bulk production and was set up through greenfield investment. Even in the auto sector, on the other hand, Toyota's production facilities in Portugal or Ireland were based on a minority joint venture or licensing due to knockdown production restricted to the domestic market of the host country. In other words, the entry mode was influenced by the significance of the site within the MNE.

Second, an examination of the non-manufacturing facilities led to further discoveries. The R&D centre and the EHQs of the car MNEs were set up by greenfield investment or by extending the existing facilities, while those of the drug MNEs were established by various modes. The EHQs of Sankyo and Yamanouchi were based on acquisition, while that of Fujisawa was a hybrid. The entry modes for the clinical test facilities vary from one company to another. Takeda originally chose a joint venture, but Yamanouchi decided to upgrade the acquired company. Sankyo chose greenfield investment, while

Fujisawa constructed a kind of double structure in Europe along with Klinge, the acquired company. The interesting point here, however, is the shift to full ownership, albeit with some exceptions[23] – this is the same conclusion as that reached by Agarwal and Ramaswami (1992), which indicates that the more experience an MNE accumulates, the more it prefers full ownership.

Concerning marketing facilities, both the car and drug MNEs generally preferred acquisition, with some exceptions such as Takeda's joint ventures and Honda's greenfield investment. The difference between the two sectors is found in the expanding process after the main business entry. The car companies chose acquisitions, while the pharmaceutical firms added new marketing companies through greenfield investment. The local firm's resources constitute a similar determinant factor for acquisition, while the difference is mainly due to the different availability of the target.

The third contribution concerns the explanation of the determinant factors of the entry mode. The factors in the previous literature are confirmed in this case study, which followed the entry mode of each firm. Joint venture is preferred, if the firm has limited financial and knowledge resources, which is typical at the early stage of internationalisation. Access to local knowledge and speedy entry give acquisitions a great advantage, while the availability of targets greatly influences acquisitions. Control over subsidiaries is the most important factor leading the MNEs to choose greenfield investment entry.

Fourth, the findings that are derived from a consideration of the differences and changes to the entry mode here have three strands. First, some exceptional cases suggest that company-specific factors influence the entry mode. Honda chose very few acquisitions or joint ventures for its marketing subsidiaries, and this is explained by its unique product line and the development of its international business, which gave experiential knowledge on Europe, and reduced the psychic distance. On the other hand, Yamanouchi's hesitation to embrace joint ventures was rooted in its own experiential knowledge gained from its failed partnership with Eli Lily in the US.

The second is that the choice of the entry mode was influenced by the entry timing, which was closely related to both the company concerned and the development of European integration. From the perspective of the internationalisation process model, an increasing amount of knowledge and information are accumulated in the MNE along with business experience. As a result, the longer the MNE conducts its international business, the less attractive the knowledge resources of a local firm become. Therefore, a shift from joint ventures or acquisitions to greenfield investment can generally be found in the course of international business. At the same time, consideration of the entry timing tells us a lot in the context of European integration. The difference in the entry mode for clinical tests and marketing between Takeda and the other three pharmaceutical MNEs is partly explained by the different level of European integration. Takeda entered the market earlier than the others, and therefore was unable to enjoy the benefit of integration in the pharmaceutical industry. The '1992' deadline forced Honda and Toyota to commence UK production by the that year. Even under such a restrictive condition, both of them chose greenfield investment, which is inferior to acquisition with regard to entry speed. This underlines the importance of control over the manufacturing subsidiary in the motor industry.

The final point, that is, the local business concern as a joint venture partner or the target of an acquisition, has been analysed less in the previous research. The availability of a local company is a precondition for a joint venture or acquisition, while the local firm must also be suitable for the business objectives of the MNE concerned. A clear contrast between the car and drug MNEs can be found in the third stage of European business, which supplements the second one. The motor MNEs could use acquisitions for obtaining marketing facilities in countries they had never covered directly. On the other hand, the pharmaceutical MNEs tended to choose greenfield investment for the same purpose. There was a difference even among those choosing acquisition in the pharmaceutical sector, and that is indicative of the varying suitability of the acquired company for the business objective of the acquiring company. The solid structure and smooth evolution is seen in the case of Yamanouchi, while Fujisawa had struggled with its follow-up development, as its double structure suggests.

6.5   CONCLUSION

This chapter has addressed the detailed questions concerning the entry mode of Japanese MNEs into the EU. A qualitative investigation on seven MNEs was undertaken, paying attention to the developmental context of the entry mode. The facts with regard to the European case and the changing pattern of internationalisation are confirmed. Some determinant factors suggested by the previous literature have been recognised more directly by studying each entry, while some ignored areas have been examined in the light of the unique approach used in this book.

These findings lead on to another theme to be addressed in the following chapter, that is, the control over subsidiaries from the pan-European perspective. The control of European subsidiaries influenced, and was influenced by, the entry mode. Even if a firm chose the best location and entry mode, this does not guarantee the best performance. If the choice did not fulfil the company's expectations, a not unusual occurrence in international business, then later development could be more complicated.

This theme, the subject of the next chapter, will complement the examination of the European strategy of Japanese MNEs.

NOTES

1. The countries where Toyota secured national distributor contracts with local companies were Denmark (1962), the Netherlands (1964), Finland (1964), the UK (1965), Greece (1965), Belgium (1966), Switzerland (1966), France (1966), Portugal (1968), Sweden (1969), Italy (1970), Germany (1970) and Austria (1970) (Toyota, 1987).
2. Nissan contracted with local companies to distribute imported Nissan cars in Finland (1962), Belgium (1964), Sweden (1966), the Netherlands (1966),Switzerland (1966), the UK (1968), France (1968), Portugal (1968), Germany (1971) and Ireland (1972) (Nissan, 1983, 1985).
3. Honda's subsidiaries established in the 1960s were in Germany (1961), Belgium (1962) France (1964) and the UK (1965) (Honda, 1975, 2000).
4. The information is from the company brochure.
5. The information is from the material provided at the interview. See also Takahashi (1988).
6. The figures on the plant productivity in Europe gives Nissan's UK plant the highest score with 99 vehicles per person in 2002, an increase from 95 in 2001, though the comparison is neither easy, nor perfect (*Financial Times*, 8 July 2003).
7. The information is from the plant's brochure.
8. The information is from Toyota's in-house news magazine.
9. Information is from the company brochure.
10. These movements should be classified as the third stage of Japanese pharmaceutical MNEs in Europe, and will be discussed further in Chapter 7. However, there was no time difference between these two stages in the case of Fujisawa, and it is acceptable to follow some of Fujisawa's attempts here.
11. The information is from the materials on the European operation provided at the interview.
12. The information is from the Yamanouchi Research Institute brochure.
13. Various issues of the *Financial Times* in 1990 and 1991 reported on the conflict between Nissan and Datsun UK.
14. The information is from the company brochure.
15. The information is from Fujisawa's in-house newspaper.
16. Beamish (1988, p. 1) begins his book on joint ventures with the statement 'Joint ventures, not wholly-owned subsidiaries', and his definition is followed here.
17. In support of this statement, Takeda had preferred a joint venture in the US at the initial stage of its main operation, although it later established a full ownership subsidiary along with the joint venture. This is an example of the 'psychic distance' influencing on the entry mode.
18. It is not always easy to acquire the joint venture from the partner, as the US case of Takeda suggests: the US partner company, Abbott, has never agreed that Takeda could buy the joint-venture company.
19. Various issues of the *Yakuji Handbook* report the dissolving of joint ventures in Japan between US or European companies on the one hand, and Japanese companies on the other.
20. The data is from the material provided at the interview.
21. The will of Soichiro Honda, the founding father of Honda, is often quoted by interviewees at Honda to justify the independent strategy. However, the real basis for supporting his word in the actual strategic decision-making lies in the business chain itself. Concerning Honda's preference for independence, see Porter and Takeuchi (2000).
22. The introduction of mass production into Europe in the middle of twentieth century also faced serious obstacles, as Tolliday (2000) reports.
23. Takeda had maintained the joint venture in Germany until 2002, however, this was at the instigation of the German partner. Takeda would have preferred to take majority control of the German subsidiary. Thus, success sometimes prevents further development, as in the case of the joint venture with Abbott in the US.

7. Pan-European Management

7.1 INTRODUCTION

Chapter 5 and 6 investigated the location and entry mode, respectively, of Japanese car and pharmaceutical MNEs into the EU. This chapter will address the important theme yet to be analysed, that is, the management aspect of European business by Japanese MNEs. These MNEs have faced obstacles and opportunities when choosing the location and the entry mode. Indeed, such choices are important decisions to make, but they are not only the factors influencing the efficient operation of European business: management may well be just as crucial.

Here, the main emphasis will be to examine the European headquarters (EHQ) of Japanese MNEs. The dynamic complexity of Europe brought by European integration under the EU raises the question of whether MNEs operate their business from a pan-European perspective. The answer is not easy, but the organisational character of Japanese MNEs supports a positive response. With the exception of Takeda, all the Japanese MNEs examined in this book have an EHQ, as seen in the previous chapters. Through the focus on the EHQ, the research on the management of MNEs can be distinguished from other popular themes, such as the transfer of Japanese management at the plant level. The latter has already been investigated (Dunning, 1986; Garrahan and Stewart, 1992; Kenney and Florida, 1993; Strange, 1993), but the interest has been limited to within the factory or the national economy rather than across national borders.

The detailed issues regarding the EHQs, which were raised in Chapter 2, should be recalled here. First, the situation and the reasons for establishing an EHQ will be confirmed, and this will highlight the uniqueness of Japanese MNEs compared with their US predecessors. A second issue is to examine the actual operation of Japanese EHQs. A point missed in previous work is how the regional headquarters co-ordinate with the non-equity business partners, and this question will also be addressed. The last matter concerns problems caused by the EHQ, and the solutions for them. This is an important issue that not been fully investigated in the literature.

This chapter is constructed as follows. The next section starts with the establishment of the EHQ (7.2), followed by an analysis of European management under the EHQ (7.3). The problems arising from the establishment of the EHQ and the solutions for them are then discussed (7.4). The final section summarises the findings, and adds concluding remarks (7.5).

7.2 ESTABLISHMENT AND OVERALL SITUATION OF THE EHQ

The establishment and situation of the EHQ of Japanese MNEs will be examined with regard to various aspects such as timing, location, size and so on. At the same time, the motives for setting up an EHQ are discussed, and this will clarify the points to be investigated in the next section on European management. Among the seven Japanese MNEs of this study, six set up an EHQ to supervise their European operations. First, the basic facts concerning the EHQ summarised in Table 7.1 are explored.

The auto MNEs set up their EHQ around the turn of the decade from the 1980s to the 1990s. In 1989, Nissan and Honda established their EHQ, Nissan Europe N.V. in Amsterdam, and Honda Motor Europe Ltd. in Reading (UK), respectively. One year later, Toyota's EHQ, Toyota Motor Europe Marketing and Engineering SA/NV (TMME), started operations in Brussels, to supervise the sales-related business and engineering operations. All of these were newly-established subsidiaries, although Japanese car MNEs had already had some business experience in these countries.

Furthermore, from the late 1990s to the early 2000s, each EHQ shows new development. First, in conjunction with the expansion of production facilities in Europe, Toyota extended the competence of its EHQ to co-ordinate its own plants in three European countries, the UK, France and Poland, and set up a new company in 1998, Toyota Motor Europe Manufacturing SA/NV (TMEM) in Brussels, with competence over manufacturing co-ordination. Toyota's organisational change proceeded in 2002, when it established Toyota Motor Europe, a holding company, which directly holds TMME and TMEM, and concentrated its strategic decision making in Europe. Thus, Toyota's EHQ has developed a unique structure, although it is still in the same building. On the other hand, Nissan and Honda changed the location of their EHQ. Honda's EHQ moved from Reading to Langley, both in the UK, and consolidated the EHQ with the UK subsidiaries for sales and marketing, and for financing moving into the same building in 2000. Nissan also moved its EHQ from Amsterdam, to Trappes, near Paris, in 2001, so that it can co-operate more closely with Renault, which has a 44.1 per cent share of Nissan. Since these recent changes are relevant to the purpose of European operation, the implications will be considered below.

Table 7.1   European headquarters of Japanese MNEs

Company	Establish-ment	Location (previous location)	Capital (mil.)	Employees
Honda	1989	Langley, UK (Reading, UK)	£340	n.a.
Nissan	1989	Trappes, near Paris (Amsterdam)	€1626	310
Toyota	1990	Brussels	€76	648
Fujisawa	1991	Munich	€14	250
Sankyo	1990 (1997) *	Munich	€16	n.a.
Yamanouchi	1991 (1994) *	Egham, near London (Leiderdorp, Netherlands)	€33.75	n.a.
Takeda	—	—	—	—

Note: * year when the name of the EHQ changed.

Sources: Annual reports, company brochures.

Japanese pharmaceutical MNEs seem to have set up their EHQ at the beginning of the 1990s, although Takeda has not established an EHQ in spite of having the longest history of European operations among the four. There were two paths to establishing an EHQ: one was based on acquisition, the other on greenfield investment. Sankyo and Yamanouchi took the first route: Sankyo acquired Luitpold, a German company in Munich, in 1990, while Yamanouchi took over Brocades Pharma, the pharmaceutical division of Royal Giest Brocades, a Dutch company in Leiderdorp, in 1991. Yamanouchi and Sankyo gradually consolidated the acquired company into the main body of their European operations, making it difficult to pinpoint the date when they established full control over the acquired company, but it is likely that it was when the acquired company took on the name of the Japanese parent.[1] The company acquired by Yamanouchi changed its name from Brocades Pharma to Yamanouchi Europe B.V. in 1994, while Luitpold changed its name to Sankyo Pharma GmbH in 1997. On the other hand, Fujisawa newly established its EHQ, Fujisawa GmbH in Munich, in 1991 despite having already acquired the majority ownership of Klinge, a German firm.

Fujisawa's method for establishing its EHQ was not a natural development from its original plan, and this suggests a difficulty concerning the configuration of competence over the subsidiaries, even if the entry mode was the same as that of the other companies.

Like the automobile MNEs, the pharmaceutical MNEs also made some changes concerning their EHQ. Fujisawa finally acquired the remaining share of Klinge in 2002, and restructured it as Fujisawa Deutschland under the EHQ. Fujisawa GmbH concentrates on the European business strategy, including new drug development. On the other hand, Fujisawa Deutschland took over the marketing not only of the drugs inherited from Klinge, but also of Prograf, which had formerly been undertaken by Fujisawa GmbH. Sankyo also consolidated its European subsidiaries under the EHQ, in 2002. Until then, the sales and marketing business was allocated to Sankyo Pharma, while the competence of new drug development process was the business of Sankyo Europe located in Düsseldorf, Germany. Although these two were still at different locations in 2003, Sankyo intends to merge them. In contrast, in 2003, Yamanouchi divided the EHQ into strategic decision making and clinical research development, and moved the former to Egham, near London, from Leiderdorp. It is noteworthy that a consideration of the implications of restructuring the EHQ does not necessarily identify general and simple direction for the pan-European business organisation.

An analysis of the reasons why Japanese MNEs established their EHQ from the late 1980s highlights the points to be examined in this chapter. Chapter 6 showed that the establishment of an EHQ is a relatively new phenomenon in the internationalisation process.[2] Both external and internal factors prompted the MNEs to jump to a new stage in their European business, although they are closely related. The fact that the European market and economy is complicated and the market integration of the EU has been making steady progress, especially from the mid-1980s, is one external factor. At the same time, the full commitment to the European market by Japanese MNEs is an internal factor. Both external and internal factors will be analysed in more detail.

The conditions in Europe made it difficult for Japanese MNEs to control operations directly from Japan. As a united market, the EU is one of the largest in the world, and almost the same size as that of the US. There are many hurdles, however, to managing their European business from Japan, for example, the geographical distance and cultural differences. Language is a serious problem even in the case of English, and more so with other languages. Therefore, some companies had formerly sent Japanese staff to European countries, not only because of their management ability and skill, but ever more because of their linguistic knowledge of the host country. The national variances, especially in market character, were much wider than the

Japanese expected, and that led to the inefficiency of direct control from Japan. One of the common complaints among those interviewed at their EHQ was that 'the parent headquarters in Japan considers the EU as a single country like the US, and expects similar results'. For those working there, Europe should be recognised as a market that should be treated more carefully than those in Japan realise, as suggested by Morrison et al. (1991), Kudo (2000) and others.

The progress of European integration under the EU is another concern. Although the EU is not a single country, even in economic terms, nevertheless the rapid progress of EU integration from the late 1980s made it difficult for Japanese companies to follow events, let alone make suitable adjustment. The SEM influenced both Japanese auto and drug MNEs, and led to the establishment of their EHQ. For Japanese car companies, which were the target of protectionist measures by the EU and the member states, it was feared that the SEM would turn the EU into a Fortress Europe against the rest of the world. Localisation was the key for Japanese MNEs to avoid exclusion from the EU market, and the establishment of an EHQ was suitable for this purpose (Yasumuro, 1992). At the same time, the SEM measures concerning the car industry would bring changes not only in the regulatory framework, but also in the actual market competition and the business operation (European Commission, 1997b). However, the SEM did not imply a Fortress Europe for the pharmaceutical firms, because there was almost no trade friction between the two sides. Rather, in the case of the pharmaceutical industry, the SEM has more impact on the new medicine development process than on any other business area. The main fruit of integration was the new drug approval system under the EMEA in London, as well as the mutual recognition system (Thompson, 1994; Wilson and Matthews, 1997), which meant that pharmaceutical companies faced the problem of choosing an appropriate method for filing a new drug. Thus, it became more difficult for Japanese MNEs in both industries to follow and adapt to the changes from Japan, and they decided to establish an EHQ.

The difficulties in Europe did not imply a lower priority in the global business of Japanese MNEs. Rather, the success in Europe had a special meaning, due to the size and character of the market. One of the interviewees in a car company commented:

> Europe is important not only because it is the largest market in the world, but also because of the difficulties. Europe is the birthplace of the motor vehicle, and has its own auto culture. The US is relatively simple compared with Europe, and 'value for money' is the standard for selling vehicles. In Europe, it used to be said that cars are more related to people's lives and sometimes reflect some social meanings. Success in Europe needs something added to 'value for money'. If European customers are satisfied and buy our cars, we can be greatly proud of it.

This statement includes some implications. Market size is one of the locational advantages, but the non-price competition is the hardest in the world. The commodity attractiveness of Japanese cars other than price is a weak point of Japanese companies, and the solution for this problem lies in recognising the European lifestyle. In other words, because of the attractiveness and the difficulties, a more detailed approach to European customers is required.

The same can be suggested in the case of the pharmaceutical industry. Since the Japanese government has restricted medical expenditure, Japanese companies need markets outside Japan. Even if European countries have also tended to reduce expenditures for healthcare due to budget restraints, the EU as a whole is nevertheless the largest market that has not yet been fully cultivated by Japanese companies. At the same time, clinical testing in Europe became as important as the market from the 1990s. In 1991, the International Conference on Harmonisation (ICH) was initiated among the US, the EU and Japan, so that pharmaceutical companies would be able to use the clinical research data collected in one of the three regions for filing a new drug in the others. The Japanese government has been increasingly willing to accept foreign data for the approval of new drugs in Japan (Ueda, 1999). Even if the US is still the most important market for Japanese drug MNEs, Europe is too large and too important for sales and clinical development, respectively, to ignore.

Therefore, Japanese MNEs increased their commitment, in itself the internal factor for establishing an EHQ, because managing European subsidiaries directly from Japan became harder. In the case of the auto industry, the internal factor was to start the supply of cars from the UK plants. Before establishing their local plants, the Japanese car industry supplied European markets mainly through exports from Japan, but exports were restricted in some countries, especially in southern Europe. As a result, the sales-related activities were conducted differently from one country to another. For example, protected markets such as France and Italy forced Japanese companies to pursue higher margins, rather than a high market share, while a high volume of sales was sought in relatively liberal markets such as Germany and the smaller countries. Thus, pan-European management was not required at that stage, and the business in each country was left to the national subsidiaries or independent national distributors. In general, the local assembly in the UK enabled Japanese MNEs to provide cars without national restriction. This was expected to increase the market share of Japanese cars in Europe, as the 'Elements of Consensus' between the EU and Japan in 1991 suggests (Mason, 1994b), although in reality there was almost no change in the market share between 1990 and 1999.

At the same time, however, local production did not automatically lead to an improvement in supply capability. For example, the lead-time from the order to the delivery of a new car to the customer initially became longer in the case of local manufacturing, due to unfamiliarity with production in Europe, the lack of main components imported from Japan, the complicated flow of the order and so on. Faced with such a situation and without any adjustment, the contribution made by local production could easily be overwhelmed by the losses caused by the confusion. Thus, the establishment of the EHQ at the turn of the decade from the 1980s to 1990s was also justified because of internal factors. Toyota's new movement a decade later was also inspired by the necessity for co-ordination among the sister plants in Europe.

The expansion of the sales network also added complexity to the operations in the pharmaceutical industry, through acquisition in the case of Sankyo and Yamanouchi or greenfield investment in the case of Fujisawa. All of them developed their own sales network for marketing from the 1990s rather than continue with licensing-out. As companies discovered that the costs of a broad and complicated operation could be reduced by establishing an EHQ and giving more competence to the local office, they could advance to a new stage of organisation. On the other hand, Takeda had restricted its subsidiaries in countries with a big domestic market through joint ventures, which were independent of each other. This enabled Takeda to avoid the obscure relationship between the group companies in Europe, though their relationships with the parent were the most complicated among the four pharmaceutical MNEs. Consequently, Takeda judged that the establishment of an EHQ would not be beneficial.

With regard to the situation of Japanese MNEs establishing EHQs, one of the main motivations for establishing a regional management structure is to rationalise and co-ordinate the existing manufacturing sites (Stopford and Wells, 1972). In the automobile industry, both Ford and GM already had some production facilities in Europe long before European integration under the EU started, but the main subsidiaries in the UK and Germany had operated independently. Faced with the development of the European Common Market in the 1960s, Ford became the forerunner for coordinating existing plants around Europe under its EHQ, Ford of Europe, which was established in the UK in 1967 – although the process of co-ordination between German and UK subsidiaries under the situation of UK exclusion from the Common Market was quite difficult, as Tolliday (1999) vividly describes. Along with setting up a Spanish plant, GM followed Ford in establishing an EHQ, GM Europe, in Switzerland in 1984, with the purpose of managing European production and other non-manufacturing operations more efficiently (Bloomfield, 1981, 1991; Dicken, 1992b).

In contrast the US cases, Japanese car and drug MNEs did not set up an EHQ to rationalise production facilities in Europe, at least, not at the beginning. Japanese MNEs had fewer manufacturing facilities than their American counterparts when they set up their EHQ.[3] Thus, there was no special need to rationalise the existing production facilities in Europe, so the initial motivation cannot be attributed to rationalisation. Indeed, the car EHQs became fully committed to production in Europe, and extended the competence to managing two or more plants in Europe, from the mid-1990s. What should be emphasised here, however, are the different relationships between the EHQ and European plants in the case of Japanese MNEs compared to their American counterparts. In other words, the single plant operation offered the possibility for more efficient operation through the EHQ. This leads to the question of how to conduct European business, and will be examined in Section 7.3.

The above finding raises the issue of another role played by the Japanese EHQ in Europe. That is, the EHQ was initially founded for the purpose of co-ordinating sales-related activities in Europe, in which there were more subsidiaries than in any other business area. It was also necessary and beneficial for MNEs to adapt to the conditions of the European markets, and the establishment of an EHQ was one of the appropriate solutions. For example, the decision to establish an EHQ sometimes reaped great benefits through a quick response to changes in market conditions. An interviewee at Nissan described this as follows.

> Faced with German unification, we were able to respond more quickly than any other Japanese car company and raised our sales in Germany in 1991 and 1992.[4] This was mainly because of the decision by Nissan Europe based on its judgement of the growth potential of the German market, especially in the small and medium-sized segment, brought by German unification. The president of Nissan Europe himself changed the production and distribution plan, in order for Nissan to provide more cars for the German market than the parent head office in Japan had initially planned.

This was one of the great successes as a result of setting up an EHQ, and giving it competence for Europe. Thus, it is undeniable that the EHQ can play a significant role through quick and appropriate decision making regarding local markets.

Furthermore, there are various other examples concerning the diversity of the market conditions between European countries in both the car and the pharmaceutical industries, as seen in Chapter 4. Customers' preferences, and the so-called 'block exemption' of the car industry from the EU's competition policy affect the car industry, while variations in the main diseases among European countries, and differences in national healthcare systems show the market segmentation in the pharmaceutical industry. National differences in market conditions justified MNEs in possessing national subsidiaries around Europe, but simultaneous expansion of the sales-related network made it difficult to control operations from Japan. As a result, establishing an EHQ became one of the solutions for internal complexity (Stopford and Wells, 1972).

What should be emphasised here is that the ownership structure of Japanese MNEs in Europe has been changing and converging since the beginning of the twenty-first century. Until the 1990s, the ownership structure of European subsidiaries was dissimilar, especially in the automobile sector. Some subsidiaries were held directly by the parent, while others were held by the EHQ or the holding company, even in the same company group. In another case, the EHQ had the same status as other national subsidiaries in the ownership hierarchy; that is, the former was fully held by the parent, but it did not hold any national subsidiary. In yet another case, the parent company and the EHQ jointly possessed some but not all of the European subsidiaries. The diversification of the ownership structure can be explained by factors such as the historical development of European business, the tax system in Japan and so on (Yasumuro, 1992). However, a change towards convergence in the ownership structure has been evident.

The first feature of change is the consolidation of ownership under the EHQ. Chapter 6 described how Japanese MNEs tended to acquire the joint venture or the formerly independent business partner such as the national distributor. Further, the national subsidiaries are fully held by the EHQ rather than by the parent in Japan. From this change, the management line in Europe becomes clearer than before, and the EHQ is poised to make strategic decisions for Europe. At the same time, this change gives the EHQ the same status as the subsidiaries in other regions such as North America. For example, some EHQ presidents are often a board member with their counterparts in North America or Asia. An EHQ president commented:

> The relationships between the parent, the EHQ, and national subsidiaries in Europe have become very clear. The competence of daily business is handed over to each national subsidiary. On the other hand, we can concentrate the important decision making, not only for European business as a whole, but also the global strategy with the other region and the parent head office in Japan. In the latter case, we are not in a parent–subsidiary relationship, but have equal status at the top of the company.

The second feature of convergence is to set up a holding company covering European subsidiaries, sometimes including the EHQ. The merit of the holding company is to reduce the tax burden through the offset of profits in some parts of the company group by the deficits in others. This is especially true for the pharmaceutical industry. The pharmaceutical companies cannot avoid the unbalanced structure of profits and deficits between business areas. R&D is not only more crucial in the pharmaceutical industry than in any other industry, but it is also time-consuming and costly, as shown in Chapter 4. On the other hand, once the medicine has been approved the company can sell it, and get a high margin until the expiry of its patent. Thus, the costs incurred by the development process can be offset by the profits of the manufacturing and sales-related subsidiaries. The holding company is the means whereby the money flows from the downstream operation subsidiaries to those upstream in the drug company. The unbalanced structure can also be true for the automobile industry, and this directional change is apparent although to a different extent.

This section has examined the situation concerning the EHQ, and considered the reasons why Japanese MNEs established an EHQ. Both the environmental and their own internal factors led Japanese MNEs to establish an EHQ, the former being the development of the EU, and the latter the extension of European business which made it difficult to maintain control from Japan.[5] However, the original purpose of the EHQ was not the same as that of the US predecessors. At the same time, the change in the ownership structure towards convergence indicates the further development of European business by Japanese MNEs. The findings in this section suggest the need to examine the pan-European management in detail, and this is the task of the next section.

7.3 EHQ MANAGEMENT OF EUROPEAN BUSINESS

Since the EHQs were set up to deal with the internal and external difficulties of direct control from Japan, the question to be further examined is what aspects of their European business Japanese MNEs manage through the EHQ, and how they achieve this. From the above investigation it is evident that there are two main considerations: collaboration in the area of the sales-related business; and realisation of the economies of scale and scope, since Japanese MNEs were poised to reap the potential benefits brought by 'multinationality' at a European level.

7.3.1 Sales-related Business Management

First, Japanese MNEs founded an EHQ to realise the collaboration and co-ordination among the sales-related operations more quickly and with deeper commitment. Because of the industry-specific characteristics, the concrete activities of the automobile and the pharmaceutical EHQs are not always the same. This subsection will examine how these EHQs co-ordinate the sales-related subsidiaries and the independent concerned parties.

The change in market conditions in Europe led Japanese car MNEs to co-ordinate their sales-related operations from a pan-European perspective. This task must be undertaken under the special circumstances in Europe, which include the SEM, the different demand cycles and patterns among European countries, the potential opportunities brought by local production, and the improvement in European and US MNEs' competitiveness.

The changing environment in Europe created both an opportunity for, and competitive pressure against Japanese car MNEs. Under such conditions, the EHQs had to not only co-ordinate with their own subsidiaries and affiliates, but also fully utilise those partners without equity relationships, such as the independent national distributors and dealer outlets. So that European customers could appreciate Japanese cars as more than just a 'pensioner's car', Japanese motor vehicle companies have been making several and mutually related attempts to improve their brand. These include consolidation of the marketing efforts from a pan-European perspective, feedback from marketing to R&D and manufacturing, improvement of after-sales services, and gathering information from all concerned parties irrespective of ownership relations. This subsection investigates how the EHQ of Japanese MNEs conducts pan-European operations in such a complicated environment.

The freer internal market of the EU with its greater sales potential made Japanese car MNEs change their marketing objective, and look for market share rather than a high monopolistic margin from the late 1980s. The establishment of the EHQ itself served this purpose (Quelch and Ikeo, 1989). In order to raise market share, Japanese MNEs began to pursue pan-European marketing through the EHQ. This does not mean that the EHQ decides and conducts all marketing-related operations. Rather, the important issue is to make clear the division of labour between the EHQ and the national distributors. The core strategic decisions are made in the EHQ, which the national distributors are allowed to adapt to local circumstances. The former includes how the company in question establishes its corporate identity and brand image. Along with the division of labour between the EHQ and the national distributors, the EHQ prepares the rough materials for marketing in Europe, ranging from printed materials such as car sales pamphlets to TV commercials, and so forth. The national distributors can and should, to some extent, modify the provided materials and the basic strategy to fit local conditions. Translating into the local language is the clearest example of adaptation of the marketing materials, but the adjustment is not restricted to such technical issues. The emphasis on the selling points of a car has to reflect customers' preferences. This can be recognised through the daily business with the dealers, which is likely to vary considerably between countries, and the most competence is given to the national distributors in this area. This is justified by the same logic by which some competence is given to the EHQ from Japan. A phrase that was frequently repeated in the interviews is: 'the local knows the local market the best'.

An attractive product is essential for success in a market, and this basic principle also applies to the auto industry. New models are still developed mainly in Japan, but adjustment of the basic model to European tastes is undertaken by the R&D facilities in Europe. The EHQs of Japanese auto MNEs, however, show some commitment to the development and adjustment process with collaboration from the sales-related subsidiaries. For development and adjustment, it is necessary to input appropriate information about the customers. Therefore, the necessary information is collected and analysed not only by the R&D facility itself, but also by the EHQ through the national distributors. At the same time, the EHQ conducts the consumer tests of new models around Europe, in order to provide Europe-specific designed cars. Introducing models geared to local preferences can be the basis for establishing a brand image, although this is not always easy.

The EHQ does not limit the information feedback from sales and marketing to R&D, but also includes that for manufacturing. This is necessary to strengthen a good reputation with customers through the reduction of lead-time, which can improve the brand image (Rhys et al., 1995). The plants of Japanese companies in the UK produce cars based on an estimate of future demand, not only of volume but also of specifications. A car has a great many variants of the latter, including right- or left-hand drive, engine size, gear type, whether it be sedan, saloon or hatch-back, colour, equipment and options, and so on. Since some important components such as the transmission are imported from Japan even today, the production plan has to be decided well before production actually starts, much earlier than it would be in Japan. In order to improve the situation, the collaboration between the national distributors and the plant is managed by the EHQ. The national distributors collect data and information on the national markets through the daily interface with the dealers, and provide these to the EHQ. The data and information obtained from public sources, such as new car registrations, GDP growth estimates and so on are necessary, but not sufficient for precise production planning. The data and information from the national distributors can supplement the public sources, but the plant itself cannot fully analyse all of the information input. Thus, the EHQ needs to sort out the appropriate information, and to indicate the rough direction for the detailed production plan. Even if the information provided for the plant is not perfect, the plant cannot supply cars as efficiently as the imports from Japan without support from the EHQ. In so far as lead-time is part of a good reputation, which contributes to improving the brand image, the role of the EHQ is significant.

There are other ways of improving reputation besides information feedback through the EHQ. The auto MNEs try to refine their image for European customers by efficient delivery of cars and parts, and better service at garages, both of which are closely related. The car and parts warehouses covering cross-border regions are established and controlled by the EHQ. Originally, each national distributor had to maintain its own stock of new cars, and the service parts and components. National distributors had to order and wait for the imports from Japan or from the local plant, even if the same product could be obtained from a neighbouring country's distributor. Through making the warehouse stock available for national distributors across the border, the warehouse can reduce both stock costs and delivery time under the control of the EHQ, and strengthen the brand.

At the same time, the greater the mechanical complexity of modern cars with, for example, electronic components, the higher must be the skill of the service personnel. The training and re-training programmes for service personnel at the garage level are provided not only by the national distributors but also by the EHQ, in order to improve customer service. For example, Toyota has its own training facility in the Brussels EHQ, offering a programme for some 500 trainees every year (Toyota, 1997, 2003). Since customers appreciate a company's service as well as its products, an improvement in sales and after-sales service improves the customers' impression of the company.

Here, it is appropriate to consider how Japanese car MNEs treat business partners that do not have an equity relationship, such as the independent national distributors and the dealer outlets. These are, in general, crucial for a sales-related business, and especially so in the EU due to the fact that the block exemption has long enabled car manufacturers to develop closer relationships with them. Each MNE has a department for dealing with independent national distributors, and all interviewees at the EHQ insisted that there was no difference between caring for the sales-related business of subsidiaries and that of non-equity partners. For example, at Toyota, which had least equity commitment for the sales-related companies until the beginning of the 2000s, a director explained the attitude of the company as follows:

> Regarding the relationship with the national distributors, Toyota values not so much full ownership, but rather close communication and discussion. We deal fairly and equally with each national distributor in Europe, irrespective of the ownership relationship.

This statement confirms the importance of the non-equity partners as well as the subsidiaries in the area of sales-related operations. Thus, establishing a good brand image would be more difficult without the co-operation of the non-equity partners.

The treatment of dealer outlets is basically the same as that for national distributors. Indeed, the daily interface with dealers is not handled directly by the EHQ, but by the national distributor for the country. The EHQ, however, plays an important role as well, since it confirms that the dealers will be conducting the business for a single manufacturer now and in the future. Because of the low market share, dealers are often anxious about the commitment of Japanese car companies to their European business. Some interviewees drew attention to such anxieties, and commented that Japanese companies take this problem very seriously, since it negatively influences the motivation of the dealers. Without the guarantee of future business, the dealers cannot persuade the final customers to purchase Japanese cars. In other words, the EHQ must ensure that the dealers actively participate in the whole strategy in Europe, irrespective of the ownership relationship.

Involvement of the dealers is never an easy task, since, at least theoretically, dealers can transfer from one manufacturer to another, because of the contractual nature of the relationship between the dealer and the manufacturer. Providing the appropriate models for the European market, which could lead to sales growth, is undoubtedly the best method to secure a dealer. This became harder in the 1990s, however, as the stagnant market share of Japanese cars in Europe suggests. Thus, Japanese car MNEs have to adopt more subtle methods to reassure dealers about the future. Establishing plants and other facilities such as the R&D centres and EHQs in Europe is a good way for the assemblers to demonstrate the seriousness of their European commitment to their dealers – it shows that the manufacturers intend to play a role as main actors rather than as niche market players.

Furthermore, Japanese car MNEs began to adopt a more direct approach, which enabled the dealers to feel more like a member of the company group, even though there was no direct capital relationship. Honda invites dealers to every ceremony for the roll-off of a new model from the Swindon plant. In order to show how seriously Honda takes its European business, the dealers are also asked to visit the Belgian warehouse in Ghent. Nissan held a pan-European meeting with 4,000 dealers from around Europe in Paris in 1998, hosted by the vice-president from Tokyo and other executives. At this meeting, Nissan previewed the new models being launched in the next three to four years in Europe. The industry norm is that the new models are shown just before a launch; previewing new models so far in advance of the norm was unique to Nissan. Toyota held a pan-European dealer meeting in Barcelona, in 1999, which was attended by the president and other executives from the Japanese parent. At this meeting, the new vice-president of TMME, a Spanish manager recruited from another auto MNE, was introduced, and dealers were shown the new strategic car being launched in European markets. Indeed, an earlier pan-European dealer meeting, attended by about 800 people had been held in Monaco in 1982 (Toyota, 1987, pp. 810–11). The Barcelona meeting was a demonstration of the company's future business direction in order to raise its market share in Europe. Even if the details vary slightly from one company to another, the basic intention among the three is the same. All of them are trying to raise the motivation of the dealers through equal treatment as group members, in order to improve the sales-related capacity at the customer interface. This may not be a dramatic approach, but it lays a firm foundation for a particular brand.

The pharmaceutical MNEs shifted their European strategy from licensing-out to self-marketing through acquisitions or joint ventures from the 1980s, and that led three of the four companies to set up a EHQ. Because of the dependence on licensing-out, the marketing operations in Europe had not been conducted by the companies themselves, in contrast with the auto MNEs. The minimal commitment to each national market before the acquisitions enabled the pharmaceutical MNEs to avoid the first hurdle that the car companies experienced: the coordination of the different marketing objectives of the sales-related activities among European countries. In this regard, the EHQ workload was less for the pharmaceutical MNEs than for the auto MNEs. This does not mean, however, that the role of the EHQ was insignificant for the sales-related business: establishing the brand and managing the collaboration with non-equity partners were also crucial tasks. The fact that the turnover for drugs with almost the same efficacy can be different, suggests the importance of sales and marketing capability (Blackett, 2001). The well-known example of this was the difference in sales performance between Zantac, sold by Glaxo Wellcome, and Tagamet, sold by SmithKline Beecham. Both medicines are used to treat gastric ulcers, and are almost identical in terms of chemical composition. In spite of this, the sales of Zantac were £1,946 million sterling in 1996, while those of Tagamet were £218 million sterling (Scrip, 1998, pp. 198, 270). Therefore, sales and marketing capacity can sometimes influence sales, along with the efficacy of the drug itself.

At the same time, the conditions surrounding the European market are also changing, in the directions of both opportunities and restrictions. The SEM plays a significant role for companies in reducing the cost of new drug application, through mutual recognition or the central approval system under the EMEA. On the other hand, an ageing society makes it highly unlikely that national healthcare systems will continue to spend as much on drugs. A series of mega-mergers and acquisitions has made European and American drug companies much bigger, and created more competitive pressure.

As in the motor industry, a pharmaceutical company cannot depend solely on its own sales-related subsidiaries and affiliates. Sales in countries without a subsidiary and affiliate have to depend entirely on licensees possessing a sales force just like European and US MNEs. At the same time, even in countries with subsidiaries, co-promotion or co-marketing with other companies is the norm in the industry.[6] The licensee has no equity relations, while the co-promoter or the co-marketer has no possess any ownership relationship with the Japanese company. The licensee or the sales partner should be carefully selected for each medicine on a case-by-case basis. Sometimes, Japanese MNEs collaborate with each other, as in the case between Takeda and Yamanouchi in Germany (Jihou, 1998).

Even if it is often very difficult to distinguish one product from another through its non-scientific character or function such as the design or after-sales services, the name of the company in question has some impact on physicians in so far as the efficacy of a drug is little different from that marketed by other companies. Thus, the role of the EHQ is to establish the brand name of the company itself. Three Japanese pharmaceutical MNEs with an EHQ entered Europe by acquiring a local company, and in varying degrees, each obtained a sales and marketing network. At the beginning of the acquisition, all of them retained the name of the acquired company. Any change of name, and its timing, have some strategic implication for brand management. Because of the heavy dependence on the domestic market, and the licensing-out of novel drugs to big US or European MNEs, Japanese drug MNEs had formerly had very little presence abroad. Since the growth of turnover in foreign markets is vital for Japanese companies faced with a shrinking domestic market, they had to improve their brand in Europe and the US. Establishing and promoting the name of the company abroad is one way to improve market presence. Indeed, the acquired company sometimes had its own brand name, which the acquiring company intended to retain. This is especially true in the case of the motor industry.[7] The acquisitions by Japanese pharmaceutical MNEs were quite different, however, since the name value of the acquired companies was limited from a global perspective due to their size and lack of innovative capacity for new drugs. Thus, Japanese companies preferred to change the name or to establish new subsidiaries using their own name.

The timing of the change was decided under consideration of improving the brand of the company itself. After entering the market through acquisitions, Japanese MNEs prepared to introduce their own new drugs on the European markets. The launch of a new drug and the following sales growth are a good tool for selling the company name, and can be the basis for future development. Yamanouchi's Harnar, an anti-dysuria, Sankyo's Noscal, an anti-diabetes drug, and Fujisawa's Prograf, an immunosuppressant, were such key drugs. When it became highly likely that a new medicine would be approved, Japanese MNEs tried to change the name of the acquired company. Yamanouchi and Sankyo succeeded, but Fujisawa did not. One of the reasons for Fujisawa's failure was opposition from the acquired company, Klinge. Although there were some negotiations on changing the name from Klinge to Fujisawa, the change was not agreed with the founding Klinge family, which owned part of the company, though not a majority, until 2001. Thus, Fujisawa had a double structure in Europe because of its inability to change the company name. Since 2000, after the full acquisition of Klinge from the founding family, and the introduction of a new medicine for atopic skin disease, Protopic, Fujisawa has largely changed its business structure in Europe: it consolidated Klinge, and changed the name to Fujisawa Deutschland, and the EHQ, Fujisawa GmbH, was concerned solely with the pan-European business. These examples show that the name of the company is crucially important for the pharmaceutical MNEs.

Along with brand management, the involvement of the non-equity partner for the co-operation of the sales-related business is also a significant factor. Because of its industry-specific character, the treatment of, and the relationship with the non-equity business partner in the pharmaceutical industry is more arm's-length than is the case in the auto industry. In countries where it has no subsidiary, the MNE licenses out to a local firm or to another MNE with a subsidiary. Once agreement has been reached, the licenser can do very little other than receive the licence fee. An interviewee at a Japanese drug MNE commented: 'we visit the licensees once a year, merely as a ceremonial matter with no strategic meaning'.

Another example of the non-equity partner being concerned with the sales-related business is through co-promotion or co-marketing. Possessing a large sales force is an easy way to increase sales, but no pharmaceutical company could afford such a strategy. This is simply because every firm has its own up-and-down cycle of sales, which is heavily influenced by the flow of new drug introductions. Thus, pharmaceutical companies maintain a sales force that matches a level somewhere below peak sales. Co-marketing or co-promotion can fill the gap between the necessary or ideal sales force and the actual one. This is especially true for Japanese MNEs, since they are newcomers and do not have a large enough portfolio of medicines for European markets to maintain the ideal scale of sales force, even though they are gradually increasing their portfolio. Thus, with the exception of Fujisawa, all Japanese MNEs chose co-marketing or co-promotion even in European countries where they have their own subsidiary. Fujisawa has not adopted co-marketing or co-promotion, because it experienced difficulty reaching an agreement on the details of its contract. In addition, it can be explained by the fact that Fujisawa's main business in Europe does not necessarily need a large sales force, due to its special therapeutic area concerning transplants.

Here, the important problems arise before the contract is secured, not after. The contents of the contract, for example, the royalty, the commission fee, the collaboration period and so on are decided in detail. As in the case of licensing, it is difficult or impossible to change the agreement after the business has been launched. Further, once co-marketing or co-promotion has began, there is a possibility that competition policy authority may well suspect close communication between the partners to be an anti-competitive measure. Therefore, preparation and negotiation before the contract is finalised are significant for success. The EHQ does not take on sole responsibility to reach an agreement, but the parent is also involved. The selection of the partner is crucial, and the points to bear in mind when choosing a partner were summarised as follows by one EHQ president:

> It is important to choose the appropriate partner for the co-promotion. The best partner is a company at the bottom of the new drug pipeline, when the new drug is about to be launched. No big company can be free from the cycle of the new drug pipeline with its ups and downs. At the bottom of new drug development process, the partner company will actively make the best effort for co-promotion, in order to safeguard the sales. Another point is that the partner should not have a drug competing with the drug for the co-promotion. Otherwise, the partner would not be eager to promote the drug in question.

Thus, despite the independent nature of the relationship with the non-equity partner, Japanese pharmaceutical MNEs attempt to indirectly motivate the co-marketing or co-promotion partner through cautious preparation before the contract is signed. Needless to say, careful observation of the market and potential partners by the EHQ can help to secure better contracts.

This subsection has examined the role of the EHQ in pursuing pan-European management. The quest to raise market presence necessitates the restructuring of the organisation, changing the company name and ensuring co-operation from a pan-European point of view. Japanese car and pharmaceutical MNEs co-ordinate the sales-related subsidiaries under the EHQ, while some autonomy is left for the national subsidiaries in the area of the daily interface with the independent partners and customers. The collaboration with non-equity partners is as important as that with the subsidiaries in both industries. The EHQs themselves demonstrate a commitment to the involvement of the non-equity business partners.

7.3.2 Cost Management

Another important task of the EHQ is to improve cost management in Europe. Every company endlessly seeks efficiency, and the subsidiaries also try hard to improve productivity. The question to be asked here, however, concerns the attempts of Japanese auto and pharmaceutical MNEs to manage costs from the viewpoint of Europe. It has already been pointed out that the complexity of European operations is one of the reasons why Japanese MNEs established their EHQ. Another side of the same coin is that there is the potential to improve efficiency, since reducing the complexity leads to a reduction in decision making time, and operation costs. Thus, efficiency can be achieved by a speedy and appropriate response in Europe to the market and its changes, through proximity of the decision making body to the local economy, as the case of Nissan Europe showed.

Here, we can add economies of scale and scope as an advantage having the European business managed by the EHQ. There are various kinds of subsidiaries of Japanese MNEs, not only the manufacturing plants but also the R&D and sales-related facilities. Even if the scale and scope economies are often suggested at the production area, they should not be limited to the manufacturing business. Therefore, this subsection addresses the following question: how do Japanese MNEs attempt their efforts to improve the cost structure through the EHQ, and in what business areas?

The operation of the EHQ for brand establishment and management, which was discussed above, simultaneously has another aspect of strengthening cost efficiency. In order to establish a common brand image around Europe, the EHQ provides the basic materials for advertisements, such as brochures and commercial films, so that national distributors can then adapt them to suit national preference and taste. This can directly reduce duplication of the jobs that had formerly been independently conducted by the national distributors, while indirectly ensuring that each national distributor will concentrate on national tasks such as the daily interface with dealer outlets. The EHQ provides the training and re-training scheme for service personnel in the garages for the same purpose, to realise economies of scale at the pan-European level, which is possible since the same basic models are introduced around Europe.

The cars and parts warehouse contributes to reducing stock costs at the European level along with the task of helping to build a good reputation for delivery, as mentioned in the previous subsection. It is quite clear that the warehouse can decrease the burden of holding stock, since the national distributors do not have to possess excess stock themselves, but can rely on the warehouse. The EHQ receives the order, and delivers the products directly to the dealer outlets or garages from a warehouse that also covers neighbouring countries. Thus, storage costs can be directly reduced and the national distributors can be free from the labour cost of delivery, which is now shifted to the warehouse and the EHQ. This enables the national distributors to concentrate more on domestic activities.

Cross-border coverage by the MNEs' warehouses became possible for two reasons: the SEM, and efforts by the MNEs. The SEM enables goods to circulate throughout EU countries without hindrance at the border. The mutual recognition of technical standards and regulations further facilitates parts delivery across borders. Crossing borders within the EU was simplified by the single document presented at customs. The MNE does not have to worry about delays caused by cross-border distribution (European Commission, 1997b). Thus, Japanese MNEs maximise the benefits brought by the SEM, by having a car and components warehouse to cover some countries across the border.

Another important point is the company's own effort to simplify the specifications for cars and components. Because of different conditions between national markets, the national distributors had formerly demanded unique specifications suitable for their own countries. The assemblers had responded to the national requests by providing various kinds of options. This was not appropriate for exploiting the benefits of the warehouse, however, because the same model with different specifications could not be exchanged among the different national markets. In order to realise the benefits of the warehouse, the carmakers unified the specifications at the European level. Through unification, the national distributors can enjoy a wider range of variants, while the assembler can produce fewer, and enjoy larger economies of scale than before. This is explained as follows.

Assume that a national distributor of Country A had 10 variants of a car, while its counterpart in Country B had 10 different variants of the same car. The assembler would have to produce 20 variants of the car in question, and could not use the stock of one country for another due to the different specifications. If the national distributor of each country gives up three variants and receives the variants of the other country, each of them can offer 14 variants of the car for domestic customers, four more than before. The assembler now has to produce less than before, and can fully utilise the benefits of the warehouse.

Even if there are differences between national markets in Europe, there is some scope for European subsidiaries to unify their business at the European level. This is because the final consumers in each country do not see or care about some business areas. The co-ordination of sales-related subsidiaries under the EHQ is intended to realise economies of scale in administrative office functions, and sometimes includes an organisational change, as the following example suggests. In 1999, Honda restructured the sales-related organisation into a threefold subregional structure. It divided the national distributors in Europe into three groups: the UK, the North and the South region group.[8] Each national distributor deals with the dealer and customer interface, and the regional groups have the direct responsibility for managing product planning and marketing. Honda's EHQ has become more focused on the pan-European strategy. The re-organisation was undertaken to pursue economies of scale through integration of the administrative office functions such as personnel and financial matters. Such integration has to be realised in the context of the national market differences within Europe, but can lead to more efficient management.

Along with the development of production in Europe, Japanese car MNEs also found opportunities for cost management in the manufacturing area. Having more than a single production facility in Europe gives the assembler an opportunity to pursue greater efficiency through a pan-European operation, like their American predecessors Ford and GM, rather than independently operating each production facility. Nissan and Toyota are attempting to turn such potential into reality through reorganisation and rationalisation. The processes at the two companies are quite different from each other, however, and will be investigated.

Nissan has had its own production facilities in the UK and Spain since the early 1980s. In spite of the relatively long history of having a two-factory operation in Europe,[9] the collaboration between the Spanish and UK plants began gradually in the early 1990s. Some marginal parts had been exported from Spain to the UK since the late 1980s, and the main components such as engines started to be exported from the British plant to its Spanish counterpart in 1992. In addition, there was some personnel collaboration. The top managing director of the UK subsidiary became the top of the Spanish plant from 1997, and afterwards became the president of Nissan's EHQ. There were also collaborations at the middle manager level, and the financial officer of the UK plant helped to improve the financial and accounting system of the Spanish subsidiary. Thus, the collaboration between the sister plants was gradually realised, although it was a relatively unilateral one from the UK to the Spanish plant, rather than reciprocal.

There was a serious delay in the collaboration at Nissan, however. The common purchase of parts and components between the two subsidiaries did not become meaningful until the mid-1990s. This was mainly due to the different types of cars produced in each plant. The UK factory assembled passenger cars on one hand, while the Spanish plant produced commercial vehicles. The EHQ and the parent, however, recognised the importance of common purchasing for parts and components, and sought to realise further synergy between the two. The company's intention was revealed in the project for the two plants to use a common platform, the basic framework of a car with an engine and chassis, in line with the trend of the auto industry. Medium-sized passenger cars and compact multi-purpose vehicles have been built on the same platform in the UK and Spanish plants, respectively, since 2000 (Gibson, 1999).

Collaboration between the UK and Spanish plants will be further advanced along with collaboration with Renault. The collaboration of the two companies ranges from R&D through manufacturing to sales and marketing. This is clearly a more comprehensive business. Even if the actual collaboration is not only in Europe and Japan, but also in the rest of the world, and will retain the brand identity of each company, the EHQ is responsible for the project in Europe under a cross-company team. Details concerning the common platform for small passenger cars and more shared procurement of parts and components have already been agreed between the two sides.

The question of how to implement the objective to realise the synergy between Nissan and Renault remains, but the benefits have already been recognised from the beginning, at least as far as Nissan is concerned. The collaboration with Renault is a big help for Nissan in many ways. Nissan can itself assess the worth of suppliers, since Renault provides the benchmark data for European procurement. One of Nissan's weaknesses is the capability to assess the prices of parts and components presented by the suppliers. Carlos Ghosn, the present chief executive officer, who was sent by Renault to overhaul Nissan, told of his business experience with Nissan in the US as the chairman of Michelin USA, and recognised Nissan's weakness in this respect (Ghosn, 2000). Thus, the benchmark for European suppliers provided by Renault strengthens Nissan's position in negotiations with suppliers. Some suppliers have voluntarily decreased the price of components without any negotiation since Nissan and Renault started their collaboration. The co-procurement with Renault can further strengthen Nissan's position in Europe, based on the much bigger size of the operation. Nissan is accelerating the rationalisation of production, not only within the group but also through its collaboration with Renault.

Along with the establishment of the continental plants, Toyota also started to rationalise operations concerning production through its EHQ in Brussels. The most visible change is to establish TMEM, the EHQ specialised to co-ordinate the manufacturing facilities in three different countries. Toyota started a French plant for small cars, and is constructing a transmission plant in Poland. The UK plants for assembly in Burnaston and engines in North Wales expanded their capacity to 200,000 vehicles and 350,000 engine units, respectively. Since the French plant started production from 2001, the actual collaboration is still in its infancy, and TMEM had a staff of 80 at the beginning of operations in 1999. When the organisation is completed the total workforce at TMEM will reach 250. As well as establishing the diesel engine plant, and consolidating the Turkish assembly plant, Toyota reorganised two EHQs in 2003: the competence controlling the engineering operation was moved from TMME to TMEM, so that the manufacturing operation can be supervised by the TMEM.

Toyota adopted a multi-plant strategy in Europe; plant operations are co-ordinated and integrated and TMEM plays a central role. The actual manufacturing process is the responsibility of each subsidiary, but the administrative office operations have gradually been absorbed by TMEM. These include procurement, financial affairs, general affairs, information systems and logistics management. Among these, the procurement of materials, parts and components is thought to be TMEM's most important task. According to an interviewee at the UK plant:

> Toyota is still a small volume producer in Europe compared with the local competitor such as Volkswagen. We cannot demand that the suppliers provide components to Toyota's own specification. Thus, we sometimes have to change the specification of cars to conform to the locally procured components.

Thus, Toyota recognised that negotiating power is one of its weaknesses in Europe, due to the small volume of production. However, through common purchasing, Toyota expects to strengthen its negotiating power with European suppliers.

Collaboration is also planned with regard to personnel exchanges between the UK and French plants, with the aim of facilitating the start of the French assembly line. The team leaders and higher-level staff in the British plant are sent to France to introduce the French staff the flexible production system, in short-term projects lasting up to six months.[10] The experience in the British plant is expected to be transplanted to the French counterpart. Initially, the exchange of experience is unilateral from the UK to France, but TMEM hopes that the collaboration will be a mutual one in the future.

Both Nissan and Toyota seek to realise economies of scale in the manufacturing process, to strengthen their negotiating power with suppliers, and to fully utilise human resources through collaboration among sister plants under the EHQ. The point to be emphasised is that Toyota's collaboration had been planned from the beginning, in contrast to Nissan's. The difference between the two MNEs is explained by the malfunctioning of the Spanish plant and the variation in the type of cars assembled between Nissan's sister plants.

Cost management is also undertaken in the pharmaceutical industry. The point here is that pan-European management under the EHQ is relatively limited in the pharmaceutical industry, but shows some unique features. Therefore, this analysis will examine not only the actual management for improving cost efficiency under the EHQ, but also the reasons why EHQ's role is restricted.

Like the auto industry, the pharmaceutical MNEs are also proceeding to harmonise administrative office operations in the area of sales-related business. Because of the different medical cultures and national regulations, the sales force conducts the interface business with physicians within each nation state individually, but not on a European basis. Nevertheless, there is some scope for economies of scale behind the scenes. Basically, data and information concerning a medicine have to be the same among European countries. Thus, the EHQ provides a common database and presentation materials to the sales force around Europe, sometimes using the same computer software system.

The unification of the administrative office business shows various interesting approaches. A Japanese pharmaceutical MNE, for example, sought to educate the sales force around Europe from a pan-European perspective. The uniqueness here is that the competence for the programme was not in the EHQ, but was delegated to the general manager of the French subsidiary. An interviewee at the EHQ commented:

> We highly appreciated the capability of the personnel manager in the French subsidiary, and intended to transfer him from the French subsidiary to the EHQ. He did not wish to leave his own country, but wanted to remain at the top of the French subsidiary. Thus, we gave up the competence for employees' education and handed it over to the manager in the French subsidiary.

Employees' education includes areas for realising economies of scale, in so far as it is conducted within the company on a pan-European basis. The interesting point here is that this MNE realigned the competence between the EHQ and a national subsidiary. This may be an exceptional case, but was justified by the pan-European utilisation of human resources in the company.

Another example concerns the tight control over the national subsidiaries, which had formerly operated independently and loosely. Another drug MNE streamlined the business practices of its subsidiaries around Europe. This MNE reconsidered the European business along with the introduction of its own novel drug, in order to have stricter control, and to establish a pan-European system of the budget. Until then, the annual plan had been decided almost independently and unsystematically by each national subsidiary, and the final budget expenditure tended to exceed the original plan at the beginning of the year. This meant that operating costs tended to be higher, while profits would be lower. With help from Japan, the EHQ made a greater commitment to establish the budget principle through an intensive one-week meeting in 1998. This problem may very well have been due to the fact that the acquired company had never fully controlled the national subsidiaries. Thus, the EHQ has to supervise the management of the national subsidiaries, in order to reduce inefficiency.

With regard to R&D cost management by the pharmaceutical MNEs, one of the most time-consuming and costly operations for a pharmaceutical company is clinical research, and Japanese MNEs need to be the most cost sensitive in this area. Japanese MNEs fully exploit the locational advantage in Europe by using the CROs. Due to the wide availability of CROs, most clinical tests are outsourced, and Japanese MNEs rely much less on their own R&D staff in Europe than in Japan. Using the CROs is already a cost-saving operation, but there are some more important questions to be examined here. Namely, how do Japanese MNEs make use of the CROs for the purpose of improving cost efficiency from the viewpoint of pan-European management, and how does the EHQ commit to supervising the CROs?

Clinical tests have to be carried out with a pan-European perspective in mind. A new drug should be launched in as many countries as possible by the MNE itself or through licensing-out, in order to maximise the sales in Europe. For scientific and marketing reasons, drug companies must collect clinical data from a wide range of countries in Europe. The efficacy and side-effects of a drug vary between ethnic groups, although the extent of the differences depends on the medicine and on the ethnic differences in Europe. Thus, it is safer to gather data from a greater number and variety of patients around Europe. At the same time, the marketing factor also influences the clinical tests, since domestic data is preferred by doctors and physicians over data from other countries. Japanese MNEs do not need to establish facilities for clinical research in European countries, but rather can contract out with one or more CROs. The task of the pharmaceutical company is to create the protocol, the basic plan for the clinical tests, with collaboration among R&D departments of the parent in Japan, and the subsidiaries in the US and Europe. Such collaboration became increasingly important in the 1990s along with the development of the ICH, under which the clinical data in one region is made available for applications in other regions. The European subsidiary concerning the clinical tests is, of course, given the competence to contract out with the CRO(s) in Europe.

Superficially, it would seem that Japanese companies are not required to invest in the development process in Europe due to the availability of the CROs. Indeed, some pharmaceutical companies acknowledged that they had sometimes used the CROs in Europe directly from Japan. However, proximity to the CROs gives the MNEs the advantage of closely supervising their operation of clinical tests. Even if the pharmaceutical company does its best to establish a protocol for the medicine in question, it cannot avoid the unpredictable results of the clinical tests because of the high uncertainties in the clinical testing process. Sometimes the company has to abandon the new drug completely, while in other cases it has to adjust and modify the plan for the clinical tests, which may well require the company to have close contact with, and provide a quick response to the CROs. At the same time, the CROs should be supervised to ensure that the clinical tests are conducted as efficiently as possible. Because of the uncertainties, the data collected by

CROs is not always ideal for the requirements of a new drug application. The weight, sex, age, ethnic group and so on, of the patients influence the efficacy and the side-effects, but patients with the ideal balance are not always available: the larger the number of patients, the more statistically significant the data. The pharmaceutical company cannot permit the CROs to collect data without any restrictions, however. On the other hand, if there is only a small number of patients, this will lead to delays in the application of the drug, and reduce the period of patent protection. The European subsidiary of a Japanese drug MNE supervises the CRO collection of minimum data for filing to the authorities with the maximum information about the efficacy and side-effects. Proximity enables the operation of the CROs to be carefully monitored, and contributes to finding new CROs, which is difficult to do from Japan.

Moreover, clinical research is the area where collaboration between the sales-related operation and R&D is possible and actually conducted. There are two methods for a pharmaceutical company to get marketing approval in the EU: mutual recognition and the central procedure under the EMEA. At first glance, the centralised system seems to be more efficient than mutual recognition, but some marketing considerations favour the latter. The central system requires the same brand name for the particular medicine through Europe. However, this might sometimes have a negative influence in some countries, because of the existence of another product with the same or similar name, an unfavourable connotation in some languages and so on. Due to the short time since 1995, there are some concerns over the uncertainty of EMEA's operation (Chaudhry and Dacin, 1997). It can be a quick option for some companies to use the marketing authorisation in one country as leverage in others through mutual recognition. The selection of the filing method for a new drug is crucial, and the drug company needs appropriate information on the national markets in order to make the selection. The EHQ is expected to collect the information and decide on the application method, through collaboration with the development department and the sales-related subsidiaries.

In addition, as the clinical tests of Phase IV, which is the follow-up data collection on the actual use of a new drug after its launch, become more and more important, collaboration is also required. In order to maintain and improve safety, it is more necessary than ever to follow up the efficacy and side-effects of a drug after marketing. The actual tests are conducted through the CROs, but the subsidiary concerned with R&D has to set and provide the protocol, as in the case of the clinical tests for applying for marketing authorisation. At the same time, independent researchers sometimes test the drugs in the interests of academic research, and the company supports such trials through funding and making the medicine available under certain conditions. The information after marketing is not limited to scientific data, but also includes patients' impressions on matters such as the frequency of the dosage. Patients' comments are not always included for a new drug because of the scientific requirements, but it is still useful information for marketing purposes.[11]

The interesting point here is that the subsidiary concerned with clinical tests is not always the EHQ, but sometimes is the R&D specialised subsidiary. Fujisawa and Yamanouchi preferred that the EHQ take responsibility for clinical tests from the beginning, while Takeda and Sankyo gave the competence for clinical trials to the R&D specialised subsidiary. In the case of Takeda, such a difference can be explained by the non-existence of the EHQ itself. On the other hand, Sankyo's slow commitment preserved the division of the EHQ and the R&D facility. In 2002, Sankyo unified the EHQ and the R&D centre, although they are still geographically separated, at Munich and Düsseldorf, respectively. There is some scope for efficiently operating the R&D business from a pan-European perspective, and all Japanese pharmaceutical MNEs pursue the benefits, irrespective of their organisational features.

Finally, production is not included in the pan-European collaboration at a pharmaceutical MNE. Production of medicines by MNEs is not controlled from a regional perspective, but from global considerations (Howells, 1992). This is also true for Japanese MNEs. Because of the scale economies, and the small cost of transportation, the production facility in Europe provides the medicine for the global market as well as the European market, irrespective of the bulk production or packaging. Moreover, since it has to match all the combined demand of its own subsidiaries, the licensee, and the co-marketing or co-promotion partners globally, the orders from all over the world are first concentrated in the parent, and then directed to the plant in Europe. In addition, the precise form and package of the medicine have already been decided, and there is little room for the EHQ or the sales-related subsidiary to feed back information from customers.

This section has examined the actual role of the EHQ in managing the sales-related operations, and in realising more efficient operation from a pan-European point of view. The establishment of the company identity is an important task of the EHQ, and all Japanese MNEs try hard to co-ordinate sales-related operations between the national subsidiaries and the EHQ, as well as with the R&D and production facilities. The co-ordination process itself includes some aspects of cost management through unification of the administrative office operations. Co-operation with the non-equity partners such as the dealers in the auto industry and the CROs in the pharmaceutical industry is also significant, and the pan-European perspective strengthens the capability of the MNE for such purposes.

7.4   PROBLEMS AND SOLUTIONS

Even if collaboration under the EHQ is crucial and necessary for efficient management in Europe, the process inevitably faces various hurdles in achieving this purpose. There is no guarantee that the expected benefits will always be realised. If only the intention and the benefits of the collaboration are emphasised, this would be a one-sided assessment of what Japanese MNEs have done in Europe. Therefore, this section will examine the problems brought by co-ordination, and the solutions of Japanese MNEs. These problems have roughly two strands: the lack of subsidiary capability and opposition to the co-ordination project itself. These are examined in turn.

7.4.1   Improving Organisational Capability

Co-ordination under the EHQ requires a higher level of operation in Europe, but the results cannot always reach the expected level. This is because the capability of the subsidiaries and the non-equity partners does not always meet the co-ordination requirements. In such a case, the absolute level of the co-ordination is reduced, or the actual collaboration between the subsidiaries should be set at a lower level.

The first type of problem can be seen in the various cases. The acquired company's incapability is an example. As seen in the last section, a Japanese pharmaceutical MNE recognised that the national subsidiaries of the acquired company could not set an appropriate annual budget and often exceeded the initially expected costs. One of the serious problems for Japanese car MNEs was that local suppliers were not familiar with the business practices of the flexible production system. The solution to these problems was relatively easy, however, since it merely required the necessary inputs for the subsidiary or the non-equity partner. The drug company provided special training for the national subsidiaries with support from Japan. Many programmes are devised by Japanese car MNEs to help their suppliers in Europe (NEDO, 1993). Thus, incapability is not fundamentally a serious hurdle, but is a sign of the need for additional inputs.

The second problem is typically seen in the case of the collaboration between the sister plants in the car industry. The collaboration needs a certain level of capacity, and this is especially true in the case of the manufacturing facilities. If the capacity of one subsidiary is not compatible with another, the collaboration is likely to be unilateral rather than mutual, which may well risk the whole European operation. For example, the collaboration of the Ford group in Europe was often disrupted in the 1970s and 1980s because of the shortcomings of Ford UK, whose production was seriously affected by conflicting labour relations (Maxcy, 1981).

Partly because of the newness of the operation, the collaboration of Japanese car MNEs in Europe is at a unilateral stage. The high level of productivity at the UK plants constrains Japanese MNEs to pursue only unilateral collaboration with their continental counterparts, as shown in the previous section. Nissan's Spanish subsidiary was long troubled with a surplus labour force until the mid-1990s, and delayed the necessary inputs of capital, technology, training and human resources. This was one of the reasons why the collaboration between the two parts actually and unilaterally started only in the early 1990s, in spite of a commitment to the Spanish subsidiary in 1980. Toyota's programme to send UK staff helps French workers to understand the flexible production system, and the French plant to roll-off cars more smoothly. Toyota cannot expect an immediate equal partnership with the sister plants, because production on the continent has only recently began.

Unilateral collaboration can be an advantage for an MNE, but it does not fully exploit the benefits of multinationality. Mutual collaboration is better, as long as the two sides do not clash with each other. The solution to realising the potential benefit of mutual collaboration is to upgrade the subsidiary now receiving the help. Nissan has already prepared for mutual collaboration through common platform production, while the interviewees at Toyota clearly suggested that Toyota intends to advance the collaboration in the future, including that from the French side to the UK.

Furthermore, organisational incapability can be negatively influenced by the employment factor. Japanese MNEs may well face the same problem of other MNEs due to being 'foreign', that is, the difficulty of recruiting high-quality staff, especially white-collar employees. An interviewee in Europe confessed: 'since this is a Japanese company, it is difficult to hire high-quality workers, who tend to prefer the top companies in their own country, or European ones'. Another commented: 'The salary and the conditions for the local staff must be relatively favourable, otherwise the company cannot recruit them'. Thus, Japanese MNEs must struggle with the trade-off between the cost and the quality of human resources.[12]

The difficulty caused by the human resources leads Japanese MNEs to employ Japanese staff. The main posts including the president of the EHQ tend to be occupied by Japanese staff, since they have not only to supervise European management, but also to co-ordinate with the parent in Japan. At the same time, Japanese staff also work in middle management, and implicitly are expected to help the local staff from behind the scene. Such help includes a wide range of jobs, from making the local staff understand the aims of the company to checking and correcting business reports, and so forth. One interviewee commented that the Japanese company calls them 'co-ordinators', and highly appreciates their role in facilitating business in

Europe.[13] Thus, the solution is the same as with the other problems – to add human resource inputs, in order to complement the weakness of the local staff in understanding and conducting the business as expected by Japanese MNEs.

In this respect, there is an interesting contrast between the car and pharmaceutical MNEs. A series of interviews has shown that the former are not always satisfied with the local staff, while the latter positively appreciate the input of European employees. The difference can be explained by the different experience of international business. The auto and pharmaceutical industries are poles apart with respect to their competitive position in the world. Since the Japanese auto industry has a long history of international operations as one of the most competitive sectors in Japan, company demands on the staff are likely to be high even on foreign soil. On the other hand, there is a strong possibility that Japanese pharmaceutical MNEs cannot fully utilise their local staff, due to their brief experience in international business. As a result, even if the quality of the employees is the same between the two industries, the assessment is likely to be more severe in the auto industry than in the pharmaceutical industry.

In order to realise the benefit of 'multinationality' at the European level through the EHQ, there are some hurdles to be overcome, for example, the incapability of subsidiaries, imbalance between sister plants, and the disadvantage caused by 'foreignness', especially with regard to human resources. These are indicative of the need to make additional inputs for more efficient operation, and the solution lies in meeting these needs.

7.4.2 Resistance and Reluctance

Another significant hurdle is the direct or indirect objection of the concerned party to the EHQ and its operation. Before the establishment of an EHQ, operations were largely left to each national subsidiary or the concerned party, which enjoyed autonomy to some extent. Once the EHQ is established, however, these operations are closely supervised by the EHQ. Some of the co-ordination programmes proposed by the EHQ or the parent inevitably led to a change in organisation and business practices, and the allocation or reduction of employees. Thus, the higher the autonomy enjoyed by the concerned party, the more likely that opposition to the EHQ would arise.

The subsidiary or the non-equity partner rarely shows direct opposition to co-ordination under the EHQ, but there are some actual cases. The frictions between Datsun UK and Nissan, and between Klinge and Fujisawa are typical examples. Datsun UK was the independent national distributor in the UK for 21 years, but its sales methods did not match up to the assembler's strategy. Datsun UK had formerly increased the market share of Nissan cars in the UK through discount pricing, but Nissan asked it to improve the brand image on the basis of high quality. The conflict between them reached a peak during 1990 and 1991. Nissan terminated its contract with Datsun UK to distribute Nissan cars, and set up its own national distributor and dealer network from scratch. Datsun UK put the case before the court, though the judge did not uphold the complaint. Disagreement on marketing methods was behind the conflict between the two companies, and the solution by the assembler was drastic.[14]

The conflict between Fujisawa and its acquired company, Klinge, was also over brand management, and similar to the Nissan case. Klinge was a family-owned firm, and it wanted to retain the company name despite Fujisawa's acquisition of a majority share in 1988, while Fujisawa wanted to change the name to enhance the company's presence in Europe along with the introduction of its own novel drug, Prograf. Unlike Nissan, there was no separation of the two, but the parallel existence of Klinge and the newly established EHQ, Fujisawa GmbH. The difference from the Nissan case is explained by Fujisawa's dependence on Klinge, whose profits are reinvested in the former to develop and launch Prograf through the holding company. Thus, the same problem does not always lead to the same solution, and the resolution is dependent on the relationship between the two sides.

Anxieties and complaints against the EHQ and/or the parent are more likely to take a milder form, such as a show of reluctance, rather than a direct clash. Because it is indirect or implicit, it is hard to recognise reluctance from outside the company. However, the existence of such a problem can be inferred from the fact that Japanese MNEs have taken a variety of actions concerning the motivation of the local staff. Co-ordination under the EHQ changes or risks the autonomy, competence and jobs of the employees. Such changes sometimes induce local staff to leave the company. As an old example, the German executives of Ford of Europe left the company in 1969 because of their opposition to centralisation under the EHQ, Ford of Europe (Suzuki, 1969). In addition, the labour market is more mobile in Europe than in Japan, and Japanese MNEs have to pay serious attention to maintaining a highly motivated local staff.

The EHQ and the parent consider and offer solutions to these problems. High wages and salaries might appear to be a good solution to raise and maintain motivation, but they have to be excluded simply because no company can afford to embark on an endless wage/salary spiral. In other words, the motivation of European staff should be maintained not only by good financial inducements, but also by more subtle methods such as giving awards and making clear the objectives for the future.

The award system for local staff is used especially by the pharmaceutical MNEs. The number of employees receiving awards, and the criteria for allocating them vary from one company to another. Yamanouchi has a long history of nominating about ten employees annually not only from the EHQ but also from the national subsidiaries, since the acquisition of Brocades Pharma. On the other hand, Takeda does not give awards on a regular basis, but just for those who fulfil certain criteria. Although there are differences between MNEs, an interesting common feature is a trip to Japan, and includes a visit to the parent headquarters. Thus, the award not only shows the high appreciation of the European staff and the actual objective, but also contributes to making them feel like a member of a big company family.

Appoint local management staff is regarded as another method of raising motivation by actually demonstrating future objectives to the local staff, and is an option open to every MNE (Yasumuro, 1992). In fact, the localisation strategy should be regarded with some reservation, since most Japanese MNEs still tend to appoint Japanese staff to the positions. However, a new policy is becoming apparent, starting with Nissan Europe, in which an Englishman was promoted from being the chief of the UK plant to EHQ's president. Judging from the availability of high-quality human resources, other MNEs will follow suit. Yamanouchi Europe also promoted a local vice-president to president and chief operating officer, and another vice-president R&D to executive vice-president R&D in March 2000. An interviewee clearly summarised the reason for such a shift:

> Assuming the high mobility of workers, it is crucial for us to actually show that the top posts are being prepared for the local staff rather than Japanese ones in the future. Paying lip-service will not stop them from moving to another company.

In addition, localisation may also contribute to more efficient management of human resources, since top Japanese executives can claim a relatively high expatriate compensation package (Yasumuro, 1992).

At the same time, localisation was not always easy, as Japanese MNEs sometimes failed in their efforts to recruit high-quality local staff of the national subsidiaries to the EHQ. The fact that a Japanese pharmaceutical MNE gave a French manager the pan-European competence for sales force training is not just an interesting case of human resource management; another side of the same coin was the failure to promote him to the EHQ. The president of another MNE admitted to a similar case of not being able to transfer the head of a national subsidiary to the EHQ, and suggested the following reason:

> He is the top manager of a national subsidiary, and can make the final decisions as far as the subsidiary is concerned. Once he moved to the EHQ, however, he would be just one of the executives. He might well have to abide by different decisions from his own in some cases.

The reluctance of staff to move from their own country to the EHQ might well be related to the cultural and national differences in Europe. Nevertheless, a high post in the EHQ is not always a satisfactory one for European managers, even if the EHQ supervises the national subsidiaries.

The real problem is whether an MNE can offer a valuable job for the local manager to fill. Honda's reorganisation of its European sales-related operation in the previous section should be interpreted in this context. Honda divided the European market into three areas in 1999, and started a sales-related operation based on this division. The manager in each area was given the competence to supervise the area concerned across national borders. Thus, the top manager of each area had greater and more extensive decision-making power than before, since the competence had formerly been restricted within the country of the national subsidiary. As a result, Honda expects that the present reorganisation may well contribute to improving the motivation by increasing the business scale: the larger the business size, the greater the opportunities and possibilities of promotion. Honda recognised that it was easier to recruit high-quality local staff along with the growth of the UK distributor, and hopes to experience a similar effect through its present reorganisation. Thus, the reorganisation is to allocate resources more efficiently, and crate more business opportunities for those with ambition.

The establishment and operation of an EHQ is aimed at more efficient pan-European management. Since both the subsidiaries and the non-equity partners of the MNE are inevitably influenced by the establishment and realignment of the competence of the EHQ, they show direct or indirect reservations concerning collaboration for the restructuring plan. Various solutions for such problems are sought by the MNE. Sometimes a direct clash led to the departure of the former business partner, as in the Nissan case. Japanese MNEs must convert the reluctance for co-ordination into motivation through awards and localisation of staff. The solution itself includes some limits, but trial and error improves MNE development in Europe, witnessed by the restructuring of Honda's marketing plan. These findings have elucidated some of the complicated difficulties of European management encountered by Japanese MNEs through their EHQ.

7.5 IMPLICATIONS FOR THE PREVIOUS LITERATURE

This chapter has examined the management aspect of Japanese MNEs in Europe by paying special attention to the EHQ. This section will summarise the findings in the light of a comparison with the previous research, thus extending our knowledge of the MNEs.

The investigation began with a picture of the EHQ of Japanese MNEs, including not only the basic facts such as the establishment date and place, but also the reasons why it was set up, and the unique feature of Japanese MNEs. The establishment of the EHQ is explained by both the external environmental factors in Europe and the internal factors of the MNE. This is supportive of the previous literature, such as Yasumuro (1992) and Shutte (1997), using different samples. The uniqueness in the case of Japanese MNEs is that the EHQ did not initially supervise the plants, since they did not operate on a multi-plant basis in Europe. This may well be characteristic of the two industries in this present book, since some MNEs in other industries, such as electrical and electronic equipment and chemicals, are similar to the US MNEs with regard to supervising and rationalising manufacturing facilities (Kudo, 2000). However, Japanese EHQs were set up mainly to co-ordinate the sales-related subsidiaries, at least, at the beginning. This is the typical difference from their US predecessors, which partly aimed at rationalising their foreign operation on a regional basis (Stopford and Wells, 1972). Such a difference could be caused by the different level of internationalisation at the time the EHQs were established. However, a new phenomenon has emerged in that some MNEs such as Toyota and Nissan are gradually following in the direction of their US counterparts.

The main purpose of management under the EHQ is twofold: the co-ordination of the sales-related business, and efficient management mainly through economies of scale and scope at the European level. These two aims are closely related, and in order to realise them the auto and pharmaceutical MNEs tried various methods under the EHQ which vary slightly according to the industry-specific features. All of the MNEs pay close attention to both pre- and post-sales activities. Even if the R&D facilities are relatively independent from the EHQ as Lehrer and Asakawa (1999) maintain, some co-ordination programmes between them are still possible.

Another unique finding here is that the non-equity partners play as a significant role as the subsidiaries of the MNE concerned, and the EHQ commits to collaboration with them along with the national subsidiaries. This is a point ignored in the literature, although the co-operation between the assembler and suppliers has often been analysed in previous research on the changing production system, especially concerning Japanese FDI (Dunning, 1986). This investigation confirms that all Japanese MNEs pay serious attention to selecting non-equity partners as important co-operators for the purpose of improving their European business. The auto industry takes a subtle approach by making the dealers feel they are part of the company group, while the pharmaceutical MNEs prepare the ground carefully before starting co-operation projects. Sullivan (1992) insists on the importance of the informal structure of the MNE's organisation, and this can be extended across company borders.

Third, the problems arising from the changes brought about by the establishment of an EHQ were analysed, and the solutions for such problems discussed. The internalisation theory insists on the superiority of the organisation over the market under certain circumstances, but the fact that the combination of the company organisation and its development could create its own difficulties cannot be ignored. One of the problems is the subsidiaries' lack of organisational capability to pursue the objectives set by the EHQ or the parent company. Because of this, Japanese MNEs provided various inputs, such as training and education, and human resources, in order to offset the shortcomings.

Another, but no less important matter is to persuade the concerned party to agree with and participate in the collaboration under the EHQ. Opposition and reluctance are often cited in the context of international management, organisational change and so on. This contribution is significant, since it explicitly examines the problems and solutions with regard to the EHQ. The separation of Datsun UK from the national distributors of the Nissan group was an example of a serious clash and a drastic solution. Most cases are less extreme, however, and require a more subtle resolution, including raising motivation levels, since the changes engendered by the EHQ may well decrease the motivation of the local staff. An increase in wages or salaries is not a final solution, because no MNE can afford to embark on a perpetual wage or salary spiral. Rather, Japanese MNEs adopt more subtle ways to motivate staff, such as the awards system and localisation.

7.6   CONCLUSION

By focusing on the EHQ, this chapter has shown that Japanese MNEs seek the benefits of 'multinationality' at the regional level under the rapidly changing environment in Europe. This reflects the strategy of the MNEs to adapt to the dynamic complexity of Europe, and is influenced by their own development from entry to expansion. The management task of the EHQ is to coordinate the sales-related business and realise economies of scale and scope at the European level through collaboration with their own subsidiaries and non-equity partners. Even if the adaptation process may well include some conflicts, Japanese MNEs attempt to input the necessary resources, and to raise motivation through various methods. Indeed, the internalisation theory suggests the superiority of the organisation to the market, but the organisation itself has its own problems to be solved. This is true for the case of the EHQ, as the investigation showed.

NOTES

1. Changing the name of the acquired company has some strategic meaning, and this will be discussed further in the next sections.
2. See Tables 6.1 and 6.2 in Chapter 6.
3. See Chapter 6 on the entry mode in the context of internationalisation.
4. German sales of Nissan cars increased from 90,000 units in 1990 to 115,000 in 1991, and 135,000 in 1992, while those of Honda and Toyota stayed at almost the same level in the same period, around 55,000 and 100,000 units, respectively. The data are from SMMT (various issues).
5. Wai-chung et al. (2001) find that MNEs establish their regional headquarters in Asia, for the same reasons.
6. Co-promotion is used commonly to sell a chemical entity under the same brand name through two or more companies, while co-marketing is used to sell the product under different brand names. Co-marketing is popular in southern European countries. This is partly due to the national legal system. For example, co-promotion is prohibited in Italy under the competition policy. Co-promotion is popular in other parts of Europe. In Germany and France, both methods can be chosen by a company. The information is from some EHQs of Japanese pharmaceutical MNEs. See also, Spilker (1994).
7. See acquisitions of Jaguar by Ford, of Saab by GM, and so on.
8. The three regional subsidiaries under the EHQ are Honda Motor Europe–UK, Honda Motor Europe–North, and Honda Motor Europe–South. The first is located in the UK, and supervises the UK, Switzerland, Sweden, Poland, the Czech Republic and Hungary. The second is in Germany, and supervises Germany, Belgium, the Netherlands and Austria. The third is in France, and supervises France, Italy, Spain and Portugal. The information is from "Honda Strengthens European Operation", the material provided at the interview. See also Harada (2000).
9. In the first half of the 1980s, Nissan had three plants in Europe including the joint venture with Alfa Romeo in Italy. The Italian plant was short-lived, however, and in 1987, Nissan sold its stake to Fiat. See Chapter 6.
10. GM also used workers from the German factory to help the start-up of the Spanish plant in 1984. *Financial Times*, 10 December 1982.
11. The frequency and method of taking a medicine greatly influences physicians' preferences for a prescription, in so far as the efficacy is similar for different medicines. Thus the drug delivery system is one of the research areas for a pharmaceutical company (Haruta, 1998, pp. 186–9).
12. The same situation of higher wages and salaries offered by MNEs than the domestic counterparts is also reported in the US (Graham and Krugman, 1991).
13. Because of their task to support the local staff from behind the scene, there has been little research on the 'co-ordinators'. However, some work suggests the informal practice for the international organisation. See, for example, Sullivan (1992).
14. The information about the conflict is from various issues of the *Financial Times* in 1990 and 1991.

8. Conclusion

8.1 INTRODUCTION

Three mutually related themes of Japanese MNEs in Europe have been analysed; the location, the entry mode and pan-European management. Each of the three was examined separately, but they are closely related with one another. Therefore, this chapter will summarise the findings, bearing the mutual relationships in mind (8.2), and consider their academic and policy implications for the MNEs in the light of regional economic integration (8.3). The final section will examine future research directions (8.4).

8.2 SUMMARY OF FINDINGS

This book has discussed three themes concerning the strategy and management of Japanese automobile and pharmaceutical MNEs in Europe. Although only seven companies were investigated, their strategic decision making and management are analysed in depth. The analysis is also conducted from the comparative perspective between the MNEs, which are positioned quite differently in the global market. Thus, both the company- and industry-specific factors influencing strategy and management can be analysed. This section will sum up the findings as a whole, paying special attention to the mutual relationships among the three themes, since a brief summary of findings was already presented at the end of each chapter.

First, the most significant finding was to show that the locational and entry strategy and the pan-European management are closely related. The location of manufacturing and non-manufacturing facilities is confirmed, and the location strategy is influenced by the elements of Porter's Diamond. At the same time, however, the entry mode is one of the key elements for the location, especially, of the pharmaceutical MNEs. Furthermore, since the facilities are not located in any one place within Europe, and the entry modes do not always lead to an ideal result, Japanese MNEs need pan-European management. This task is conducted by the EHQ, whose establishment and location also reflect MNEs' strategy. Indeed, the mutual relationships among the strategy, organisation, structure, and management and operation are not a new academic interest (Chandler, 1962, 1977), but they continue to attract theoretical and practical attention (Rugman and Hodgetts, 2003). The work in this book will make a contribution to the understanding of MNEs' strategy and management.

Second, the changes in both strategy setting, and pan-European management in a time series are made clear, and the internal and external factors of MNEs are pointed out as the driving force. Here, it is worth emphasising that the internal factors of MNEs advancing the changes are not always positive, for example, the growth of sales, but can also be negative, for example, conflicts with the concerned party, and poor business performance. The changes concerning the EHQ typically demonstrate this point. Toyota expanded its scale and competence, while Nissan moved the location in order to have close communication with Renault, which injected capital into Nissan. Yamanouchi's smooth entry led the establishment of its own EHQ, while Fujisawa had long maintained the double structure consisting of the acquired company and the EHQ. The present situation of a firm is the result of their historical development, and this is suggested as an evolutionary process (Nelson and Winter, 1982). This concept has recently been applied to the research on MNEs (Kogut and Zander, 1993), although the internationalisation process model (Johanson and Wiedersheim-Paul, 1975; Johanson and Vahlne, 1977) can be used likewise. This book does not employ the term 'evolution', while the dynamic changing process of MNEs' strategy and management can be demonstrated.[1]

The factors forcing MNEs to reconsider their strategy and management are not only internal, but also external. One of the most critical external factors is the development of European integration under the EU. Indeed, in comparison with developed countries in the global economy, European integration is the most significant element to distinguish it from other regions. This is also true for the specific case of MNEs, due to the fact that locational conditions influence the FDI decision (Dunning, 1988, 2003). These effects of European integration in both the pharmaceutical and automobile industries are confirmed. Japanese pharmaceutical MNEs especially follow the development of the new drug marketing approval system, including the establishment of the EMEA. Japanese motor MNEs also exploit the benefits of the SEM, for example, to ease the smooth circulation of cars, parts and components across national borders both for local production and for distribution. Thus, as much previous research has suggested (Yannopoulos, 1990; Thomsen and Woolcock 1993; United Nations 1993; European Commission, 1998), it is confirmed that European integration is the accelerator of FDI and the MNEs' change of direction in Europe.

At the same time, European integration under the EU is not intended to create a bigger and single economic entity from the group of nation states.

Some aspects of the European economy such as the circulation of goods, services and factors become increasingly integrated, while others such as the quality of demand, and issues concerning the labour force, remain less than fully integrated. This investigation has shown that Japanese MNEs appreciate this asymmetrical feature of European economy. Therefore, they take advantage of European integration, and also carefully treat the disintegration at the national level. The most diversified locational pattern of the sales-related subsidiaries suggests that the quality of demand in each national market is still very important, despite the SEM. The location and relocation of R&D facilities reflects the limits of people's mobility in Europe, and Japanese MNEs themselves tend to move close to where talented human resources accumulate. While some previous research has already mentioned the aspect of disintegration under the EU (Hood and Young 1983; Whitley, 1992; Niss, 1994), this investigation has added many examples of all MNE operations.

Furthermore, the development of the EU itself changes the locational conditions, alongside the combination of integration and disintegration. In the light of these dynamics, the MNEs review, adjust and adopt their strategy and management. For example, Takeda's different entry strategy is explained by the different level of EU integration at that time. The dynamics of European integration heavily influences the strategy and management of Japanese MNEs, in spite of their relatively short experience in Europe compared with the indigenous and US MNEs. In sum, with regard to the external factor, the important element affecting Japanese MNEs is the asymmetrical and dynamic nature of European integration, rather than integration or disintegration alone.

From this unique comparison, the importance of the industry-specific factors on the strategy and management is also evidenced. The comparison is based on the different position of Japanese automobile and pharmaceutical industries in the global economy. The former is a comparatively advantaged sector, while the latter is disadvantaged. Since the previous literature has tended to examine the comparatively advantaged sector of Japan, that is, automobiles, and electric and electronic equipment, the investigation of Japanese pharmaceutical MNEs is itself a valuable contribution, and it is shown that the development of competitive products and the adoption of a suitable strategy enables them to cultivate the European market. At the same time, because of its competitive position, resulting in protectionism, the auto FDI is relatively reactive to European conditions, including the fear of a 'Fortress Europe'. However, domestic factors, such as a change in the national healthcare system, are likely to force Japanese companies abroad, as well as factors such as the attractiveness of Europe with its SEM, the availability of CROs and the ICH. Other industry-specific factors affecting strategy and management are the different importance and nature of R&D and production. The R&D of Japanese pharmaceutical MNEs in Europe requires collaboration with external parties such as a university and a CRO, while the auto MNEs tend to act independently. The location of car plants is closely related to the transferability of the flexible production system, but pharmaceutical plants are attracted by the government factor, especially low corporate tax.

Finally, through the detailed examination at each company, it has been shown that the company-specific factors are no less important for strategy and management. They contain many elements ranging from company performance, to company history, to the experience acquired from other regions. Even if Japanese MNEs face the same situation in Europe, the reaction varies considerably. This can be explained by the company-specific factor. For example, Yamanouchi avoids joint ventures as a result of its unfavourable co-operation with Eli Lily in the US before expanding its European business. Another example is that, despite having a similar sales size as Toyota, Nissan's poor performance as a whole in the 1990s restricts plant diversification in Europe, while the capital injection from and collaboration with Renault makes it unnecessary for Nissan to extend the plants by itself. The company-specific factor is confirmed in the previous chapters, and this throws light on the determinants of strategy and management.

This summary of the findings lead to a consideration of the implications, which is the task of the next section.

8.3 IMPLICATIONS

As mentioned in the methodology, the analysis is qualitative, rather than quantitative, and the number of MNEs sampled has been limited to seven. This enables a detailed investigation of Japanese MNEs in Europe to be carried out, but makes it difficult to generalise the findings. Nevertheless, the findings provide both support for some models and the previous work, and disagreement with, or suggestion for making changes in others. Thus, the work of this book can be the basis for our understanding of MNEs, as such, this qualitative examination is no less significant than the statistical empirical studies (Miles and Huberman, 1994) and can be used as a building block for more general theory in the future (Eisenhardt, 1989).

The findings on investing in a regionally integrating area have special implications for the 'globalisation/regionalisation' argument. Levitt (1983) uses the term 'globalisation' rather than 'internationalisation'. Kogut (1997) suggests that such a shift in terminology is based on the shift from the interdependent to the integrated world economy. He also explains globalisation from the perspective of FDI and MNEs, but the arguments sometimes focus on different aspects which bypass one another. This is because globalisation can be seen, for example, from the trade or the financial capital flow angle (IMF, 1997). However, two main issues can be highlighted: the actual situation of globalisation, and the impact of globalisation. Our findings can contribute to this argument.

Concerning the first matter, that is, the actual globalisation situation, it cannot be rejected that there is a tendency for the world economy to move from interdependence to integration. It is also true that the international flow of trade, capital and FDI has been increasing since the 1980s. However, for various reasons, scholars do not agree on the concept of globalisation. From a historical comparison, some are sceptical of the new phase of the world economy represented by the term of 'globalisation' (Hirst and Thompson, 1999). Others refer to the international circulation of goods, services and factors within each region such as Europe, North America and Asia, rather than on a global basis. The relationships between the regions are much less close than that in each region, and 'regionalisation' is a more suitable description for the present situation of the world economy (Rugman, 2001; Rugman and Hodgetts, 2003). The findings in this book show the importance of regional considerations for strategy setting and management more than global considerations. Indeed, Japanese MNEs in Europe are still dependent on the parent for the development of the basic model of cars, for example, and bear other regions in mind for the production of medicine, but the main efforts are directed towards Europe. This is especially true for the case of EHQ, which plays a permanent rather than a transitional role. Thus, the actual globalisation situation is not a fully integrated world economy, but a world economy consisting of the regionally integrated units, whose level of integration, of course, is different from one region to another.

The second issue is the impact of globalisation. It is often stated that freer circulation of goods, services and factors, especially capital, forces the differences among national economies to converge, and the MNEs play a main part in this convergence process (Levitt, 1983; Yip, 1992). The same can be said, or more so, of the EU, since it has been reducing national barriers against trade and factor mobility among the member states to a greater extent than the world economy (Siebert, 1990; Sadler, 1995). On the other hand, along with those objecting to the actual globalisation situation, there are other scholars who reject the above argument on its unifying effects (Whitley, 1999; Woolcock, 1997). We can appreciate this issue from the whole analysis in this book.

Japanese MNEs invested in Europe to obtain not only markets but also local resources, including talented human resources, the scientific, technical and market knowledge, and so on. At the same time, they transfer their own resources to Europe, in order to keep their competitive edge in the local market. Through this process, Japanese MNEs can maximise benefits through the configuration of the resources transferred from home, and obtained from the host country. This does not mean, however, that the MNEs work to integrate the national economy or business system into the European one. The significant point is that the European conditions have been, and will be changing through the asymmetrical development of the EU. Even if European integration is not the sole factor influencing Japanese MNEs, some of their decisions and operations could not be realised without the development of the EU. Thus, MNEs look at both the national and European conditions, and utilise them along with their own business strategy. In other words, Japanese MNEs are neither a force wiping out national character, nor a simple reactor to locational conditions and their changes, but are mindful users of the asymmetrical structure of European economic integration.

In addition to the academic implications, the findings also have some implication for policy-making. It is rational to discuss them from the viewpoint of the asymmetrical dynamics of European economy, since this is given special attention. Concerning economic policy, one of the most critical and controversial issues is the receiving of FDI, because most countries, both developed and developing, have come to regard inward FDI as the development tool for the local and national economy. This is especially true within the EU, since the SEM attracts inward FDI, while at the same time raises concerns about the relocation of MNEs' facilities (UN, 1993). The analysis suggests that the locational decision of MNEs is not dependent on a single factor such as cheap labour, and the industry-, company- and operation-specific factors also play a significant part. This means that efforts by the local and national governments to attract FDI need to be precise and appropriate for the target MNEs.

Moreover, receiving the FDI is not the final, but the starting point for MNEs' influence on the local and national economies. Much research has shown that the impact of inward FDI is heavily affected by the strategy and management of the MNE in question (Amin, 1993; Barnes and Kaplinsky, 2000). This book also shows that Japanese MNEs operate their business from a pan-European perspective. For example, Honda's reorganisation and restructuring of its sales subsidiary network has sometimes occurred across national borders, while the international human resource management is actually planned and conducted at a European level. As a result, the expected effects may well spill over to areas other than the local or national economy. Another side of the same coin is that spillover effects from inward FDI in other locations are probable, although the extent of such effects is unclear. Therefore, local and national governments should neither over- or underestimate the impact of MNEs.

The last, but not least, issue is the implication for European integration. The development of European integration often leads to a fear of divergence among the local economies, and this consideration is the basis for giving support to the less-advanced area within the EU (Kaldor, 1970; Krugman, 1987). However, others such as Dluhosch (2000) reject both the divergence among locals within the EU, and the redistributive policy by the EU. In so far as MNEs are involved in the relocation of resources within the EU, it may be fair to draw inferences concerning what MNEs mean to the EU. Although this research is based on just seven MNEs, it shows both the concentration in some, for example, the production in the early days, and the divergence in others, for example, the sales-related subsidiaries. At the same time, the operation is conducted across the national border of the reception country, which may well anticipate development-enhancing effects. These findings suggest that the effects of MNEs both for and against convergence are likely to be over expectation, and the impacts of MNEs on the balanced development of the EU economy should be appreciated more carefully.

Some academic and policy implications can be obtained from the whole analysis in this book, but there are some limitations. This is the basis for the future research direction, which will be given in the final section.

8.4   FUTURE RESEARCH DIRECTIONS

The final task is to point out future research directions, which should be derived from both the strengths and the weakness of the findings.

The close investigation at the company level, which provided unique information, albeit with a small number of samples, could offer a firm benchmark for a study of MNEs within a regionally integrated area. There are generally two directions for future research: to supplement the weakness due to the small number of samples, and to compare the findings with other cases. The sample MNEs are few, but the companies represent the major part of FDI in each industry. Other Japanese industries are also investing in Europe, however, such as electrical and electronic equipment, and chemicals. As suggested, the industry-specific factors influenced the FDI and foreign management, and an investigation of other industries would contribute to an understanding of the relationships between the MNEs and European integration. At the same time, MNEs in the car and pharmaceutical sectors from countries other than Japan, especially the US, would further strengthen our knowledge, since US firms have a longer and wider experience than their Japanese counterparts.

On the other hand, Japanese MNEs are operating in other areas where a regional economic integration programme is advancing, though to a lesser extent than in the EU. The North American Free Trade Area, Mercosur and the Association of South East Asian Nations are following the EU in reducing internal barriers. Japanese car MNEs have invested in these regions, as well as in Europe, while the pharmaceutical MNEs are also engaged in the US and some Asian countries. The locational conditions, the differences from Europe, and the dynamic changes of both the MNEs and the regional economic integration certainly influence the strategy and operation of the MNEs. Therefore, research concerning cases in these regions and comparison with the findings here would enhance our insights on the MNEs in the integrating area.

Finally, Europe itself will continue to change under the development of the EU, and Japanese MNEs should transform themselves accordingly. Among the various areas of the EU that are advancing the integration programme, two are particularly noteworthy: the EMU, including the introduction of euro notes and coins from 2002, and the enlargement of the EU to Central and East European countries in 2004. The single currency was introduced for interbank transactions from 1999, but the circulation of notes and coins from 2002 inevitably increased the competitive pressure among the euro-zone countries. The general public can compare the prices of goods and services more directly than before, and this enables them to check the claim of consumer groups that some of the price differences in the EU are artificially produced by the MNEs or EU policies such as the block exemption in the car industry. Moreover, the non-membership of some member states such as the UK in the EMU will continue to strengthen the asymmetrical structure of the EU, and MNEs have to adapt to this situation, as when Toyota set up its second plant not in the UK but in France. In other words, the EMU and the opt-out from it are likely to require that MNEs adopt a more precise strategy and operation than before.

Central and East European countries became member states of the EU in 2004, thus providing an increasing variety of locational conditions for MNEs. The market size of each country is small, due to the relatively small population except for Poland, and they have a low level of per capita GDP. In addition, because of the historical legacy of planned economies, the social framework is not as strong as in West European countries. The potential for future growth is high, however, and wage costs are much lower than in the West. Even if the cheap labour is not always attractive, the enlargement of the EU will surely offer wider investment opportunities for MNEs. Indeed, some MNEs are already actively seeking new business chances, such as the establishment of plants by Toyota. Needless to say, the difficulty for MNEs to exploit 'multinationality' will also be intensified. It is still not clear what will happen in the process, but the continuing changes in the EU and the reaction of the MNEs should be closely monitored. Our obligation in the future is to reassess the results of this book in the light of new developments in Europe.

NOTE

1. Nelson and Winter (1982) claim that the concept of 'evolution' should be based on 'genes' to explain the firm's behaviour and structure, and in their work the 'genes' are represented by 'routine'. In this book it was not appropriate to use the term 'genes', which is why the term 'evolution' is not used.

Bibliography

Aaron, C. (1999), *The Political Economy of Japanese Foreign Direct Investment in the UK and the US*, London: Macmillan.

Abraham, J. and G. Lewis (2003), 'Europeanization of Medicines Regulation', in Abraham, J. and H.L. Smith (eds), *Regulation of the Pharmaceutical Industry*, Basingstoke: Palgrave, pp. 42–81.

Agarwal, S. and S. Ramaswami (1992), 'Choice of Foreign Entry Mode: Impact of Ownership, Location, and Internalisation Factors', *Journal of International Business Studies*, vol. 23, pp. 1–27.

Altshuler, A., M. Anderson, D. Jones, D. Roos and J. Womack (1984), *The Future of the Automobile: The Report of MIT's International Automobile Program*, London: George Allen & Unwin.

Amin, A. (1993), 'The Globalisation of the Economy, An Erosion of Regional Network', in Grabher, G. (ed.), *The Embedded Firm: On the Socioeconomics of Industrial Networks*, London: Routledge, pp. 278–95.

Amin, A. and I. Smith (1991), 'Vertical Integration or Disintegration? The Case of the UK Car Parts Industry', in Law, C.M. (ed.), *Restructuring the Global Automobile Industry: National and Regional Impacts*, London: Routledge, pp. 169–99.

Andersen, O. (1993), 'On the Internationalization Process of Firms: A Critical Analysis', *Journal of International Business Studies*, vol. 24, no. 2, pp. 209–31.

Ando, K. (1997), 'The Single European Market and the Location Strategy of Foreign Car Multinationals', in Macharzian, K., M.J. Oesterle and J. Wolf (eds), *Global Business in the Information Age: Proceedings of the 23rd Annual EIBA Conference Stuttgart, December 14–16, 1997*, vol. 1. Stuttgart: European International Business Academy, pp. 433–54.

Azuma, E. (1991), *Sekai ni Kateruka Fujisawa Yakuhin, Yamanouchi Seiyaku* (Can Fujisawa and Yamanouchi Compete in the World), Tokyo: Niki Shuppan.

Baden-Fuller, C.W.F. and J.M. Stopford (1991), 'Globalisation Frustrated: The Case of White Goods', *Strategic Management Journal*, vol. 12, pp. 493–507.

Baldwin, R.E. (1994), *Towards an Integrated Europe*, London: Centre for Economic Policy Research.

Ballance, R., J. Pogany and H. Forstner (1992), *The World's Pharmaceutical Industry: An International Perspective on Innovation, Competition and Policy*, Aldershot, UK and Brookfield, US: Edward Elgar.

Barnes, J. and Kaplinsky, R.M. (2000), 'Globalisation and the Death of the Local Firm? The Automobile Components Sector in South Africa', *Regional Studies*, vol. 34, no. 9, pp. 797–812.

Bartlett, C.A. and S. Ghoshal (1989), *Managing Across Borders: The Transnational Solution*, London: Hutchinson Business.

Basu, D. and V. Miroshnik (2000), *Japanese Foreign Investments 1970–1998*, Armonk, NY: M.E. Sharpe.

Beamish, P.W. (1988), *Multinational Joint Ventures in Developing Countries*, London: Routledge.

Beamish, P.W. and J.C. Banks (1987), 'Equity Joint Ventures and the Theory of the Multinational Enterprise', *Journal of International Business Studies*, Summer, pp. 1–16.

Bhaskar, K. (1979), *The Future of the UK Motor Industry*, London: Kogan Page.

Bhaskar, K. (1989), *Innovation in the EC Automotive Industry: An Analysis from the Perspective of State Aid Policy*, Luxembourg: Office for Official Publications of the European Communities.

Bhaskar, K. (1990), *The Effects of Different State Aid Measures on Intra-Community Competition: Exemplified by the Case of the Automotive Industry*, Luxembourg: Office for Official Publications of the European Communities.

Blackett, T. (2001), 'Branding and its Potential within the Pharmaceutical Industry', in Blackett, T. and R. Robins (eds), *Brand Medicine: the Role of Branding in the Pharmaceutical Industry*, Basingstoke: Palgrave, pp. 9–26.

Blackwell, N., J.P. Bizet, P. Child and D. Hensley (1991), 'Shaping a Pan-European Organization', *The McKinsey Quarterly*, vol. 2, pp. 94–111.

Bloomfield, G.T. (1981), 'The Changing Spatial Organization of Multinational Corporations in the World Automotive Industry', in Hamilton, F.E.I. and G.J.R. Linge (eds), *Spatial Analysis, Industry and the Environment*, vol. II, Chichester: John Wiley, pp. 357–94.

Bloomfield, G.T. (1991), 'The World Automotive Industry in Transition', in Law, C.M. (ed.), *Restructuring the Global Automobile Industry: National and Regional Impacts*, London: Routledge, pp.19–60.

Bordenave, G. and Y. Lung (1996), 'New Spatial Configurations in the European Automobile Industry', *European Urban and Regional Studies*, vol. 3, no. 4, pp. 305–21.

Bresman, H., J. Birkinshaw and R. Nobel (1999), 'Knowledge Transfer in International Acquisitions', *Journal of International Business Studies*, vol. 30, no. 3, pp. 439–62.

Buckley, P. (1983), 'Macroeconomic versus International Business Approach to Direct Foreign Investment: A Comment on Professor Kojima's Interpretation', *Hitotsubashi Journal of Economics*, vol. 24. no. 1 (June), pp. 95–100.

Buckley, P.J. and M. Casson (1976), *The Future of the Multinational Enterprise*, London: Macmillan.

Buckley, P.J. and M. Casson (1998), 'Analysing Foreign Market Entry Strategies: Extending the Internalization Approach', *Journal of International Business Studies*, vol. 29, no. 3, pp. 539–62.

Burstall, M. (1990), *1992 and the Pharmaceutical Industry*, London: IEA Health and Welfare Unit.

Burstall, M.L., J.H. Dunning and A. Lake (1981), *Multinational Enterprises, Governments and Technology: Pharmaceutical Industry*, Paris: OECD.

Burstall, M.L. and I.S.T. Senior (1985), *The Community's Pharmaceutical Industry*, Luxembourg: Office for Official Publications of the European Communities.

Cantwell, J., S. Iammarino and C. Noonan (2001), 'Sticky Places in Slippery Space – the Location of Innovation by MNCs in the European Regions', in Pain, N. (ed.), *Inward Investment, Technological Change and Growth: The Impact of Multinational Corporations of the UK Economy*, New York: Palgrave, pp. 210–39.

Casson, M. (1990), *Enterprise and Competitiveness: A Systems View of International Business*, Oxford: Clarendon.

Caves, R. (1996), *Multinational Enterprise and Economic Analysis*, 2nd edn, Cambridge: Cambridge University Press.

Caves, R.E. and S.K. Mehra (1986), 'Entry of Foreign Multinationals into US Manufacturing Industry', in Porter, M. (ed.), *Competition in Global Industries*, Boston, MA: Harvard Business School Press, pp. 449–81

Cecchini, P. (1988), *The European Challenge: The Benefits of a Single Market* (Cecchini Report), Aldershot: Wildwood House.

Chandler, A.D. (1962), *Strategy and Structure, Chapters in the History of the Industrial Enterprise*, Cambridge, MA: MIT Press.

Chandler, A.D. (1977), *The Visible Hand: The Managerial Revolution in American Business*, Cambridge, MA: Harvard University Press.

Chandler, A.D. (1990), *Scale and Scope: The Dynamics of Industrial Capitalism*, Cambridge, MA: Harvard University Press.

Chaudhry, P. and P. Dacin (1997), 'Strategic Planning in a Regulated Trade Bloc: The Pharmaceutical Industry in the European Union', *European Management Journal*, vol. 15, no. 6, pp. 686–97.

Chaudhry, P., P. Dacin and J.P. Peter (1994), 'The Pharmaceutical Industry and European Community Integration', *European Management Journal*, vol. 12, no. 4, pp. 442–53.

Church, R. (1986), 'The Effects of American Multinationals on the British Motor Industry: 1911–83', in Teichova, A., M. Levy-Leboyer and H. Nussbaum (eds), *Multinational Enterprise in Historical Perspective*, Cambridge: Cambridge University Press, pp. 116–30.

Church, R. (1994), *The Rise and Decline of the British Motor Industry*, Cambridge: Cambridge University Press.

Clegg, J. and S. Scott-Green (1999), 'The Determinants of New FDI Capital Flows into the EC: A Statistical Comparison of the USA and Japan', *Journal of Common Market Studies*, vol. 37, pp. 597–616.

Coase, R.H. (1937), 'The Nature of the Firm', *Economica*, vol. 4, pp. 386–405.

Commission of the European Communities (1985), *Completing the Internal Market*, White Paper from the Commission to the European Council (Milan, 28 and 29 June 1985), (COM(85), 310), Luxembourg: Commission of the European Communities.

Commission Regulation 123/85 on the Application of Article 85 (3) of the Treaty to Certain Categories of Motor Vehicle Distribution and Servicing Agreements, Official Journal of the European Communities, L 15.

Commission Regulation, 1475/95 on the Application of Article 85 (3) of the Treaty to Certain Categories of Motor Vehicle Distribution and Servicing Agreements, Official Journal of the European Communities, L 145.

Commission Regulation, 1400/2002 on the application of Article 81(3) of the Treaty to categories of vertical agreements and concerted practices in the motor vehicle sector, Official Journal of the European Communities, L 203.

Corstjens, M. (1991), *Marketing Strategy in the Pharmaceutical Industry*, London: Chapman & Hall.

Cusmano, M.A. (1989), *The Japanese Automobile Industry: Technology and Management at Nissan and Toyota*, Cambridge, MA: Harvard University Press.

Dalton, D.H. and M.G. Serapio Jr. (1998), 'Foreign R&D Facilities in the United States', in Woodward, D. and D. Nigh (eds), *Foreign Ownership and the Consequences of Direct Investment in the United States, Beyond Us and Them*, Westport, CT: Quorum, pp. 163–80.

Darby, J. (1996), 'Less Successful Strategies: Japanese Manufacturing in Southern Europe', *South European Society and Politics*, vol. 1, no. 1, pp. 24–46.

Darby, J. (1997), 'The Environmental Crisis in Japan and the Origins of Japanese Manufacturing in Europe', *Business History*, vol. 39, pp. 94–114.

Dassbach, C.H.A.C. (1989), *Global Enterprises and the World Economy*, New York: Garland.

Davidson W.H. (1980), 'The Location of Foreign Direct Investment Activity: Country Characteristics and Experience Effects', *Journal of International*

Business Studies, vol. 11, pp. 9–22.

De Koning, A.J., P. Verdin and P. Williamson (1996), 'Managing Regional Integration: Lessons from Europe', INSEAD Working Paper Series, 96/93/SM.

de Meyer, A. (1989), 'Ford of Europe, Product Research and Development', in Davidson, W.H. and J. de la Torre (eds), *Managing the Global Corporation: Case Studies in Strategy and Management*, New York: McGraw-Hill, pp. 478–88.

de Wolf, P. (1994), 'The Pharmaceutical Industry', in Sachwald, F. (ed.), *European Integration and Competitiveness*. Aldershot, UK and Brookfield, US: Edward Elgar, pp. 277–317.

Délégation à l'Aménagement du Territoire et à l'Action Régionale (DATAR) (1997), *DATAR Japan News Letter*, no. 84.

Department of Trade and Industry (DTI) (1999), *The UK R&D Scoreboard, 1999*, London: DTI.

Derbyshire County Council (1996), *Toyota at Burnaston*, Derby: Derbyshire Structure Plan Review.

Deutsch, K.G. (1999), *The Politics of Freer Trade in Europe: Three-level Games in the Common Commercial Policy of the EU, 1985–1997*, New York: St. Martin's Press.

Dicken, P. (1992a), 'European 1992 and Strategic Change in the International Automobile Industry', *Environment and Planning, A*, vol. 24, pp. 11–31.

Dicken, P. (1992b), *Global Shift: The Internationalization of Economic Activities*, 2nd edn, London: Paul Chapman.

Dicken, P. (1998), *Global Shift, Transforming the World Economy*, 3rd edn, New York: Guilford Press.

Dluhosch, B (2000), *Industrial Location and Economic Integration: Centrifugal and Centripetal Forces in the New Europe*, Cheltenham, UK and Northampton, MA, USA: Edward Elgar.

Dunning, J.H. (1986), *Japanese Participation in British Industry*, London: Croom Helm.

Dunning, J.H. (1988), *Explaining International Production*, London: Unwin Hyman.

Dunning, J.H. (1993), *Multinational Enterprises and the Global Economy*, Wokingham: Addison-Wesley.

Dunning, J.H. (1997), 'The European Internal Market Programme and Inbound Foreign Direct Investment', *Journal of Common Market Studies*, vol. 35, no. 1&2, pp. 1–30, 190–223.

Dunning, J.H. (2003), 'Location and the Multinational Enterprise: A Neglected Factor?', in Brewer, T.L., S. Young and S.E. Guisinger (eds), *The New Economic Analysis of Multinationals, An Agenda for Management, Policy and Research*, Cheltenham, UK and Northampton,

MA, USA: Edward Elgar, pp. 45–69.

Dunning, J.H. and J.A. Cantwell (1991), 'Japanese Direct Investment in Europe', in Bourgenmeier, B. and J.L. Mucchielli (eds), *Multinationals and Europe 1992: Strategies for the Future*, London: Routledge, pp. 155–84.

Dymock, E. (1995), *Honda, the UK Story*, Sutton Veny: Dove.

Eastwood, K. and L. Hunt (1993), *The Automotive Components Sector in Thamesdown*, Thamesdown: Borough of Thamesdown.

Economist Intelligence Unit (1999), 'Price Harmonisation in Europe: Prospects and Implications by Manufacturer', *Motor Business Europe*, November, pp. 124–36.

Edwardes, M. (1983), *Back from the Brink*, London: Pan Books.

Eisenhardt, K.M. (1989), 'Building Theories from Case Study Research', *Academy of Management Review*, vol. 14, no. 4, pp. 532–50.

El-Agraa, A.E. (1994), 'The Economics of the Single Market', in El-Agraa, A.E. (ed.), *The Economics of the European Community*, 4th edn, Hemel Hempstead: Harvester Wheatsheaf, pp. 155–69.

Emerson, M. (1992), *One Market, One Money: An Evaluation of the Potential Benefits and Costs of Forming an Economic and Monetary Union*, Oxford: Oxford University Press.

Enderwick, P. (1996), 'Transnational Corporations and Human Resources', in Dunning J.H. (ed.), *Transnational Corporations and World Development*, London: International Thomson Business Press, pp. 215–49.

Eriksson, K., J. Johanson, A. Majkgard and D. Sharma (1996), 'Time and Experience in the Internationalization Process', mimeo.

Eriksson, K., J. Johanson, A. Majkgard and D. Sharma (1997), 'Experiential Knowledge and Cost in the Internationalization Process', *Journal of International Business Studies*, vol. 28, pp.337–60.

Eriksson, K. and A. Majkgard (1998), 'Path Dependence in the Internationalization Process', mimeo.

Ernst & Young (1992), *Doing Business in the Republic of Ireland* (Japanese edition), Tokyo: Ernst & Young.

European Commission (1996), *The Single Market and Tomorrow's Europe: A Progress Report from the European Commission*, Luxembourg: Office for Official Publications of the European Communities.

European Commission (1997a), *The Single Market Review: Impact on Manufacturing, Pharmaceutical Products*, Luxembourg: Office for Official Publications of the European Communities.

European Commission (1997b), *The Single Market Review: Impact on Manufacturing, Motor Vehicles*, Luxembourg: Office for Official Publications of the European Communities

European Commission (1997c), *The Single Market Review: Impact on Trade and Investment, Foreign Direct Investment*, Luxembourg: Office for Official Publications of the European Communities.

European Commission (1998), 'Commission Communication on the Single Market in Pharmaceuticals', COM (98), 588 final.

European Commission (2000a), *Evaluation of Operation of Community Procedures for the Authorisation of Medical Products*, Brussels: European Commission.

European Commission (2000b), *Pharmaceuticals in the European Union*, Luxembourg: Office for Official Publications of the European Communities.

European Commission (2001), 'Car Prices in European Union: Still No Clear Trend towards a Substantial Reduction of Price Differentials', News Release, 19 February.

Foley, P., J. Hutchinson, B. Herbone and G. Tait (1996), 'The Impact of Toyota on Derbyshire Local Economy and Labour Market', *Tijdschrift voor Economische en Sociale Geografie*, vol. 87, no. 1, pp. 19–31.

Forum on the European Automobile Industry (1994), *Forum on the European Automobile Industry, Brussels, Palais de Congres, 1 March 1994: Written proceedings/European Commission, European Parliament*, Luxembourg: Office for Official Publications of the European Communities.

Freyssenet, M., A. Mair, K. Shimizu and G. Volpato (eds) (1998), *One Best Way? Trajectories and Industrial Models of the World's Automobile Producers*, Oxford: Oxford University Press.

Fridenson, P. (1995), 'Fordism and Quality: The French Case, 1919–93', in Shiomi, H. and K. Wada (eds), *Fordism Transformed: The Development of Production Method in the Automobile Industry*, Oxford: Oxford University Press, pp. 160–83.

Friedman, J., D.A. Gerlowski and J. Silberman (1992), 'What Attracts Foreign Multinational Corporations? Evidence from Branch Plant Location in the United States', *Journal of Regional Science*, vol. 32, no. 4, pp. 403–18.

Fujimoto, T. (1999), *The Evolution of a Manufacturing System at Toyota*, Oxford: Oxford University Press.

Gambardella, A., L. Orsenigo and F. Pammolli (2000), *Global Competitiveness in Pharmaceuticals: A European Perspective*, Brussels: European Commission.

Garrahan, P. and P. Stewart (1992), *The Nissan Enigma: Flexibility at Work in a Local Economy*, London: Mansell.

General Policy Review Staff (1975), *The Future of the British Car Industry*, London: HMSO.

George, S. (1985), *Politics and Policy in the European Community*, Oxford: Oxford University Press.

Ghosn, C. (2000), 'Watashi ha Nissan no Napoleon ni arazu' (I am not Napoleon of Nissan, interview article with Carlos Ghosn), *Bungeishunju*, January, pp. 124–36.

Gibson, I. (1999), 'Face to Face: with Sir Ian Gibson of Nissan Europe', *Motor Business Europe*, August, pp. 1–15.

Giga, S., K. Ueda and Y. Kuramoto (1996), *Takeda Yakuhin, Banyuu Seiyaku (Merck)*, (Takeda Phamaceutical Company and Banyuu Pharmaceutical; Merck), Tokyo: Ohtsuki Shoten.

Gillingham, J. (2003), *European Integration 1950–2000: Superstate or New Market Economy?*, Cambridge: Cambridge University Press.

Grabowski, H. and J. Vernon (1990), 'A New Look at the Returns and Risks of Pharmaceutical R&D', *Management Science*, vol. 36, pp. 804–21.

Graham, E.M. and P. Krugman (1991), *Foreign Direct Investment in the United States,* 2nd edn, Washington, DC: Institute for International Economics.

Harada, M. (2000), 'On the Record: with Minoru Harada, President of Honda Motor Europe', *Motor Business Europe*, February, pp. 17–27.

Haruta, E. (1998), *Iyakuhin Gyoukai* (Pharmaceutical Industry), Tokyo: Kanki Shuppan.

Head, K., J. Ries and D. Swenson (1995), 'Agglomeration Benefits and Location Choice: Evidence from Japanese Manufacturing Investments in the United States', *Journal of International Economics*, vol. 38, pp. 223–47.

Heater, D. (1992), *The Idea of European Unity*, Leicester and London: Leicester University Press.

Hennart, J.F. (1982), *A Theory of Multinational Enterprise*, Ann Arbor, MI: University of Michigan Press.

Hennart, J.F. (1991), 'The Transaction Costs Theory of Joint Ventures: An Empirical Study of Japanese Subsidiaries in the United States', *Management Science*, vol. 37, pp. 483–97.

Hennart, J.F. and G.M. Kryda (1998), 'Why Do Traders Invest in Manufacturing?', in Jones, G. (ed.), *The Multinational Traders*, London: Routledge, pp. 213 –27.

Hennart, J.F. and Y.R. Park (1993), 'Greenfield vs. Acquisition: The Strategy of Japanese Investors in the United States', *Management Science*, vol. 39, pp. 1054–70.

Hill, S. and M. Munday (1992), 'The UK Regional Distribution of Foreign Direct Investment: Analysis and Determinants', *Regional Studies*, vol. 26, no. 6, pp. 535–44.

Hine, R. C. (1985), *The Political Economy of European Trade: An Introduction to the Trade Policies of the EEC*, Brighton: Wheatsheaf.

Hirst, P. and G. Thompson (1999), *Globalization in Question: The*

International Economy and the Possibilities of Governance, Cambridge: Polity.

Hoffmann, S. (1989), 'The European Community and 1992', *Foreign Affairs*, vol. 69, Fall, pp. 27–47.

Honda (1975), *Honda no Ayumi 1948–1975* (The Steps of Honda between 1948 and 1975), Tokyo: Honda.

Honda (2000), *Honda Shashi, 50-nen Shi* (The Company History of Honda, a 50-year History), Tokyo: Honda.

Hood, N. and S. Young (1983), *Multinational Investment Strategies in the British Isles: A Study of MNEs in the Assisted Areas and in the Republic of Ireland*, London: HMSO.

Howells, J. (1990), 'The Internationalization of R&D and the Development of Global Network', *Regional Studies*, vol. 24, pp. 495–512.

Howells, J. (1992), 'Pharmaceutical and Europe 1992: the Dynamics of Industrial Change', *Environment and Planning, A*, vol. 24, pp. 33–48.

Howells, J. (1997), 'Research and Development Externalisation, Outsourcing and Contract Research', Paper presented at the 'Collaboration and Competition in R&D and Innovation Programme: Lessons for the Public and Business Sectors' Conference, Judge Institute of Management Studies, Cambridge, 9–11 June 1997.

Howells, J. and I. Neary (1995), *Intervention and Technological Innovation: Government and the Pharmaceutical Industry in the UK and Japan*, London: Macmillan.

Hu, Y.S. (1973), *Impact of US Investment in Europe: A Case Study of the Automotive and Computer Industries*, New York: Praeger.

Hudson, R. (1995), 'The Japanese, the European Market and the Automobile Industry in the United Kingdom', in Hudson, R. and E.W. Schamp (eds), *Towards a New Map of Automobile Manufacturing in Europe? New Production Concept and Spatial Restructuring*, Berlin: Springer, pp. 63–91.

Hymer, S.H. (1976), *The International Operations of National Firms: A Study of Direct Foreign Investment*, Cambridge, MA: MIT Press.

International Monetary Fund (IMF) (1997), 'Globalization in Historical Perspective', in IMF, *World Economic Outlook*, May 1997, Washington, DC: IMF, pp. 112–16.

International Monetary Fund (IMF) (2000), *International Financial Statistics, Yearbook, 2000*, New York: IMF.

Japan Automobile Manufacturers Association (JAMA) (annually), *Shuyoukoku Jidousha Toukei* (The Statistics of the Automobile in Main Countries), Tokyo: JAMA.

Japan Automobile Manufacturers Association (JAMA) (2000), *Nippon no Jidousha Kougyou* (The Motor Industry of Japan), Tokyo: JAMA.

Japan External Trade Organization (JETRO) (2002), *Shinshutsu Kigyou Jittai Chousa, Oushuu Toruko hen, Nikkei Kigyou no Katsudou Joukyou, 2002 nen-ban* (Survey of Operation of Japanese Companies in the Manufacturing Sector, 2002 edn), Tokyo: JETRO.

Japan Pharmaceutical Manufacturers Association (JPMA) (1997), *Data Book 1997–98*, Tokyo: JPMA.

Japan Pharmaceutical Manufacturers Association (JPMA) (2000), *Data Book 2000*, Tokyo: JPMA.

Japan Pharmaceutical Manufacturers Association (JPMA) (2001), *Data Book 2001*, Tokyo: JPMA.

Japan Pharmaceutical Manufacturers Association (JPMA) (2003), *Data Book 2003*, Tokyo: JPMA.

Jihou (1994), *Yakuji Handbook, 1994* (Handbook on the Pharmaceutical Industry, 1994), Tokyo: Jihou.

Jihou (1998), *Yakuji Handbook, 1998* (Handbook on the Pharmaceutical Industry, 1998), Tokyo: Jihou.

Jihou (2000), *Yakuji Handbook 2000* (Handbook on the Pharmaceutical Industry, 2000), Tokyo: Jihou.

Jihou (2003), *Yakuji Handbook 2003* (Handbook on the Pharmaceutical Industry, 2003), Tokyo: Jihou.

Johanson, J. and J.E. Vahlne (1977), 'The Internationalization Process of the Firm: A Model of Knowledge Development and Increasing Foreign Market Commitment', *Journal of International Business Studies*, vol. 8, no. 1, pp. 23–32.

Johanson, J. and F. Wiedersheim-Paul (1975), 'The Internationalization of the Firm, Four Swedish Cases', *Journal of Management Studies*, vol. 12, no. 3, pp. 305–22.

Johnson, D. and C. Turner (2000), *European Business: Policy Challenges for the New Commercial Environment*, London: Routledge.

Jones, D.T. (1994), 'The Auto Industry in Transition: From Scale to Process', *Journal of the Economics of Business*, vol. 1, no. 1, pp. 139–50.

Jones, D.T. and S.T. Prais (1978), 'Plant Size and Productivity in the Motor Industry: Some International Comparisons', *Oxford Bulletin of Economics and Statistics*, vol. 40, no. 2, pp. 131–51.

Jones, G. (1993), *British Multinational Banking 1830–1990*, Oxford: Clarendon.

Kaldor, N. (1970), 'The Case for Regional Policies', *Scottish Journal of Political Economy*, vol. 17, pp. 337–48.

Kanavos, P. (1996), *American and Japanese (Bio)pharmaceutical Presence in Europe*, Luxembourg: European Parliament.

Keller, M. (1993), *Collision: GM, Toyota, Volkswagen and the Race to Own the 21st Century*, New York: Currency & Doubleday.

Kenney, M. and R. Florida (1993), *Beyond Mass Production: The Japanese System and its Transfer to the U.S.*, Oxford: Oxford University Press.

Kogut, B. (1983), 'Foreign Direct Investment as a Sequential Process', in Kindleberger, C.P. and D. Andretsch (eds), *The Multinational Corporation in the 1980s,* Cambridge, MA: MIT Press, pp. 38–56.

Kogut, B. (1997), 'Globalization', in Warner, M. (ed.), *Concise International Encyclopedia of Business and Management*, London: International Thomson Business Press, pp. 219–33.

Kogut B. and H. Singh (1988), 'The Effects of National Culture on the Choice of Entry Mode', *Journal of International Business Studies*, vol. 19, pp. 411–32.

Kogut, B. and U. Zander (1993), 'Knowledge of the Firm and the Evolutionary Theory of the Multinational Corporation', *Journal of International Business Studies*, vol. 24, pp. 624–45.

Kojima, K. (1978), *Direct Foreign Investment: A Japanese Model of Multinational Business Operation*, London: Croom Helm.

Komiya, R., M. Okuno and K. Suzumura (eds) (1988), *Industrial Policy of Japan*, New York: Academic Press.

Kravis, I.B. and R.E. Lipsey (1982), 'The Location of Overseas Production and Production for Export by U.S. Multinational Firms', *Journal of International Economics*, vol. 12, pp. 201–23.

Krugman, P. (1987), 'Economic Integration in Europe: Some Conceptual Issues', Padoa-Schioppa, T. (ed.), *Efficiency, Stability and Equity*, Oxford: Oxford University Press, pp. 117–40.

Krugman, P. (1990), *Geography and Trade*, Cambridge, MA: MIT Press.

Kudo, A. (2000), 'Nippon Kigyou no Tai EC/EU Senryaku' (Japanese, EC/EU Strategy of Japanese Companies), mimeo, paper presented to Nippon Keiei-shi Gakkai (Japan Business History Association), at Seijou University, Tokyo, 23–24 September.

Lall, S. (1996), 'Transnational Corporations and Economic Development', in Dunning J.H. (ed.), *Transnational Corporations and World Development.* London: International Thomson Business Press, pp. 44–72.

Lane, C. (1989), *Management and Labour in Europe: The Industrial Enterprise in Germany, Britain and France*, Aldershot: Gower.

Lane, C. (1995), *Industry and Society in Europe: Stability and Change in Britain, Germany, and France*, Aldershot, UK and Bookfield, US: Edward Elger.

Laux, J. (1992), *The European Automobile Industry*, New York: Twayne.

Law, C.M. (1991), *Restructuring the Global Automobile Industry: National and Regional Impacts*, London: Routledge.

Lehmann, J.P. (1992), 'France, Japan, Europe and Industrial Competition: The Automotive Case', *International Affairs*, vol. 68, no. 1, pp. 37–53.

Lehrer, M. and K. Asakawa (1999), 'Unbundling European Operations: Regional Management and Corporate Flexibility in American and Japanese MNCS', *Journal of World Business*, vol. 34, no. 3, pp. 265–86.

Levitt, T. (1983), 'The Globalization of Markets', *Harvard Business Review*, May–June, pp. 92–102.

Liebenau, J. (1984), 'Industrial R&D in Pharmaceutical Firms in the Early Twentieth Century', *Business History*, vol. 26, pp. 329–46.

Loewendahl, H.B. (2001), *Bargaining with Multinationals: The Investment of Siemens and Nissan in North-East England*, New York: Palgrave.

Lucarelli, B (1999), *The Origins and Evolution of the Single Market in Europe*, Aldershot: Ashgate.

Macarthur, D. (1991), *Japanese Pharmaceutical Expansion into Europe: Strategies and Prospects*, London: Financial Times Business Information.

Mair, A. (1994), *Honda's Global Local Corporation*, London: Macmillan.

Majkgard, A. and D. Sharma (1997), 'Client-following and Market-seeking Strategies in the Internationalization of Service Firms', mimeo.

Markusen, A. (1985), *Profit Cycles, Oligopoly and Regional Development*, Cambridge, MA: MIT Press.

Markusen, J.R. (1995), 'The Boundaries of Multinational Enterprises and the Theory of International Trade', *Journal of Economic Perspectives*, vol. 9, pp. 169–89.

Mason, M. (1994a), 'Historical Perspectives on Japanese Direct Investment in Europe', in Mason, M. and D. Encarnation (eds), *Does Ownership Matter? Japanese Multinationals in Europe*, Oxford: Clarendon, pp. 3–38.

Mason, M. (1994b), 'The Political Economy of Japanese Automobile Investment in Europe', in Mason, M. and D. Encarnation (eds), *Does Ownership Matter? Japanese Multinationals in Europe*, Oxford: Clarendon, pp. 411–34.

Mason, M. (1997), *Europe and the Japanese Challenge: The Regulation of Multinational in Comparative Perspective*, Oxford: Oxford University Press.

Matray, J.S. (2001), *Japan's Emergence as a Global Power*, Westport, CT: Greenwood Press.

Mattoo, A. and P.C. Mavroidis (1995), 'The EC–Japan Consensus on Cars: Interaction between Trade and Competition Policy', *The World Economy*, vol. 18, no. 3, pp. 345–65.

Maxcy, G. (1981), *The Multinational Motor Industry*, London: Croom Helm.

Mead, R. (1998), *International Management: Cross-Cultural Dimensions*, 2nd edn, Oxford: Blackwell.

Meeusen, W. (1999), *Economic Policy in the European Union: Current Perspectives*, Cheltenham, UK and Northampton, MA, USA: Edward Elgar.

Methe, D.T. and J. Penner-Hahn (1999), 'Globalization of Pharmaceutical Research and Development in Japanese Companies, Organizational Learning and the Parent–Subsidiary Relationship', in Beechler L.S. and A. Bird (eds), *Japanese Multinationals Abroad*, Oxford: Oxford University Press, pp. 192–210.

Miles, M.B. and A.M. Huberman (1994), *Qualitative Data Analysis: An Expanded Sourcebook*, 2nd edn, Thousand Oaks, CA: Sage.

Monti, M. (2000), 'Beyond the EU's Block Exemption', speech delivered at Forum Europe Conference: 'Who will be in the Driver's Seat?', *Competition Policy Newsletter*, no. 2, pp. 1–7.

Morris, J. (1991), 'Globalization and Global Localization: Explaining Trends in Japanese Foreign Manufacturing Investment', in Morris J. (ed.), *Japan and the Global Economy: Issues and Trends in the 1990s*, London: Routledge, pp. 1–13.

Morris, J. (1992), '1992 Elements of Consensus: Trouble and Strife between the EC and Japanese Automobile Industries', *European Access*, February, pp. 17–18.

Morrison, A.J., D.A. Ricks and K. Roth (1991), 'Globalization versus Regionalization: Which Way for the Multinational?', *Organization Dynamics*, vol. 19, no. 3, pp. 17–29.

Morrison, A. and K. Roth (1992), 'The Regional Solution: An Alternative to Globalization', *Transnational Corporations*, vol. 1, no. 2, pp. 37–55.

Motor Industry Local Authority Network (MILAN) (1992), *Local Authorities and Japanese Investors in the Motor Industry Exchange of Experience*, Warwick: MILAN.

Motor Industry Local Authority Network (MILAN) (1996), 'Plant Visit to Honda Assembly Plant Swindon', *Briefing Note Series* MB29, Warwick: MILAN.

Mullineux, N (1995), *Car Retailing in Europe: Opportunity for the Next Decade*, London: Pearson Professional.

Musso, S. (1995), 'Production Methods and Industrial Relations at Fiat (1930–90)', in Shiomi, H. and K. Wada (eds), *Fordism Transformed: The Development of Production Method in the Automobile Industry*, Oxford: Oxford University Press, pp. 243–68.

Mutou, H. (1988), 'Automobile Industry', in Komiya, R., M. Okuno and K. Suzumura (eds), *Industrial Policy of Japan*, New York: Academic Press, ch. 11.

National Economic Development Office (NEDO) (1993), *The Experience of Nissan Suppliers: Lessons for the United Kingdom Engineering Industry*, London: NEDO.

Neal, L. and D. Barbezat (1997), *The Economics of the European Union and the Economies of Europe*, Oxford: Oxford University Press.

Nelson, R.R. and S.G. Winter (1982), *An Evolutionary Theory of Economic Change*, Cambridge, MA: Belknap Press of Harvard University Press.

Nicholson, F. and R. East (1987), *From the Six to the Twelve: The Enlargement of the European Communities*, Harlow: Longman.

Nicolas, F. (1995), 'The Expansion of Foreign Direct Investment', in Sachwald, F. (ed.), *Japanese Firms in Europe*, Luxembourg: Harwood Academic Publishers, pp. 5–44.

Nikkei Business (1997), 'Leader no Kenkyu' (Study on the Leader), *Nikkei Business*, 5 December, pp. 88–92.

Nikkei Business (2000a), 'Case Study, Sankyo', *Nikkei Business*, 10 June, pp. 58–64.

Nikkei Business (2000b), 'Toyota ga Nanfutsu ni Design Kyoten wo Oku Riyuu' (The reason why Toyota is locating its design studio in southern France), *Nikkei Business*, 28 August, p. 12.

Nippon Keizai Shinbunsha (Japan Economic Journal) (2000), *Kishi Kaisei* (Can Nissan Restructure?), Tokyo: Nippon Keizai Shinbunsha.

Nippon Yakushi Gakkai (Academic Association for the History of the Japanese Pharmaceutical Industry) (1995), *Nippon Iyakuhin Sangyou-shi* (The History of the Pharmaceutical Industry in Japan), Tokyo: Yakuji Nippou.

Niss, H. (1994), 'European Cultural Diversity and Its Implications for Pan-European Advertising', in Zetterholm, S. (ed.), *National Culture and European Integration: Exploratory Essays on Cultural Diversity and Common Policies*, Oxford: Berg, pp. 161–72.

Nissan (1983), *21 Seiki heno Michi, Nissan Jidousha 50 Nen shi* (The Road to the 21st Century, 50-year Company History of Nissan), Tokyo: Nissan.

Nissan (1985), *Nissan Jidousha Shashi, 1974–1983* (The Company History of Nissan, 1974–1983), Tokyo: Nissan.

Nissan (1996), *Nissan no Globalisation* (Globalisation of Nissan), Tokyo: Nissan.

Nissan Motor Manufacturing (UK) Ltd. (1999), *Information Pack*, Sunderland: Nissan Motor Manufacturing (UK) Ltd.

Noelk, M. and R. Taylor (1981), *EEC Protectionism: Present Practice and Future Trends*, Brussels: European Research Associates.

O'Donnell, R. (1991), 'Fiscal and Taxation Policy', in Keatinge, P. (ed.), *Ireland and EC Membership Evaluated*, London: Pinter, pp. 126–35.

Odagiri, H. and H. Yasuda (1997), 'Overseas R&D Activities of Japanese Firms', in Goto, A. and H. Odagiri (eds), *Innovation in Japan*, Oxford: Clarendon, pp. 204–28.

Organisation for Economic Co-operation and Development (OECD) (1998), *Trends in International Migration*, SOPEMI Annual Report, 1998 edn, Paris: OECD.

Owen, N. (1983), *Economies of Scale, Competitiveness, and Trade Patterns within the European Community*, Oxford: Clarendon.

Padmanabhan, P. and K.R. Cho (1999), 'Decision Specific Experience in Foreign Ownership and Establishment Strategies: Evidence from Japanese Firms', *Journal of International Business Studies*, vol. 30, no. 1, pp. 25–44.

Pallares-Barbera, M. (1996), 'Nissan Motor Iberica in Spain and Japanese Production Systems', in Darby, J. (ed.), *Japan and the European Periphery*, London: Macmillan, pp. 180–91.

Pearce, R. (1992), 'Factors Influencing the Internationalization of Research and Development in Multinational Enterprises', in Buckley, P.J. and M. Casson (eds), *Multinational Enterprises in the World Economy: Essays in Honour of John Dunning*, Aldershot, UK and Brookfield, US: Edward Elgar, pp. 75–95.

Pearce, R. (1997), *Global Competition and Technology: Essays in the Creation and Application of Knowledge by Multinationals*, London: Macmillan.

Pearce, R. and M. Papanastassiou (1996), *The Technological Competitiveness of Japanese Multinationals: The European Dimension*, Ann Arbor, MI: University of Michigan Press.

Pelkmans, J. (2001), *European Integration, Methods and Economic Analysis*, 2nd edn, Harlow: Pearson Education.

Penner-Hahn, J.D. (1998), 'Firm and Environmental Influences on the Mode and Sequence of Foreign Research and Development Activities', *Strategic Management Journal*, vol. 19, pp. 149–68.

Penrose, E. (1959), *The Theory of the Growth of the Firm*, Oxford: Basil Blackwell.

Peters, L.S. (1998), 'Strategies of Foreign Corporate R&D Investment and Sourcing in the United States', in Woodward, D. and D. Nigh (eds), *Foreign Ownership and the Consequences of Direct Investment in the United States: Beyond Us and Them*, Westport, CT: Quorum, pp. 207–29.

Porter, M.E. (1985), *Competitive Advantage*, New York: Free Press.

Porter, M.E. (1990), *Competitive Advantage of Nations*, New York: Free Press.

Porter, M.E. and H. Takeuchi (2000), *Can Japan Compete?*, Tokyo: Diamond-sha.

Prentis, R.A., Y. Lis and S.R. Walker (1988), 'Pharmaceutical Innovation by the Seven UK Owned Pharmaceutical Companies (1964–85)', *British Journal of Clinical Pharmacology*, vol. 25, pp. 387–96.

Preston, P.W (2000), *Understanding Modern Japan: A Political Economy of Development, Culture and Global Power*, London: Sage.

Quelch, J.A. and K. Ikeo (1989), 'Nissan Motor Co. Ltd.: Marketing Strategy for the European Market', in Bartlett, C.A. and S. Ghoshal (eds), *Transnational Management: Text, Cases and Readings in Cross Border Management*, Chicago: Irwin, pp. 151–69.

Raines, P. and R. Brown (eds) (1999), *Policy Competition and Foreign Direct Investment in Europe*, Brookfield, VT: Ashgate.

Reich, M.R. (1990), 'Why the Japanese Don't Export More Pharmaceuticals', *California Management Review*, Winter, pp. 125–50.

Reis-Arnd, E. (1987), 'A Quarter of a Century of Pharmaceutical Research: New Drug Entities, 1961–1985', *Drugs Made in Germany*, vol. 30, pp. 105–12.

Rhys, D.G. (1989), *The Motor Industry in the European Community*, Hertford, UK: Institute of the Motor Industry.

Rhys, D.G., P. Nieuwenhuis and P. Wells (1995), *The Future of Car Retailing in Western Europe*, London: Economist Intelligence Unit.

Ringe, M.J. (1992), *The Contract Research Business in the United Kingdom: The European Dimension*, Luxembourg: Office for Official Publications of the European Communities.

Robson, P. (1987), *The Economics of International Integration,* 3rd edn, London: Unwin Hyman.

Root, F.R. (1987), *Entry Strategies for International Markets*, Lexington, MA: Lexington Books.

Rugman, A.M. (1981), *Inside the Multinationals*, London: Croom Helm.

Rugman, A.M. (2001), *The End of Globalization: Why Global Strategy is a Myth and How to Profit from the Realities of Regional Markets*, New York: Amacom.

Rugman, A. and R.M. Hodgetts (2003), *International Business*, 3rd edn, Harlow: Pearson Education.

Sachwald, F. (1995a), 'The Automobile Industry: The Transplantation of the Japanese System Abroad', in Sachwald, F. (ed.), *Japanese Firms in Europe*, Luxembourg: Harwood Academic Publishers, pp. 169–210.

Sachwald, F. (1995b), 'Japanese Chemical Firms: A Limited Internationalization', in Sachwald, F. (ed.), *Japanese Firms in Europe*, Luxembourg: Harwood Academic Publishers, pp. 211–34.

Sadler, D. (1995), 'National and International Regulatory Framework: The Politics of European Automobile Production and Trade', in Hudson, R. and E.W. Schamp (eds), *Towards a New Map of Automobile Manufacturing in Europe? New Production Concept and Spatial Restructuring*, Berlin: Springer, pp. 21–37.

Salvadori, D. (1991), 'The Automobile Industry', in Mayes, D. (ed.), *The European Challenge: Industry's Response to the 1992 Programme*, London: Harvester Wheatsheaf, pp. 28–91.

Sankyo (1979), *Sankyo Hachiju-nen Shi* (80-year History of Sankyo), Tokyo: Sankyo.

Sankyo (2000), *Sankyo 100-nen Shi* (100-year Company History of Sankyo), Tokyo: Sankyo.

Sapienza, A.M. (1993), 'Assessing the R&D Capability of the Japanese Pharmaceutical Industry', *R&D Management*, vol. 23, pp. 3–16.

Sato, M. (2000), *Jidousha Gasshou Renkou no Sekai* (Automobiles, the World of Unity and Integration), Tokyo: Bungei Shunju.

Scrip (1998), *Scrip's 1998 Yearbook*, vol. I, Richmond: PJB Publications.

Scrip (1999), *Scrip's 1999 Yearbook*, Richmond: PJB Publications.

Scrip (2003), *Scrip's 2003 Yearbook*, Richmond: PJB Publications.

Sekiguchi, S. (1979), *Japanese Direct Foreign Investment*, London: Macmillan.

Seo, T. (1987), *Iyakuhin (Pharmaceuticals)*, Tokyo: Nippon Keizai Shinbun.

Shahou Fujisawa (the in-house company news magazine) (1998), January.

Shirai, T. (1994), 'Face to Face: with the President of Nissan Europe', *European Motor Business*, 2nd quarter, pp. 6–20.

Shutte, H. (1997), 'Regional Headquarters in Action: Empirical Evidence and Model Building', in Macharzina, K., M.-J. Oesterle and J. Wolf (eds), *Global Business in the Information Age: Proceedings of the 23rd Annual EIBA Conference, December 14–16, 1997*, vol. 21, Stuttgart: European International Business Academy, pp. 541–71.

Siebert, H. (1990), 'The Harmonization Issue in Europe: Prior Agreement or a Competitive Process', in Siebert, H. (ed.), *The Completion of the Internal Market, Symposium 1989*, Tübingen: Mohr, pp. 53–75.

Sloan, A. (1965), *My Years with General Motors*, London: Sidgwick & Jackson.

Smith, A. and A.J. Venables (1990), 'Automobile', in Hufbauer, G.G. (ed.), *Europe 1992: An American Perspective*, Washington, DC: Brookings Institution, pp. 119–58.

Society of Motor Manufacturers and Traders (SMMT) (annually), *Motor Industry of Great Britain: World Automotive Statistics*, London: SMMT.

Spilker, B. (1994), *Multinational Pharmaceutical Companies: Principles and Practices*, 2nd edn, New York: Raven Press.

Starkey, K. and A. McKinlay (1993), *Strategy and the Human Resource: Ford and the Search for Competitive Advantage*, Oxford: Blackwell.

Stopford, J.M. and L.T. Wells (1972), *Managing the Multinational Enterprise: Organization of the Firm and Ownership of the Subsidiaries*, London: Longman.

Strange, R. (1993), *Japanese Manufacturing Investment in Europe: Its Impact on the UK Economy*, London: Routledge.

Sullivan, D. (1992), 'Organisation in American MNCs: The Perspective of the European Regional Headquarters', *Management International Review*, vol. 32, pp. 238–50.

Sun, J.M. and J. Pelkmans (1995), 'Regulatory Competition in the Single Market', *Journal of Common Market Studies*, vol. 33, no. 1, pp. 67–89.

Suzuki, T. (1969), 'Horon, 64-nen ikou no Ford no Senryaku' (Appendix: the Strategy of Ford after 1964), in *Ford no Kaigai Senryaku*, Tokyo: Ogawa-shuppan, pp. 537–45 (Japanese translated edition of Wilkins, M. and F.E. Hill (1964), *American Business Abroad: Ford on Six Continents*, Detroit: Wayne State University Press).

Swann, D. (2000), *The Economics of Europe: From Common Market to European Union*, 9th edn London: Penguin Books.

Taggart, J.H. (1993), *The World Pharmaceutical Industry*, London: Routledge.

Takahashi, F. (1988), *Yamanouchi Seiyaku, Kokusaikigyou ni shoujun* (Yamanouchi Pharmaceutical, Focusing on the International Corporation), Tokyo: Asahi Annai Community.

Takahashi, T. (1997), 'On the Record: with the Managing Director of Toyota Motor Europe', *EIU Motor Business Europe*, vol. 1997, 1st quarter, pp. 21–33.

Takeda (1983), *Takeda 200-nen Shi* (The Company History of Takeda, a 200-year History), Osaka: Takeda.

Thiran, J.M. and H. Yamawaki (1996), 'Patterns of Japanese Manufacturing Employment in the European Regions', in Darby, J. (ed.), *Japan and the European Periphery*, London: Macmillan, pp. 37–51.

Thomas, I.L.G. (2001), *The Japanese Pharmaceutical Industry: The New Drug Lag and the Failure of Industrial Policy*, Cheltenham, UK and Northampton, MA, USA: Edward Elgar.

Thompson, R. (1994), *The Single Market for Pharmaceuticals*, London: Butterworths.

Thomsen, S. and P. Nicolaides (1991), *The Evolution of Japanese Direct Investment in Europe, Death of a Transistor Salesman*, London: Harvester Wheatsheaf.

Thomsen, S. and S. Woolcock (1993), *Direct Investment and European Integration: Competition among Firms and Governments*, London: Pinter.

Tolliday, S. (1999), 'American Multinationals and the Impact of the Common Market: Cars and Integrated Market, 1954–67', in Amatori, F. and A. Colli (eds), *Industrialization and Reindustrialization in Europe*, Milan: Franco Angeli, pp. 383–93.

Tolliday, S. (2000), 'Transplanting the American Model? US Automobile Companies and the Transfer of Technology and Management to Britain, France, and Germany, 1928–1962', in Zeitlin, J. and G. Herrigel (eds),

Americanization and Its Limits: Reworking US Technology and Management in Post-War Europe and Japan, Oxford: Oxford University Press, pp. 76–119.

Toyota (1987), *Sozo Kagiri Naku, Toyota Jidousha 50-nen shi* (Unlimited Creation, a 50-year History of Toyota), Toyota, Japan: Toyota.

Toyota (1997), *The Automobile Industry, Toyota and the World*, Toyota: Japan.

Toyota (1998), *Creation*, March.

Toyota (2003), *Toyota in Europe 2003*, Brussels: Toyota Motor Europe.

Tsoukalis, L. and M. White (eds) (1982), *Japan and Western Europe: Conflict and Cooperation*, London: Frances Pinter.

Tung, R.L. (1990), 'International Human Resource Management Policies and Practices: A Comparative Analysis', in *Research in Personnel and Human Resource Management*, Supplement 2. Greenwich, CT: JAI Press, pp. 171–86.

Turner, L., D. Ray and T. Hayward (1997), *The British Research of Japanese Companies*, London: Insight Japan.

Ueda, K. (1999), *Iyakuhin Kisei Harmonization Suishin Kokusai Kyoudou Kenkyuu* (International Studies on the Harmonisation of Pharmaceutical Regulation), Tokyo: Ministry of Health and Welfare.

United Nations (UN) (1993), *From the Common Market to EC 92: Regional Economic Integration in the European Community and Transnational Corporations*, New York: UN.

United Nations (UN) (1998), *World Investment Report 1998: Trends and Determinants*, New York: UN.

United Nations (UN) (2000), *World Investment Report 2000: Cross-border Mergers and Acquisitions and Development*, New York: UN.

United Nations (UN) (2002), *World Investment Report 2002: Transnational Corporations and Export Competitiveness*, New York: UN.

United Nations (UN) (2003), *World Investment Report 2003: FDI Policies for Development: National and International Perspective*, New York: UN.

Urwin, D. (1991), *The Community of Europe: A History of European Integration since 1945*, London: Longman.

US Department of Commerce (1986), *A Competitive Assessment of the US Pharmaceutical Industry*, Boulder, CO: Westview Press.

Valencia, M. (2000), 'A Survey of European Business, Lean, Mean, European', *The Economist*, 29 April, p. 18.

Vasconcellos, G.M. and R.J. Kish (1998), 'Cross-border Mergers and Acquisitions: the European–US Experience', *Journal of Multinational Financial Management*, vol. 8, pp. 431–50.

Venables, A. (1995), 'Economic Integration and the Location of Firms', *American Economic Association*, vol. 85, no. 2, pp. 296–300.

Vernon, R. (1966), 'International Investment and International Trade in the Product Cycle', *Quarterly Journal of Economics*, vol. 80, pp. 190–207.

Vernon, R. (1979), 'The Product Cycle Hypothesis in the New International Environment', *Oxford Bulletin of Economics and Statistics*, vol. 41, pp. 255–67.

Veugelers, R. (1991), 'Locational Determinants and Ranking of Host Countries: An Empirical Assessment', *Kyklos*, vol. 44, pp. 363–82.

Viner, J. (1950), *The Customs Union Issue*, London: Stevens & Sons.

Wada, M. (1997), *Iyaku Sangyo Ron* (The Pharmaceutical Industry), Tokyo: Gyousei.

Wai-chung, H., J. Poon and M. Perry (2001), 'Towards a Regional Strategy: The Role of Regional Headquarters of Foreign Firms in Singapore', *Urban Studies*, vol. 38, no. 1, pp. 157–83.

Wells, P. and M. Rawlinson (1992), 'New Procurement Regimes and the Spatial Distribution of Suppliers: The Case of Ford in Europe', *Area*, vol. 24, pp. 380–90.

Wheeler, D. and A. Mody (1992), 'International Investment Location Decisions: The Case of U.S. Firms', *Journal of International Economics*, vol. 33, pp. 57–76.

Whisler, T.R. (1999), *The British Motor Industry 1945–1994: A Case Study in Industrial Decline*, Oxford: Oxford University Press.

Whitley, R. (1992), 'Society, Firms and Markets: The Social Structuring of Business System', in Whitley, R. (ed.), *European Business System: Firms and Markets in their National Context*, London: Sage, pp. 5–45.

Whitley, R. (1999), *Divergent Capitalisms: The Social Structuring and Change of Business Systems*, Oxford: Oxford University Press.

Wickens, P. (1987), *The Road to Nissan: Flexibility, Quality, Teamwork*, London: Macmillan.

Wilkins, M. (1974), *The Maturing of Multinational Enterprise: American Business Abroad from 1914 to 1970*, Cambridge, MA: Harvard University Press.

Wilkins, M. and F.E. Hill (1964), *American Business Abroad: Ford on Six Continents*, Detroit: Wayne State University Press.

Williamson, O.E. (1975), *Markets and Hierarchies*, New York: Free Press.

Williamson, O.E. (1985), *The Economic Institutions of Capitalism*, New York: Free Press.

Wilson, B.D. (1980), 'The Propensity of Multinational Companies to Expand through Acquisitions', *Journal of International Business Studies*, vol. 11, pp. 59–65.

Wilson, C. and D. Matthews (1997), 'The Evolution of Rules for the Single European Market in Pharmaceuticals', National Institute of Economic and

Social Research, Discussion Paper no.125, London: National Institute of Economic and Social Research.

Womack, J.P., D.T. Jones and D. Roos (1990), *The Machine that Changed the World*, New York: Rawson Associates.

Woodcock, P.C., P.W. Beamish and S. Makino (1994), 'Ownership-based Entry Mode Strategies and International Performance', *Journal of International Business Studies*, vol. 25, pp. 253–73.

Woolcock, S. (1997), 'Competition among Rules in the European Union', in Mayes, D.G. (ed.), *The Evolution of the Single European Market*, Cheltenham, UK and Northampton, USA: Edward Elgar, pp. 66–86.

Yamanouchi (1999), *Annual Report*, Tokyo: Yamanouchi.

Yamawaki, H. (1993), 'Location Decision of Japanese Multinational Firms in European Manufacturing Industries', in Hughes, K.S. (ed.), *European Competitiveness*, Cambridge: Cambridge University Press, pp. 11–28.

Yamawaki, H. (1994), 'Entry Patterns of Japanese Multinationals in US and European Manufacturing', in Mason, M. and D. Encarnation (eds), *Does Ownership Matter? Japanese Multinationals in Europe*, Oxford: Clarendon, pp. 91–121.

Yannopoulos, G.N. (1990), 'Foreign Direct Investment and European Integration: The Evidence from the Formative Years of the European Community', *Journal of Common Market Studies*, vol. 28, no. 3, pp. 235–59.

Yasumuro, K. (1992), *Global Keiei-ron* (On Global Management), Tokyo: Chikura Shobou.

Yip, G.S. (1992), *Total Global Strategy: Managing for Worldwide Competitive Advantage*, Englewood Cliffs, NJ: Prentice-Hall.

Zejan, M.C. (1990), 'New Ventures or Acquisitions: The Choice of Swedish Multinational Enterprises', *Journal of Industrial Economics*, vol. 38, pp. 349–55.

Index

Stopford, J.M. 5, 11, 19, 25, 84, 121,
    134, 136, 161
Strange, R. 9, 66, 128
subsidiaries
    controlling 13–14, 120–23
    increase in 2
    managing 18–22
Sullivan, D. 22, 161, 163
Sun, J.M. 5
supporting industries 10, 66
Suzuki, T. 158

Taggart, J.H. 59
Takahashi, F. 58, 59, 112, 127
Takahashi, T. 111
Takeda
    acquisitions 105
    EHQ not established 130, 134
    entry to Europe 109
        initial stage 96
        main stage 101
        subsequent developments 105
    joint ventures 58, 101, 111–13
    licensing 96
    production locations 62, 68
    R&D, basic research 81
    US presence 58
Takeuchi, H. 99, 127
tariff reductions 43–4
Taylor, R. 97
Thiran, J.M. 9
Thomas, I.L.G. 55
Thompson, G. 20, 59, 168
Thompson, R. 82, 132
Thomsen, S. 8, 9, 97, 165
TMEM *see* Toyota Motor Europe
    Manufacturing
TMME *see* Toyota Motor Europe
    Marketing and Engineering
Tolliday, S. 127, 134
Toyota
    acquisitions 104
    continental locations 69–70
    dealer relations 141–2
    diversification of production 61–3,
        69–70
    EHQ establishment 129–30
    entry to Europe 108
        initial stage 94–5
        main stage 100

    subsequent developments 105
    Ireland 95
    joint ventures 111, 113–14
    pan-European management 149–50
    performance 2
    production locations 61–3
    R&D, basic research 80–82
    relative size 50–51
    UK plants 100
    US presence 54
    warehouses 75–6
Toyota Motor Europe Manufacturing
    (TMEM) 129, 149–50
Toyota Motor Europe Marketing and
    Engineering (TMME) 129, 149–50
Tsoukalis, L. 97
Tung, R.L. 25
Turner, C. 59
Turner, L. 80

Ueda, K. 133
UK
    automobile demand 66
    automobile production   61–8, 99–100
    EMEA attracting FDI 83–4
    government intervention 66–7
    industrial relations 65–6
    pharmaceutical EHQs 84, 86
    presence of supporting industries 66
    R&D, pharmaceuticals 79
    SEM and FDI 100
    wages 63
universities 80–81, 106
Urwin, D. 3

Vahlne, J.E. 15, 98, 113, 165
Valencia, M. 3
Vasconcellos, G.M. 13, 116
Venables, A.J. 9, 59
Vernon, J. 59
Vernon-Kojima model 63–4, 69–70, 88
Vernon, R. 8, 88
Veugelers, R. 10, 12
Viner, J. 9

Wada, M. 47
wages 63–4, 67
Wai-chung, H. 163
Wells, L.T. 5, 19, 25, 84, 121, 134, 136,
    161